EXPLORING REALITY

EXPLORING REALITY

Michael Leahy   *Michael Irwin*

Krishan Kumar   *R. B. Freedman*

Stephen Bann   *Lewis Ryder*

Ben Brewster   *Dan Cohn-Sherbok*

London
ALLEN & UNWIN
Boston   Sydney   Wellington

Allen & Unwin, the academic imprint of
Unwin Hyman Ltd,
PO Box 18, Park Lane, Hemel Hempstead, Herts HP2 4TE, UK
40 Museum Street, London WC1A 1LU, UK
37/39 Queen Elizabeth Street, London SE1 2QB, UK

Allen & Unwin Inc.,
8 Winchester Place, Winchester, Mass 01890, USA

Allen & Unwin (Australia) Ltd,
8 Napier Street, North Sydney, NSW 2060, Australia

Allen & Unwin (New Zealand) Ltd in association with the Port
Nicholson Press Ltd,
60 Cambridge Terrace, Wellington, New Zealand

First published in 1987

British Library Cataloguing in Publication Data

Exploring reality.
1. Humanities – Study and teaching (Higher) – Great Britain
2. Interdisciplinary approach in education – Great Britain
3. Education, Higher – Great Britain – Philosophy
I. Leahy, Michael
001.3'07'1141   LB2365.H8
ISBN 0–04–100049–8
ISBN 0–04–100050–1 Pbk

Library of Congress Cataloging-in-Publication Data

Exploring reality.
Bibliography: p.
Filmography: p.
Includes index.
1. Humanities. 2. Interdisciplinary approach to knowledge.
I. Leahy, Michael.
AZ201.E97 1987 001.3   86–28862
ISBN 0–04–100049–8 (alk. paper)
ISBN 0–04–100050–1 (pbk.: alk. paper)

Typeset in 10 on 11 point Sabon by Computape (Pickering) Limited,
and printed in Great Britain by
St. Edmundsbury Press, Suffolk

To Ian Gregor, who began the exploration

Contents

Notes on Contributors

Michael Leahy is a Senior Lecturer in Philosophy at Kent. He has published articles in several areas of the subject but is particularly interested in aesthetics and conceptual issues surrounding the psychology of animals. He has also taught at the Universities of Durham, in the UK, and at Penn State, Cornell, New Hampshire and Allegheny College, in the USA.

Michael Irwin is Professor of English Literature at the University of Kent. His academic work includes a study of Henry Fielding and *Picturing: Description and Illusion in the Nineteenth-Century Novel*. He has also written two novels, the more recent *Striker* (1985).

Krishan Kumar is Reader in Sociology at the University of Kent. Has also been a producer in the Talks and Documentaries Department of the BBC, Visiting Fellow at Harvard University, and Visiting Professor of Sociology at the University of Colorado at Boulder. Author of *Prophecy and Progress: The Sociology of Industrial and Post-Industrial Society* (1978) and *Utopia and Anti-Utopia in Modern Times* (1986).

Robert Freedman came to the Biological Laboratory at the University of Kent in 1971 and is now Reader in Protein Biochemistry. From 1986 to 1988 he was seconded to the Science and Engineering Research Council to manage a multi-centre university/industry research programme. For ten years he was biochemistry consultant to *New Scientist*, he is currently a member of the editorial board of *The Biochemical Journal*, and he has lectured frequently to schools and BAYS groups on biochemical topics. His first degree was in chemistry, and his major interests have been in the properties and biological functions of proteins, particularly in how they fold up into their active three-dimensional conformation after their synthesis.

xi

Stephen Bann is Reader in Modern Cultural Studies and Chairman of the Board of Studies in History and Theory of Art at Kent. His most recent book is *The Clothing of Clio* (1984) and he is preparing for publication a collection of essays on the American painter Stephen Edlich, entitled *Collage as Carving*.

Lewis Ryder lectures in Theoretical Physics at the University of Kent. He is interested in the theory of fundamental particles and pursues research into the mathematical structure of gauge theories, which are believed to describe the nuclear and electromagnetic interactions of these particles. He is also interested in relativity and cosmology, and in the possible connections between relativity and particle physics. He has written two books on elementary particle physics, which have been translated into Russian and Chinese.

Ben Brewster is a lecturer in Film Studies at the University of Kent and a former editor of *Screen* magazine. He has written articles on cinema semiotics, Russian montage theory and early film history, and is currently working on a study of the one-reel fiction film in the 1910s.

Dan Cohn-Sherbok was born in Denver, Colorado and educated at Williams College and the University of Cambridge. He was ordained a liberal rabbi at the Hebrew Union College and has served congregations in the United States, Australia, England and South Africa. He was appointed Lecturer in Theology at the University of Kent in 1975 where he is also Director of the Centre for the Study of Religion and Society. He is the author and editor of several books and has contributed numerous articles to scholarly journals.

Plates

Preface

This book sets out to do something simple and challenging which academic compartmentalism has tended to prevent. It derives from a multidisciplinary course mounted for first-year Humanities students at the University of Kent. The original aim seemed straightforward: to get lecturers from a variety of subjects to describe, in terms accessible to non-specialists, how their respective disciplines engage with 'reality'. It so happened that each of these individuals not only carried out the original brief but tried to take students to the far edge of the discipline concerned, to areas where the 'explorer' begins to lose his bearings, where accepted truths collapse into paradox or are exposed as conventions. The result has been a surprising degree of coherence and continuity in a course that on paper looked like a succession of self-contained units. Certain basic conceptual dilemmas have repeatedly re-emerged.

The course works well. Undergraduates find it refreshing to step outside conventional subject boundaries and think in comparative terms about principles, objectives and limitations. They seem pleased to discover that they can grasp central issues in subjects new to them, such as philosophy or film theory, and can even understand, in outline, some of the theoretical problems confronting the physicist or the biologist. The teachers have regularly attended one another's lectures and responded with keen interest. Each lecture is followed by a seminar and the course concludes with two symposia, one conducted by the students and the other by the staff.

This book in effect represents the 'lecture' side of the course. As such, we hope it may give rise to lively seminars in many another institution. Each of the contributors advances propositions familiar enough within his own discipline. There may be idiosyncrasy in illustration or presentation, but the writer would hope to provide a reasonably representative account of his subject. The level of argument is pitched quite high but in no case does the writer assume any prior knowledge of the discipline concerned. The interested general reader should be able not only to keep up with the play, but to join in the game.

Each chapter was circulated in draft form to all the contributors. Our various responses and general reflections were collected in the form of a long tape-recorded discussion and numerous memoranda. The final chapter represents an attempt to digest this material into more or less coherent form. It is deliberately miscellaneous and open-ended, offering questions rather than answers. Opposed viewpoints have been preserved side by side; it is for the reader to adjudicate. All the contributors are represented in this final section, but the editors, who assembled it, must take responsibility for it.

The book is intended as much for teaching purposes as for general reading. It asks fundamental questions and proposes bold comparisons. Only a university like Kent, with a strong interdisciplinary tradition, could have mounted a course that juxtaposed such a variety of subjects. Teachers and students elsewhere should find the cross-relationships as intriguing as we did. The theme is, of course, inexhaustible. Space permitting, we would have been delighted to include a chapter by an economist, a musician, a political scientist, a historian, a palaeontologist ... The issues concerned are fundamental to every discipline – indeed to education itself – but are all too often left in the background. We hope readers will find it stimulating to tackle them directly.

Michael Irwin
Dan Cohn-Sherbok

Plate 1.1 Chiang Yee, *Cows in Derwentwater*, 1936. Brush and Ink

Plate 1.2 Anonymous, *Derwentwater, looking toward Borrowdale*, 1826. Lithograph

Chapter One

Introduction

MICHAEL LEAHY

'Now, what I want is, Facts. Teach these boys and girls nothing but Facts. Facts alone are wanted in life. Plant nothing else, and root out everything else. You can only form the minds of reasoning animals upon Facts: nothing else will ever be of any service to them ... Stick to Facts, Sir!'

Charles Dickens, *Hard Times*, [1854] 1907, p. 1

The Gradgrind Theory –
A Starting Point

Your first contact with this book will probably have been through the title, *Exploring Reality*. It is equally probable that the temptation to proceed further will have been prompted by a curiosity tinged with unease rather than instant interest. This reaction is more than what the several authors expect, it is what they hope for, since it is a sign of the conceptual alertness which will be needed to engage with the controversies raised. Titles like *Exploring Alaska* or *Exploring the Great Wall of China on Horseback*, fascinating though they may be, should provoke no such difficulties because the subject matter is clear to anyone with only the slightest knowledge of the world's geography. But a proposed confrontation with reality raises expectations which might well vacillate between what is almost too obvious and what is chillingly esoteric. What are we proposing to talk about? What does the title *mean*?

Thomas Gradgrind, the schoolmaster in Dickens's *Hard Times*, although not everyone's idea of a kindly educationist, clearly prompts answers of the almost-too-obvious variety which would meet with considerable approval. Reality is literally staring us in the face, it is the world we see, touch, smell and hear; it is the world of 'Facts'. The view is influential in contemporary theories about education which put the emphasis on subjects like economics, the natural sciences and mathematics as best suited to prepare children with the facts necessary for adulthood. This view of reality will be our starting-point. To do it justice, for it is an important view with a distinguished history, I shall elaborate it in four steps:

(1) Reality consists of *facts*. These are apprehended by the senses or discovered by calculation; for example, the Mediterranean is blue, the sun is 865,000 miles in diameter, human beings never live to be 300.

(2) Novelists, poets, theologians, historians, scientists and indeed all of us in the humdrum of everyday life attempt to be 'true' to facts. The very words 'common sense' suggest that the sharp end of experience is often a more reliable guide than pompous theorizing. This can be generalized: respectable or important beliefs and statements are those which correspond to facts. For example: does theology (literally, an account of God) *really* tell us anything? The answer given is that if God's existence can either be seen, felt, or otherwise sensed, or proved by acceptable calculation, then yes; otherwise it is well-meaning quackery.[1]

(3) Accounts of facts can only be true if the personality of the writer or speaker does not intrude. The facts must be communicated in undiluted form. If they are 'coloured' by a narrator in any way then reality is *automatically* distorted and the account at risk. Facts, it is often said, are *given*. Mr Gradgrind's pupils are ideally suited to meet this requirement. His class is an 'inclined plane of little vessels then and there arranged in order, ready to have imperial gallons of facts poured into them until they were full to the brim' (Dickens, 1907, p. 2).

2

(4) The accounts which are pre-eminent in satisfying all of the above requirements are those of mathematics and the experimental sciences like physics and chemistry.

Putting Gradgrind to Work

Our bare outline is completed. Let us pursue, at this stage somewhat haphazardly, some of its implications. If scientists are successful in depicting reality by giving us facts, then some of the other contenders would seem to make a pretty miserable job of it. What about novelists, painters and film-makers, the subjects of three of our chapters? It is undoubtedly the case that some people gain great comfort from the apparent realism of the arts. Eighteenth-century portraits or nineteenth-century landscapes are generally preferred to late Picasso or even Cézanne; the novels of Thomas Hardy or Graham Greene are more widely read than those of James Joyce or Vladimir Nabokov (except, perhaps, for *Lolita*). The same trend, which owes a great deal to theories about the arts in ancient Greece over two thousand years ago, is even more marked in the world of film where the dominance of the Hollywood epic style is almost complete. Most people hardly know what avant-garde cinema *is*, even after a regular diet of the films on British or American television.

The counter-argument to these tastes for realism is initially devastating. Realism in the arts is the effect of cunning artifice aided and abetted by the ingrained habits of lazy audiences. The verisimilitude is illusory. Even the most deceptive paintings are two-dimensional representations of solid subjects and novels, however enthralling, recount the lives and loves of people *who never really existed*. Even where the writer has used models from 'real life' these will be well camouflaged and readapted by selection of circumstance in the finished product. What we have are *fictions*: a term which if used of an account by a scientist or historian would amount to a charge of telling lies. In chapter 7 Ben Brewster will show how similar arguments can undermine the claim that what makes the style of the Hollywood epic so universal is that it gives us an uncontroversial carbon copy of what we see and hear.

Positivism

The view suggested by Mr Gradgrind, to which I have been attempting to do justice, in the process having shown apparent scant regard for theology, literature, painting and film, is called *positivism*. It is a view with which I disagree; a disagreement shared by most, if not all, of the contributors to this book, including the scientists. Yet it strikes many people as intuitively persuasive and has traditionally been a fruitful corrective to woolly-mindedness across the spectrum of academic disciplines. The term 'positivism' was coined by the French philosopher Auguste Comte (1798–1857) as a label for his account of the evolution of knowledge ([1830–42] 1974). Comte listed three ascending stages. The least advanced was the 'theological': here reality is grasped in terms of the creations and conflicts of gods and spirits which he saw as the mere repetition of superstition and prejudice. Attempts to transcend these by abstraction and generality, the usual hallmarks of rational inquiry, mark the second stage, the 'metaphysical'. The results, in Comte's view, were also unsatisfactory since, like phlogiston in early theories of combustion, they were in no way corroborated by experience or evidence. The defects of theological and metaphysical attempts to capture reality are remedied by the final, the so-called 'positive', stage. Appeals, Comte claimed, must only be made to simple quantitative descriptions of sensory phenomena. The result should be something which is *measurable*; 'quantitative' implying that numerical units are involved.

Positivism had far-reaching implications. Intellectual energy naturally gravitated towards those sciences which deal obviously in the measurable. It also sparked enthusiasm to introduce quantitative methods into disciplines like economics, political science, sociology and even history as a pre-condition of respectability. An updated version of positivism surfaced in Vienna one hundred years later. That movement, known as *logical* positivism, was introduced to the English-speaking world by A. J. Ayer's *cause célèbre* in 1936, *Language, Truth and Logic*.

Let us return to the fourfold outline. It is intended to do no more than represent the mainstream of positivistic thought. How can we begin to expose confusions and contradictions in it? There

4

are two converging lines of attack. First many factual accounts cited by those in sympathy with positivism are despite appearances dependent upon the active participation of the observer and so offend the third requirement; namely, that facts are *given*. Secondly the professed neutrality of scientific accounts becomes, upon inspection, equally suspect. The development of this attack will occupy most of the remainder of this introduction. It will provide a mere foretaste of the arguments to follow from the various contributors.

Complications about Facts

The controversial nature of allegedly factual accounts is illustrated in three examples:

Explanations in history A popular form of science fiction involves time travel. The successful voyager emerges from his time machine with, let us say, a first-hand knowledge of the American Civil War.[2] (The future can also be involved but let us ignore that.) In the nineteenth century, mainly as a result of positivistic fervour, some historians actually claimed that they ought to be able to communicate the reality of the past much as it would reveal itself to the time traveller. (They did not use the example of time travel, of course.) Their claim would now be dismissed as a naive misunderstanding. History is written by *historians*, creatures of their time like anyone else; contemporary assessments are made of past events, contemporary interest in the past rigorously pursued, irrelevant material ignored. History is now seen to involve a *manipulation* of the data available; its practitioners are not passive observers but creators of a past in an image of the present.[3] Yet this suggests an obvious breach of the historian's neutrality.

Realistic painting I referred earlier to the fact that the most life-like paintings, including the genre known as *trompe-l'oeil* which can deceive even attentive viewers, involve skilled artifice. Ernst Gombrich in *Art and Illusion* ([1960] 1977), a work of great importance, explains why this *must* be so. The apparently accurate rendering of the natural world in drawing, painting and even photography depends upon the assimilation of *styles*. These styles are relative to times and cultures. Presented with the juxta-position of a landscape by the Chinese painter Chiang Yee (1937, p. 45) and an anonymous British lithograph from the last century, westerners will almost certainly judge the lithograph, whatever its quality, to be the more realistic (see Plates 1.1 and 1.2 above). An oriental audience would think differently; a curious anomaly that Gombrich discusses at length (1977, pp. 55–78). Judged by the fourfold criteria of positivism it is out of the question that both groups could be right; indeed, the disquieting conclusion might be that *no* pictorial representation is truly realistic.

Colour judgements The first example of a fact apprehended by the senses was of a blue sea. The judgement seems to satisfy the requirements of positivism so obviously as to defy further dis-cussion; such examples are called paradigms. Yet it *is* conten-tious. Our ability to agree about colours depends upon anatomi-cal similarities within the eye and these, in their turn, can depend upon geographical location. Colour vocabularies are often notor-iously difficult to translate; between ancient Greek and English, for example. The conclusion usually drawn is that for the Greeks the world was indeed coloured differently. But if facts are *given* (the third requirement) it seems wrong to say this. So is, at the very best, only one of us right? If so, which one?

The discussion of colour judgements brings to light a basic ambiguity in Comte's disarmingly transparent requirement, namely, the 'simple quantitative descriptions of sensory phenom-ena'. The problem is that what we sense is, for example, green or loud. But these are *qualitative* states. The quantitative equiv-alents, that which is measurable, will be light waves or decibels. Somehow a subtle translation needs to be completed which rules out as straightforwardly factual what was originally a paradigm.

Complications about Science

Let us now ask some questions about the status of scientific explanations, in particular the central notions of experiment, hypothesis and laws.[4] The vocabulary of much science is also controversial.

Experiment What makes science particularly authoritative is the possibility of testing its results experimentally. Yet it is frequently overlooked that in many cases this is not possible. In economics, for example, the result of an increase in money supply does not have experimental validity because of the impossibility of controlling other variables and the absence of what is called a 'control group'; namely, a group similar in all respects to that experimented upon except for the variable under scrutiny, which in this case would be the increase in money supply. Such problems are the stock in trade of the social sciences. But the natural sciences face similar difficulties. Medicine is hampered by the ethical objections to using human beings in the laboratory and many theories in astronomy and physics must wait for decades or longer to be tested; the existence of intelligent life on other planets, for example, or predictions about the arrival of a comet.

Hypothesis Experiments are devised to test hypotheses. Hypotheses are provisional solutions to problems. Robert Freedman and Lewis Ryder, in the chapters on biology and physics respectively, will show how the role of theories and hypotheses in their respective areas is very subtle. Far from simply reflecting inert and given facts they are better seen as constitutive of what are, for the science in question, *acceptable* facts. There is a marked similarity between theory and hypothesis in the different sciences and the artistic styles of various traditions of painting mentioned earlier.

Laws The third paradigm of a fact was that human beings never live to be 300. Yet it is a curious fact. Although it might state that all human beings to date have failed to reach 300, it implies *more* than this; there are implications for people yet to come. None the less we can be confident of its truth despite the impossibility of examining all future generations. Such statements are *law-like* and are typical of science. Yet in going beyond the observations by which they are established they offend the strictures of positivism.

Vocabulary The continually evolving concepts of science are both more rarefied and more restricted than the reference to the *senses*, in the first criterion of positivism, would seem to require. How then is science pre-eminent? We have moved on from the times when bright schoolchildren could bemuse their parents with the revelation that the relatively stable kitchen furniture was *in reality* atoms and molecules in constant motion, more space that solidity. Atoms and molecules are themselves composed of more basic particles and ever more esoteric ones are discovered regularly. It would be a massive act of faith, some physicists might call it obstinacy, to think that the analysis of the microcosm, the search for ever more 'basic' entities, will ever be regarded as completed once and for all. The search will simply be frustrated in various ways; or cease to be interesting or worth paying for. So how can it be correct to assert, in positivistic vein, that the kitchen chair is *in reality* composed of particles which are themselves, at least in theory, capable of ever further resolution? The difficulty disappears if we drop the qualification 'in reality'; indeed the chair *is* composed of atoms and molecules, or a book of individual pages. But by dropping the qualification we are ceasing to acknowledge the positivist's justification for the unique status of science, namely that it is somehow more *real* than other disciplines. In so doing we have forgotten what this book is all about.

The Sceptic's Defence of Positivism

Not surprisingly, in a slim volume devoted to a topic of almost breath-taking scope, we have covered a lot of ground in a few pages. Not only is it difficult ground, and likely to become more so, but it must also be stressed that it is controversial and disputed ground. Although in some areas academic opinion is more or less unanimous, in others it is sharply divided and this is one of them.[5]

Here is the position so far. The fourfold theory of positivism, adapted to serve the multidisciplinary aims of this book, will have struck most readers as very plausible. Indeed it embodies ways of thinking so deeply rooted in our idioms and culture as to be almost irresistible. The outline arguments against positivism have been deliberately devised to undermine it from within; to show that what apparently satisfies one axis of the theory fails to satisfy one of the others. In particular we have attempted to show that the observer, whether novelist, historian, or scientist, intrudes upon paradigm factual judgements to the overall impoverishment of the theory. It is tempting to draw the sceptical conclusion that the various examples and arguments cited to discredit common-sense positivism show that the arts and sciences in question therefore fail to get to grips with true facts, and hence with reality, at all! This is a valiant attempt to preserve the positivistic position but it pays an enormous cost. It will not only confirm the suspect nature of literature and painting as unreliable sources of true facts but condemn likewise both the previously irreproachable disciplines of history and physics as well as everyday judgements about colours and perhaps similar properties.[6]

Scepticism Undermined

It is true that people can appear to be radical sceptics about traditional sources of knowledge. But they do so almost invariably for limited purposes. It is, for example, a useful rhetorical device for deriding the pretensions of an intellectual establishment and it is also to the fore in many statements of religious belief such as the Catholic Mass and the Testaments. But if we pursue further and consider what would become of such iconoclasm were it applied generally and consistently there are paradoxical results. The hater of intellectual pretension none the less uses the products of applied science, such as central heating and electric guitars, since he knows that they make life more pleasant. The devout Christian, interested in estate management in the nineteenth century, will read historians such as Thompson (1963) and Asa Briggs (1954) rather than Dickens or George Eliot, reserving the novels for diversion. If our sceptics meet with an accident they will consult an MD rather than an exponent of voodoo or acupuncture and would consider it most unwise to do otherwise. Yet surely the point of attempting to sever the link between reality and disciplines like history and the sciences is intended to cast doubt upon the reliability of such activities, so that their facts become only so-called; otherwise the operation seems pointless.

The conduct of people's lives, be they ferocious sceptics in their *talk*, betrays the recognition that our needs require that we consult experts, or consume the results of expertise from a variety of disciplines, and that it is rational and proper to do so. This being so, the wrangles over the supremacy of history over literature or of medicine over voodoo or astrology seem relatively untouched. The only casualty seems to have been the word, but better to call it the *concept*, of 'reality'. Scepticism, of the sort described, subverts itself in practice and it is difficult to see how it could do otherwise.

Reality Created – The Beginnings of a New Theory

Given the inconsistencies of positivism and the failure of the sceptical alternative to get to grips with the problem, since 'reality' re-emerges in another guise, we must be prepared to countenance a more radical possibility.

Most of the problems with the positivistic model of reality arose because of its requirement that the observer must be completely passive. The metaphor of mirroring is frequently used to describe that model's role of the ideal observer since mirrors seem to reproduce what is before them without distortion. This, as it happens, is a false belief. The image that you see in the mirror when you look at your face is precisely half the size of your head (Gombrich, 1977, pp. 4–8). People *are* deceived by mirrors but not for long. They are also deceived by tailors' dummies.

But human beings are in any case not mirrors. Historians will try to prove each other wrong, scientific explanations make reference to abstract entities like laws and theoretical particles, or, more generally, to perceive the world we need sense organs as intermediaries. An alternative theory of reality, if it is to avoid the unsatisfactory outcome of the positivistic model, must take seriously the role of *participating* observer, not the merely passive. An active observer becomes essential to reality rather than militating against it or frustrating it. Reality can then cease to be viewed as some elusive bedrock of experience systematically resisting all attempts to discover it and forcing its baffled explorers into scepticism or mysticism. Indeed it will be seen as misleading to describe it as a *discovery* since the beliefs, abstract entities and points of view of its investigators become part of it. On this view reality is at least as much a *creation* as a discovery. But for creations we need creators. The perplexities of positivism can only be erased by recognizing that the role of the observer changes from that of passive audience to protagonist on stage.

The contributors to this book are all creators in the sense described, although they might not all be self-consciously so. They happen to be operating in the contexts of familiar academic disciplines. But it is important to reiterate that we are all of us, in everyday life, engaging in rational debate, acting on the basis of beliefs that we believe to be true, or claiming that others are in the wrong. Reality, frequently in the form of a reference to 'the facts', has a part to play in this everyday experience in which everyone is, in part, also a creator.

The process involved is far more complex than my apparently straightforward account suggests. It will be developed in the sequel. In particular it will be necessary to forestall the objection that the theory is ridiculously permissive in appearing to justify any account as being as realistic as any other. Indeed were that so the new theory would be as unhelpful as the sceptical retreat from positivism was seen to be. Scepticism dismissed all attempts to capture reality as equally *un*realistic. This, it was argued, fails to do justice to the obvious facts of life which demonstrate that it is rational to trust some accounts more than others. A theory which implied that all accounts were equally *realistic* would fail to match the facts of experience to precisely the same degree.

Notes

1 Even at this early stage it is worthwhile to recommend the incomparable writings of the British philosopher David Hume (1711–76) which proceed in this vein. His two essays, 'Of a particular providence and of a future state' and 'Of miracles' (Hume, [1784] 1902) are matched by very little on the topic written since.

2 In Ward Moore's *Bring the Jubilee* (1955) such a trip is actually made by an historian anxious to solve a knotty problem. Unfortunately he interferes with the outcome of the war and is thereby prevented from returning to complete his research. If you carefully consider the matter that is more of a problem than it seems!

3 Two relevant and approachable sources are E. H. Carr's *What is History?* (1961, pp. 7–30) and Karl Popper's *The Open Society and its Enemies* (1966, esp. Vol. 2, pp. 259–80). The latter is also useful on the comparison between history and science.

4 Two stimulating collections of articles are required reading for anyone who wishes to pursue these important issues further. The articles are in most cases approachable by non-scientists. *The Philosophy of Science*, edited by P. H. Nidditch (1968), and *Scientific Revolutions*, edited by Ian Hacking (1981), are best looked at in that order.

5 Discussion has intensified in recent years with the publication of Richard Rorty's *Philosophy and the Mirror of Nature* (1980) and his *Consequences of Pragmatism* (1982). For a contrary view see Bernard Williams (1985, pp. 132–55) who puts the debate into perspective. See also Hacking (1981).

6 So, of course, the theory is no longer really intact without radical revision of the first criterion, to exclude colour and law-like judgements, and of the fourth, to exclude physics and perhaps by parity of reasoning other sciences as well. Such wholesale demolition of normal sources of information has a history; it is explicit in Plato (427–347 BC), one of the most celebrated of all philosophers. It has also been a convenient device for religious philosophers such as René Descartes (1596–1650) and George Berkeley (1685–1753); creating a pregnant vacuum for an eternal being to fill with his own reality. Traditionally of the sciences only mathematics retained respectability since it provided certain formal links with what becomes for such writers a very arcane reality indeed.

Chapter Two

Facts and Fictions

MICHAEL IRWIN

> At times her whimsical fancy would intensify natural pro-
> cesses around her till they seemed a part of her own story.
> Rather they became a part of it; for the world is only a
> psychological phenomenon, and what they seemed they
> were.
>
> Thomas Hardy, *Tess of the d'Urbervilles*

The argument that follows is divided into three sections, each of
which is concerned with a quite distinct literary issue. What the
sections have in common is their bearing upon a problem that has
challenged writers in every age: how is the author, confined
within his or her own subjectivity, to reach towards a reality that
seems to lie beyond it?

I
Poetry and Facts

Robinson Crusoe finds very little to say about the beauties of his
desert island. Indeed he seems to have no aesthetic response to it.
He sees it rather as a collection of potential resources, something
between a larder and a builder's yard. There are goats to provide
milk, meat and clothing, trees to provide the raw materials for
boats, fences and utensils. This utilitarian attitude might reasonably be shared by those of us living much further from the brute

struggle for physical survival. For us, too, the physical world is the sole resource-centre, providing directly or indirectly the houses we live in, the cars we drive, everything we eat or wear.

Oddly enough, however, Crusoe's response is so far from typical as to be freakish. In Western tradition, certainly, what we call 'nature' has not merely been *used* as an assemblage of physical phenomena, but apprehended, with love and awe, as a mysterious totality of which we ourselves are part. Anyone who has felt exhilarated by a fine spring day, or been comforted, in time of grief, by walking at night beneath the stars, has shared in this experience. The exploration of this response is one of the great themes of literature and has produced that ancient genre the pastoral idyll, which pictures man living in perfect harmony with nature. The typical subject is an actual shepherd, contentedly tending his flock under blue skies. Birds sing, flowers bloom, gentle breezes blow; man and nature are at one. It is a vision that can easily decline into triteness and insipidity, but it derives from an impulse that most of us would recognize.

In this charmed environment the shepherd is characteristically shown tuning his lay or wooing his mistress – or tuning his lay in order to woo his mistress. In other words the beauty and harmony of the scene engender Art and Love. Characteristically, too, there are divinities about, the gods of trees and rivers – perhaps Pan himself. The vision is a religious one. In a sense the supreme pastoral idyll is the account of the Garden of Eden before the Fall.

One aspect of this idealized view has become known (the term was coined by Ruskin) as 'the pathetic fallacy' – the suggestion that animals, birds and even plants might share our joys and sorrows. In the pastoral elegy, where the death of a shepherd is lamented, breezes sigh, birds sing mournful ditties and the clouds weep rain. Nature sympathizes with human suffering.

In the first half of the eighteenth century some of the best English poets were writing pastoral verse but producing (on the whole) lifeless imitations of Greek or Latin originals. Pope's work in this mode seems merely a matter of formula – as, for example, in the lament for Daphne in the Fourth Pastoral:

14

> For her, the Flocks refuse their verdant Food,
> The thirsty Heifers seek the gliding Flood.
> The silver Swans her hapless Fate bemoan,
> In Notes more sad than when they sing their own.
>
> (ll. 37–40)

The writer shows a knowledge of classical poetry rather than a feeling for nature.

The emergence of the Romantic movement, towards the end of that century, was centrally involved with an attempt to re-establish from a basis of personal experience the pastoral tradition that had so declined. Wordsworth in particular was to assert again and again that the idea of sympathy in nature was no metaphor. Man, animals, plants, even inanimate matter, are spiritually interrelated. The same 'motions' or 'presences' inform the whole of creation. Nature can speak to us, can soothe, fortify, instruct. In *The Tables Turned* the poet advises his friend to put down his book and learn from nature:

> One impulse from a vernal wood
> May teach you more of man,
> Of moral evil and of good,
> Than all the sages can.
>
> (ll. 21–4)

In his long autobiographical poem *The Prelude* he was to show how his own character, beliefs and morality had been shaped by his response to the majestic scenery of the Lake District, where he spent his boyhood. The great project of Wordsworth's own exploration of reality was his sustained attempt to demonstrate that nature had a soul, that there was a ghost in the machine.

The story of that project is very relevant to this essay but it is a complex one. For my immediate purposes it is simpler to consider the work of John Clare, whose early beliefs and occasional doubts were closely akin to those of Wordsworth. Like Wordsworth he revels in the 'facts' of nature but strives to go beyond them.

Clare was born in 1793 into the uneducated family of a cottage-farmer. He spent a childhood of extreme poverty in the village of Helpstone, in Northamptonshire. Somehow he managed to acquire not only a deep and intimate love of nature but also, against extraordinary odds, a passion for poetry. While scraping a living as an agricultural labourer he wrote poems of his own, and in 1820 was fortunate enough to have a volume of them published. Briefly he enjoyed celebrity as a peasant-poet. But he fell out of fashion as abruptly as he had fallen into it. Later volumes of verse were financial failures. He fell prey to depression and delusions and was eventually certified insane. The last twenty years of his life were spent in the Northampton General Lunatic Asylum. He died in 1864.

Through all these vicissitudes Clare remained a poet. His verse is the record of a lifelong engagement with nature. Here is a typical descriptive poem, *Mouse's Nest*:

> I found a ball of grass among the hay
> And progged it as I passed and went away;
> And when I looked I fancied something stirred,
> And turned agen and hoped to catch the bird –
> When out an old mouse bolted in the wheats
> With all her young ones hanging at her teats;
> She looked so odd and so grotesque to me,
> I ran and wondered what the thing could be,
> And pushed the knapweed bunches where I stood;
> Then the mouse hurried from the craking brood.
> The young ones squeaked, and as I went away
> She found her nest again among the hay.
> The water o'er the pebbles scarce could run
> And broad old cesspools glittered in the sun.

This simple-looking record of an inconclusive encounter could be an entry in a nature diary, the sort of 'country note' still to be read in the *Guardian*. But Clare has rendered it into a poem – in fact into a simplified sonnet. The 'poetic' element is as unobtrusive as it could well be. The rhyme-scheme is the straightforward *aabb*. There are no figures of speech – not so much as a metaphor. The grammar is rudimentary, the clauses being crudely hooked together by the 'and', ten times repeated. The vocabulary, largely monosyllabic, is that of ordinary conversation. Clare has also contrived to preserve the word-order of natural speech. The only oddity in the poem is the final couplet, perhaps to be interpreted as a footnote to provide perspective: 'This is the sort of day it was.' Otherwise all the writer's effort seems to have been directed towards a scrupulous recording of facts.

Since I none the less find the work strongly and immediately appealing I ask myself whether I am responding to it *as a poem*. Is my reaction merely a version of what I would feel if I saw the mouse's nest myself, or if I read a good prose account by somebody who had seen one? As it happens a convenient prose comparison exists, in the shape of a passage by Gilbert White, the eighteenth-century naturalist, in his *Natural History of Selborne* (1788):

I have procured some of the mice mentioned in my former letters, a young one and a female with young, both of which I have preserved in brandy. From the colour, shape, size, and manner of nesting, I make no doubt but that the species is nondescript. They are much smaller and more slender than the *mus domesticus medius* of Ray; and have more of the squirrel or dormouse colour: their belly is white, a straight line along their sides divides the shades of their back and belly. They never enter into houses; are carried into ricks and barns with the sheaves; abound in harvest, and build their nests amidst the straws of the corn above the ground, and sometimes in thistles. They breed as many as eight at a litter, in a little round nest composed of the blades of grass or wheat.

One of these nests I procured this autumn, most artificially platted, and composed of the blades of wheat; perfectly round, and about the size of a cricket-ball; with the aperture so ingeniously closed, that there was no discovering to what part it belonged. It was so compact and well filled, that it would roll across the table without being discomposed, though it contained eight little mice that were naked and blind. As this nest was perfectly full, how could the dam come at her litter respectively so as to administer a teat to each? Perhaps she opens different places for that purpose, adjusting them again when the business is over: but she could not possibly be contained herself in the ball with her young,

17

which moreover would be daily increasing in bulk. This wonderful procreant cradle, an elegant instance of the efforts of instinct, was found in a wheat-field, suspended in the head of a thistle.

(November 4, 1767)

White's approach is the scientific one, inquiring and speculative. His account offers more information than does Clare's poem. But there is no question of arid detachment; on the contrary, the passage is charmingly animated and appreciative. What, if anything, does Clare's poem offer which White's prose does not? I think that when reading it I respond at three levels. First I am interested in the 'facts' themselves as I am when reading White's description. Second I am aware of an *encounter*. I see not only the mouse and her nest but also the observing poet, curious and intrigued. I respond to his response. Finally I am influenced by the fact that he has chosen not simply to describe his experience but to describe it in a poem, somehow to dignify it. Involved in the sonnet are nature, man's appreciation of nature, and the sense that nature and art are interrelated.

The scrupulous literalism of *Mouse's Nest* is typical. Clare always seems passionately anxious to *record* accurately. For instance, in his many poems about birds' nests he is very precise about the colour of the eggs. The pewit's are 'of dingy dirty green,/ Deep blotched with splashy spots of chocolate stain'. The nightingale's are 'of deadened green, or rather olive-brown'. Again my pleasure in such descriptions is more than pleasure in the facts presented; a colour photograph of a nightingale's nest would be no substitute for Clare's poem. The skill of the poet's word-painting goes beyond the depiction of facts to become an expression of Clare's own joy. Repeatedly his work is an effusion of delight. Even 'House or Window Flies' can give him pleasure:

These little indoor dwellers, in cottages and halls, were always entertaining to me; after dancing in the window all day from sunrise to sunset they would sip of the tea, drink of the beer, and eat of the sugar, and be welcome all summer long. They look like things of mind or fairies . . .

18

A favourite expression is 'I love': 'I love ... To see the startled frog', 'I love at eventide to walk alone', 'I love to hear the evening crows go by'. The poet's copious use of 'old' seems to express affection: 'the old hare', 'the old fox', 'the old cock', 'the old grunting badger'.

Among the facts of nature, then, Clare is inspired by love. But does he find it or merely import it? In *The Progress of Rhyme* he claims to find it:

> For everything I felt a love,
> The weeds below, the birds above;
> And weeds that bloomed in summer's hours
> I thought they should be reckoned flowers;
> They made a garden free for all,
> And so I loved them great and small,
> And sung of some that pleased my eye,
> Nor could I pass the thistle by,
> But paused and thought it could not be
> A weed in nature's poesy.
> No matter for protecting wall,
> No matter though they chance to fall
> Where sheep and cows and oxen lie,
> The kindly rain when they're adry
> Falls on them with as plenteous showers
> As when it waters garden flowers;
> They look up with a blushing eye
> Upon a tender watching sky,
> And still enjoy the kindling smile
> Of sunshine though they live with toil,
> As garden flowers with all their care,
> For nature's love is ever there.

(ll. 83ff.)

Clare relates his own feelings towards what he sees to a love that suffuses the whole of nature. A 'tender' sky refreshes the flowers with 'kindly rain'; the sunshine smiles. This love, this mutual regard, transforms what would otherwise be a wilderness into a garden. Nature is both lover and artist, producing her own 'poesy'.

But if this love is really inherent in nature itself how is it that Clare can lose all sense of it, as he sometimes does? In *Decay*, for example, he laments the loss of his former joys:

> Ay, Poesy hath passed away,
>   And Fancy's visions undeceive us;
> The night hath ta'en the place of day
>   And why should passing shadows grieve us?
> I thought the flowers upon the hills
>   Were flowers from Adam's open gardens;
> But I have had my summer thrills,
>   And I have had my heart's rewardings.
>   So Poesy is on the wane,
>   I hardly know her face again.

(ll. 61ff.)

If the love derives from the poet's own mind its origins may be suspect. In the introduction to his *Selected Poems of John Clare* James Reeves (1954) advances two claims that seem to be in contradiction. At one point he emphasizes Clare's extraordinary empathy with nature:

> It is the mark of a lover, in the purest sense, that he can, at least temporarily, lose his identity in the contemplation of the object of his love. This happened to Clare habitually ... He loses himself in nature.

Later there comes a rather different claim:

> When Clare writes from his sympathy with small and helpless creatures, he is really thinking of himself. He projects his own nature on to the defenceless snail, the bee searching wearily for honey, the happy lark, the timid water bird, and, when he was feeling beaten and persecuted, the hunted badger.

The loss of identity in contemplation becomes, on this reckoning, an illusion. Even Clare, the arch-empathizer, the loving observer, in a vital sense cannot see beyond himself. The 'meanings' he sees in nature are solipsism in disguise.

The great English Romantic poets consciously encountered the same problem. In *Dejection: a Letter* Coleridge laments that he cannot respond to the loveliness of the moon and stars: 'I see, not feel, how beautiful they are.' He fears that the mountains, woods

20

and lakes that once gave him joy 'are not now to me the Things, which once they were'. He has come to see that joy as the product of his own intellect, his own mood:

> O Sara! We receive but what we give,
> And in *our* life alone does Nature live.
>
> (ll. 296–7)

Keats dramatizes a similar lapse of mood in his *Ode to a Nightingale*. Eager to partake of the happiness of the singing bird he has joined it 'on the viewless wings of Poesy'. In contrast to the pain and brevity of human life the nightingale stands for beauty and immortality. Keats associates it with the surrounding sensuous darkness, with the sweet scent of spring flowers, with remote lands and ancient legend. But his blissful reverie is cut short by what seems an incidental use of the word 'forlorn'. The poet is reminded that the ideas that made the bird seem immortal are after all the product of his own sad mind. He is returned to his 'sole self', wondering whether his experience has been truly 'a vision' or merely 'a waking dream'.

It is Wordsworth, however, who suffers most often and most keenly from this sense of being trapped within his own subjectivity. At his most confident he will speak boldly of the mysterious powers in nature:

> And I have felt
> A presence that disturbs me with the joy
> Of elevated thoughts; a sense sublime
> Of something far more deeply interfused,
> Whose dwelling is the light of setting suns,
> And the round ocean, and the living air,
> And the blue sky, and in the mind of man,
> A motion and a spirit, that impels
> All thinking things, all objects of all thought,
> And rolls through all things.
>
> (*Tintern Abbey*, ll. 94ff.)

But in the *Immortality* ode the poet laments the loss of this transcendent response:

21

> Turn wheresoe'er I may,
>   By night or day,
> The things which I have seen I now can see no more.

(ll. 7ff.)

In the same spirit as Coleridge and Keats he asks:

> Whither is fled the visionary gleam?
> Where is it now, the glory and the dream?

(ll. 56–7)

The facts of nature are unchanged, but Wordsworth *sees* differently. The inference is that 'the glory and the dream' derived from himself and are not intrinsic in physical creation. Again, arguably, the mystery declines into projection, a version of the pathetic fallacy.

But Wordsworth has an interesting fall-back position. In the section of *Tintern Abbey* from which I quote above, he goes on to speak of his love for

> the mighty world
> Of eye and ear, both what they half create,
> And what perceive . . .

(ll. 106ff.)

In the lines prefaced to *The Excursion* he refers to

> these emotions, whencesoe'er they come,
> Whether from breath of outward circumstance,
> Or from the Soul – an impulse to herself . . .

(ll. 10ff.)

Even if the sense of mystery that he celebrates is the creation of the human mind or soul is it not a great mystery still? Is it not marvellous that not only poets but man in general, if we except the occasional Crusoe, should respond to his natural surroundings, that concatenation of physical facts, with awe and love? Is it not miracle enough that we should be spiritually attuned to our environment? In some moods Wordsworth, like many of us would say 'Yes'. In others he, like most of us, would seem hungry for external certitudes, for the possibility, at least, of an escape from the confinement of subjectivity.

II
Seeing Double – the Self-Conscious Narrator

This problem of subjectivity has also been a crucial issue in the evolution of the novel. Nineteenth-century British fiction generally purported to be realistic, to offer a faithful representation of real life. The great novelists of that period found it convenient to proceed as though the achievement of verisimilitude was a straightforward matter. They expected and obtained the assent of their readers. People were ready to 'believe in' Sam Weller or Oliver Twist. The author claimed and was granted the authority to describe and define his or her characters, to pass moral judgements on them, to decide their fate. Towards the end of the century, however, the confidence that underlay these conventions began to be eroded. The very conception of 'character' was increasingly called into question. Who could claim complete knowledge of another human being – even a fictional one? Who would presume to pass absolute judgement on someone else's moral failings, or, if doing so, would expect to command general agreement? Characterization became more tentative. Authors less readily claimed omniscience. Behind all these changes lurked the acknowledgement that, after all, the 'realities' portrayed in a novel were mere inventions – products of a single mind and expressive of the limitations, as well as of the breadth, of that mind.

Most of the great modernist novels of the early part of this century, novels written in reaction to the realist tradition, were markedly autobiographical: *Buddenbrooks, A la recherche du temps perdu, Sons and Lovers, A Portrait of the Artist as a Young Man, Ulysses.* If the rationale for this trend had been spelt out, the writers concerned would have probably made the following points. 'It seems increasingly unlikely that one can ever comprehend another human being. I shall therefore write about the individual I know best – namely myself. Narrowly considered, *all*

23

fiction is transcribed autobiography, a refraction of the author's own personality. I will achieve greater candour and directness by staying within the limits of my actual experience. Again, my aim is to present a view of the world, a view inevitably subjective. To assess it adequately you will need to know a great deal about me. Accordingly I will tell you who I am, and how my mind, my emotions, my sensibilities developed. In short I will show you not only the world as I perceive it, but also the instrument of perception – my own personality. The reader can thus allow for prejudice and distortion. He or she will be enabled to see double, to contemplate simultaneously the work of art and the artist.'

A Portrait of the Artist as a Young Man is perhaps the most thorough enterprise of this kind. The title is in a sense misleading: 'the artist' is not pictured simply as a 'young man'. Joyce provides an account of his career from babyhood until the acceptance of his vocation. On first reading the narrative seems strangely discontinuous, riddled with omissions. But this is no ordinary biography; all the emphasis is on those episodes and circum-stances that have helped, directly or indirectly, to mould the character of the young artist, Stephen Dedalus. His literary evolution is further revealed by means of a remarkable technical innovation: at each stage of the story the vocabulary and style Joyce deploys are those that would have been available to Stephen himself at that point in his development. The technique is readily apparent in the opening sentences of the book, which show the infant Stephen emerging from non-verbal consciousness into baby-talk:

> Once upon a time and a very good time it was there was a moocow coming down along the road and this moocow that was coming down along the road met a nicens little boy named baby tuckoo ...

But this deliberate limitation is just as significant, though far less obvious, as Stephen moves into precocious adolescence. The style is that of a brilliant but self-conscious student, steeped in the language of Pater, Shelley, Newman and Byron.

Joyce's novel, then, is a thorough and complex exercise in detachment. His younger self is separated out, defined on its own terms, allocated its own characteristic modes of speech and thought. At first glance the author seems to have achieved the ideal that Stephen proposes: 'The artist, like the God of the creation, remains within or behind or beyond or above his handiwork, invisible, refined out of existence, indifferent, paring his fingernails.' If a writer is to extricate himself from his own subjective responses in order to 'get at' reality – in this case the accessible reality of his own former self – then perhaps these are the means to adopt.

But on reflection certain difficulties and dilemmas emerge. One problem concerns exposition. Joyce is telling the story in terms of Stephen's responses and Stephen would not reflect upon information he took for granted. But this information includes such matters as his own appearance, his age at various key junctures, the personality of his mother, the names and even the number of his brothers and sisters, and so on. Without such knowledge the reader can hardly 'place' various minor incidents, the full force of which depends crucially on such placing. The same holds true of those revelatory moments Joyce called 'epiphanies', around which the novel is constructed. These moments, derived from his own experience, can be intriguing as transcribed in the novel. But their full impact must depend upon a knowledge of the context in which they occurred – knowledge available to Joyce, and by extension to Stephen, but not to the reader. The objective account demands subjective embellishment.

On the level of style there is further difficulty. The James Joyce who writes *Portrait of the Artist* is to be distinguished from the portrayed Stephen, who comes to luxuriate in a sensuous romantic style of writing and even of thinking. But this vocabulary of Stephen's was, of course, to evolve into the vocabulary of the mature Joyce. Joyce incorporates Stephen and Stephen's experiences. It isn't easy to see where the 'Young Man' ends and the author who writes about him begins. In an obvious sense, of course, the distinction is a false one: Joyce *is*, or rather has been, Stephen. But by the same token the possibility of detachment or objectivity looks dubious. The famous climactic passage in which Stephen rhapsodizes at the sight of a girl on the sea-shore has been seen alternatively as a wonderful example of Joycean prose and as a skilfully ironic exposure of Stephen's self-conscious poeticizing. Whatever view one takes on this issue, the fact that the dispute exists shows the difficulty, for Joyce, of extricating the 'reality' of his past self from his mature personality.

In any case there is a major dilemma, ultimately inescapable, at the theoretical level. Joyce's novel might be thought to go beyond 'realism' in showing both what Stephen sees and the sensibilities of the perceiver. 'This', says Joyce in effect, 'is the person I was.' But looking back on his past to make that assessment and write his novel has involved a further set of perceptions, those of the mature Joyce, which will incorporate a further element of bias. In short the novelist's sensibility, his instrument of perception, he can assess solely by the exercise of that very instrument. He cannot step outside himself.

In this absolute sense all literature *is* doomed to be self-portraiture. Fortunately we do not usually choose to think in absolutes. I have considered *Portrait of the Artist*, an extraordinary work, only from a very narrow point of view: Joyce was far from being solely concerned with the attempt to achieve detachment. Indeed he builds into his novel a number of reminders that the detachment Stephen seeks is illusory. Nor were the great nineteenth-century novelists naive, as they are fashionably accused of being, in their adherence to realism. They were not adopting a philosophical position but working within a literary convention – 'Let us proceed *as though* reality could be straightforwardly reproduced' – which proved astonishingly fruitful. But to the extent that various literary modes are pushed towards a logical conclusion – and there will be writers and critics in every age who do push in this direction – we are obliged to acknowledge this problem of subjectivity. It is graphically represented in an image which both Escher and Steinberg have sketched in their very different styles: a hand holds a pencil which is drawing a hand which is holding a pencil which is drawing the original hand. The artist creates a work of art and the work of art displays the artist. We can imagine only what we have it in us to imagine. In the words of the aphorism: 'If the triangles invented a god, it would have three sides.'

III
Working Models:
the Novelist as Toy-Maker

The first section of this chapter dealt with the dilemma encountered by the poet who tries to explore the mystery apparently inherent in nature. The second tried to show from a different point of view how the writer is confined within his own consciousness. He is not, however, condemned to struggle endlessly and hopelessly with these insoluble problems. He may, of course, choose to ignore them. He can also contemplate them, interrogate them, play with them. This final section will glance at the work of two recent writers of fiction who experimented in this mode.

One is Isak Dinesen, who is known chiefly for her short stories. Characteristically these tales are set in remote times and exotic locales. From the opening sentence there will be a flavour of legend, or of high romance:

> On a full-moon night of 1863 a dhow was on its way from Lamu to Zanzibar, following the coast about a mile out. (*The Dreamers*)

> 'Ce pauvre Jean,' said an old Russian General with a dyed beard on a summer evening of 1875 in the drawing-room of a hotel at Baden-Baden. (*The Invincible Slave-owners*)

The cast is usually picturesque – kings, cardinals, poets, beggars, actors, seafarers. An extravagant plot is likely to be diversified with interpolated stories, poetic descriptions of nature and stylized conversations, heavy with aphorism. This artificial, even whimsical, art seems at first glance remote from 'reality', but is in fact able to comment profoundly on the great issues of life – love, salvation, courage, creativity, order.

Typically in a Dinesen story a character tries to get towards truth by a kind of trick. He or she will attempt to stage-manage a sequence of events, to impose a fiction on life. At the point where that fiction goes awry a larger pattern is revealed. It is as though God has been forced to show his hand by concluding the story as he sees fit. He is the supreme story-teller: our fictions feebly emulate his.

This abstract programme is best explained by analysis of a particular story. *Sorrow-acre* is a convenient and particularly impressive example. Set in Denmark, in the late eighteenth century, it tells how the lord of a country estate sets a challenge to one of his peasants, Anne-Marie. Her son is in danger of imprisonment. The old lord will have him released if the mother can mow, between sunrise and sunset, a field that normally provides three days' mowing for a man. She accepts his terms and labours all day while her master, clad in lace and brocade and tended by footmen, keeps watch. She just succeeds, but dies in the moment of success.

This drama is witnessed by a young man named Adam, potentially heir to the estate. Adam has travelled widely in Europe and absorbed the new ideas of romanticism and reform. He is appalled by the challenge and his protests oblige his uncle to defend the feudal tradition that he represents. The old man argues that he has given his word. He and Anne-Marie are both committed to a system in which the lord's word is absolute. If he relented through pity he would seem to mock the woman's efforts. His implacability gives the task definition, as his courteous presence gives it dignity.

But this argument from tradition is less important than a second line of defence. When Adam pleads, justly, that the original ultimatum had been merely a matter of whim or caprice, the old man replies that the Word of God might, for all we know, have been similarly capricious but has none the less become 'the principle of our world, its law and gravitation'. The lord's arbitrariness is a version of God's arbitrariness. Anne-Marie's heroism and eventual triumph is its vindication.

Her story, however, is framed by a wider one. Adam will inherit only if his uncle fails to produce an heir. The old man has recently taken a young bride in the hope of continuing the line. While he sips his morning chocolate in the field his wife stands naked before her mirror and sees how her beautiful body has been marked by whalebone and garter, the constraints of tradition. She comes of aristocratic stock, but when 'the hunting instincts of her breed' are aroused it is only in the interest of catching a flea that is biting her leg. The old way of life is declining towards decadence and absurdity. As the day goes by, the old lord seems to age and dwindle. The story hints that at his death Adam will marry the young widow and reform the estate.

In the course of the day, curiously enough, the nephew has recovered from his revulsion and reached a reconciliation with the old man. After threatening to go to America, the new world, he changes his mind and tells his uncle that he will stay. What moves him is the realization that if the lord has created a fiction in which Anne-Marie becomes a character, so equally is the lord a character in the wider story that is told by God. The old man has already lost a son but has accepted that blow and the impending demise of the family with dignity and courage. In a sense he asks no more of Anne-Marie than has been asked of himself. But Adam has been enabled to glimpse this wider story, in which his uncle plays the tragic role, only by means of the fiction that the old man capriciously composed.

In its strategy, if not its subject-matter, *Sorrow-acre* is a typical Dinesen tale. It is a strategy that sheds an interesting light on the subjectivity problem. It suggests that there need be no stable, higher reality beyond the reach of the human mind. Our lives, our aspirations, are essentially no more substantial, no more serious, than those of characters in the stories we tell and read. 'Meaning' is to be found by accepting one's destiny, playing out with conviction the role assigned in the life one is involved with. As a writer exclaims in *The Young Man with the Carnation*: 'Almighty God, as the heavens are higher than the earth, so are thy short stories higher than our short stories.'

There has not been space here to convey the *quality* of *Sorrow-acre*, but simply to say something of the method of the story and of the ideas that the method implies. My account of Nabokov's *Pale Fire* must be sketchier still since this is a full-length novel and a notorious puzzle-piece that has generated volumes of explanation and counter-explanation. What the work has in common with Dinesen's tales is the element of conscious artifice, almost of sport. *Sorrow-acre* tells the story of an old man who initiates a kind of game; *Pale Fire* is, in effect, a game – which the reader is invited, or challenged, to play.

The account that is to follow will not make full sense without some explanatory words about the author. Vladimir Nabokov was born in 1899, in St Petersburg. His father was a lawyer and a courageous liberal politician. The family was prosperous. The boy had a happy childhood and was brought up trilingual, fluent in Russian, English and French. In 1919, as a consequence of the revolution, the Nabokovs were obliged to leave Russia. The father was assassinated in Berlin, in 1922.

After studying at Cambridge Nabokov spent the years 1925–40 in France and Germany. He published, in Russian, eight novels and a number of short stories and plays. In 1940 he went to the United States, where he found employment as a professor of literature. He began to write in English and achieved notoriety with *Lolita* in the late 1950s. *Pale Fire* appeared in 1962 and confirmed his reputation as a major writer. He eventually retired to Switzerland, where he died in 1977.

As a boy he practised conjuring. He was an excellent games player and sportsman – a cyclist, a horseman, a soccer goal-keeper. In Berlin he kept himself for a time by tennis coaching. He composed what he claims were the first Russian crossword puzzles, for an émigré newspaper. By his own account he 'devoted a prodigious amount of time' to devising chess problems. He translated *Alice in Wonderland* into Russian. All these activities may have had a bearing on his interest in the novel as an exercise in trickery, puzzlement, or sport – though *Through the Looking-Glass* would be the more obvious antecedent to *Pale Fire*.

The dizzying complexity of this novel only gradually becomes apparent. The book consists of four parts, a foreword, a 999-line poem in heroic couplets, called 'Pale Fire', by a poet named John Shade, an extensive commentary on that poem and an index. The foreword is by Charles Kinbote, a lecturer at Wordsmith College, where Shade had been a colleague. In it he explains how he came to know Shade and how he acquired the manuscript when the poet was shot, a few months previously.

The poem is straightforward, often conversational, in style. Shade writes personally and anecdotally about his own experi-ences and in particular about his relationships with his wife and with his sad, plain daughter who committed suicide. Essentially the theme is death and the possibility or otherwise of an afterlife.

It quickly becomes apparent that Kinbote's commentary on Shade's poem is ludicrously subjective. He uses the text as a starting-point for his own revelations. His personality is unwittingly revealed. He is a large, boring, bearded, unhappy, paranoid, lonely, vegetarian homosexual with bad breath. Having arrived in Wordsmith College in the spring he proceeded to hang around Shade, cornering him at every opportunity to pester him with reminiscences about his native country, Zembla, and in particular with stories about Zembla's exiled king, Charles the Beloved. His hope and belief had been that 'Pale Fire', which he had watched Shade writing all summer, would celebrate this deposed monarch. His notes reflect a growing petulance and distress at its failure to do so.

The index is hilariously wilful and freakish. Typically the entry for 'Kinbote' is far longer than the entry for 'Shade'. Various of Kinbote's college enemies are insulted or omitted.

At a fairly early point in the commentary the alert reader, proud to be ahead of the game, will guess that Kinbote is himself Charles the Beloved. The stories he has been telling Shade about that monarch's Zemblan past – stories that he retells in his notes – are autobiographical. The homosexual king has settled in America under an alias because he fears his political opponents. His fears are justified because, as he goes on to explain, Shade was shot in error by Jakob Gradus, a Zemblan extremist, who had come to assassinate King Charles.

But before reaching the account of the killing the same alert reader will have come to another conclusion. Odd hints in the foreword have been confirmed by various details in the commentary: Kinbote is mad. He is 'really' Professor Botkin, an 'American scholar of Russian descent', referred to only incidentally in the commentary. The manic editor has been diagnosed as suffering from 'cerebral sclerosis'. Shade was 'really' killed by an escaped homicidal maniac named Jack Grey, who mistook him for Judge Goldsworth (in whose house Shade was staying) who had passed the sentence of imprisonment.

Zembla, it would seem, is all fantasy. Just as Alice's normal world of nursery rhymes, chess games, governesses and aunts is transformed in a dream-like way behind the looking-glass, so Zembla is a transcription of New Wye, where Botkin lives. Various aspects of the town and the college are recognizable in their transposed form. For example, Gerald Emerald, a lecturer who had spurned 'Kinbote's' advances, features in Zembla as

Izumrudov, one of the leaders of the regicide group. If Botkin, as the index suggests, has a Russian past, then no doubt that, too, provides ingredients for the imaginary Zembla.

But the reader who has gone this far is beginning to skid down a slippery slope. What *is* 'real' in *Pale Fire*? If 'Kinbote' can invent Zembla might he not equally have invented Shade and Shade's poem? There are critics who read the novel in just this way. Of the two main characters only Kinbote 'exists'; Shade is a figment of his fantasy. But this reading can be turned on its head. Many hold the view that Shade is the author not only of the poem, but of the whole book, foreword, commentary and all.

I have to leave on one side the arguments as to *why* either of these characters should have felt a need, or desire, to invent the other and to assemble this complex structure. Suffice it to say that plausible arguments as to motive can be mounted for either case. The immediate point to grasp concerns the nature of the game Nabokov invites the reader to play. His book is an extraordinary latticework of clues, counter-clues, contra-dictions, confirmations and false trails. The cross-referencing is so intricate that the novel has to be read twice to be read at all and should be read several more times by those who are seri-ously interested in exploring its secrets. Whatever truth or 'reality' it may eventually prove to contain, it manifestly con-tains falsehoods. The reader must begin by adjudicating between the more obviously contradictory claims – as to who murdered Shade, for example. There is evidence to marshal and assess. The early moves in the game can be made confidently enough. Later the going gets harder. I'd advise the reader who wants to try to crack the code to look out particularly for references to wheelbarrows, trucks and the girl in the black leotard. Passages that repay close attention include lines 609–16 of the poem, and the long note to lines 433–4.

But my concern here is neither to offer an explication of the novel nor to attempt a critical assessment. *Pale Fire* is a very specialized taste. Those who, in a literary sense, prefer football to chess will prefer to read, say, *Great Expectations* or *Anna Karenina*. What is important, and interesting, is seeing the *point* of the elaborate game that Nabokov has invented.

The opening lines of Shade's poem are crucial:

> I was the shadow of the waxwing slain
> By the false azure in the windowpane;
> I was the smudge of ashen fluff – and I
> Lived on, flew on, in the reflected sky.

The bird with which the poet identifies hits the window and falls, deceived by the reflection of the sky in the glass. But the suggestion is that the bird's soul, or the idea of the bird, penetrates the pane and flies on through the imagined blue. The image is directly relevant to the poet's discussion of the possibility of life after death: the body fails, but the spirit survives in some abstract world. More central to the novel as a whole, however, is a second meaning of the image, which links *Pale Fire* with that great proto-modernist work *Through the Looking-Glass*. In broad terms the glass stands for consciousness. On one side of it lies the 'real' world of people and phenomena. On the other side is the mental or imaginative life into which these 'facts' are translated. That translation may result in fantasy, in maniacal delusion, or in a work of art. In trying to guess which is the 'actual' world of *Pale Fire* and which the imagined world we are induced to wonder whether the former is in effect any more 'real' than the latter. The madman or the artist may find his private vision more substantial than the experiences that have given rise to it. The external world is in any case resistant, as we have seen, to simple description or definition. What adjustment can be achieved between the inner and the outer vision?

Ultimately, of course, whether Shade is real and Kinbote fantasy, or vice versa, both are inventions. It is easy to see how either character might speak for his creator. Nabokov was a Russian who became an American, a poet who became an editor (of Pushkin's *Eugene Onegin*, for which he provided a notoriously wide-ranging and idiosyncratic commentary). The psychological equilibrium that either of his characters might achieve by inventing the other, he perhaps achieves by inventing both of them. He has found a means of imaginatively fusing impressions of his academic life in America with romanticized recollections of his Russian boyhood. What is finally 'real' is the work of art thus created.

In *Through the Looking-Glass* Alice has an intriguing

argument with Tweedledum and Tweedledee when the three of them come upon the Red King, who is lying asleep:

'He's dreaming now,' said Tweedledee: 'and what do you think he's dreaming about?'

Alice said: 'Nobody can guess that.'

'Why, about *you*!' Tweedledee exclaimed, clapping his hands triumphantly. 'And if he left off dreaming about you, where do you suppose you'd be?'

'Where I am now, of course,' said Alice.

'Not you!' Tweedledee retorted contemptuously. 'You'd be nowhere. Why, you're only a sort of thing in his dream!'

'If that there King was to wake,' added Tweedledum, 'you'd go out – bang! – just like a candle!'

'I shouldn't!' Alice exclaimed indignantly. 'Besides, if *I'm* only a sort of thing in his dream, what are *you*, I should like to know?'

'Ditto,' said Tweedledum.

'Ditto, ditto!' cried Tweedledee.

He shouted this so loud that Alice couldn't help saying 'Hush! You'll be waking him, I'm afraid, if you make so much noise.'

'Well, it's no use *your* talking about waking him,' said Tweedledum, 'when you're only one of the things in his dream. You know very well you're not real.'

'I *am* real!' said Alice, and began to cry.

This famous argument has many applications. Implicit in it is the question: 'Have we invented – dreamed up – the god that we believe invented us?' As Martin Gardner (1965) remarks in a comment in *The Annotated Alice*: 'An odd sort of infinite regress is involved here ... Alice dreams of the King, who is dreaming of Alice, who is dreaming of the King, and so on.' Carroll himself was evidently interested in the dilemma, for he returns to it at the very end of his book. Alice asks her kitten whether it was she herself or the Red King who 'dreamed it all'. Carroll passes the question to his readers: 'Which do you think it was?' Well, it could hardly have been the Red King; animated chessmen don't exist. But then again the Alice of the story is not 'real', although she is based upon the real-life Alice Pleasance Liddell. The true dreamer is Lewis Carroll. But Carroll is 'really' Charles Lutwidge Dodgson. The notion of 'fact' retreats like the horizon-line as one fiction melts into another.

What Nabokov and Dinesen propose, in their different ways, is a consolation not too remote from what I described earlier as Wordsworth's fall-back position. Instead of striving after some fixed, objective, external truth we should find comfort in a sort of relativity. A few years ago a book was published called *Masquerade*, which presented a series of puzzles in words and pictures. When solved, these puzzles gave sufficient information to enable the solver to recover a valuable piece of jewellery that had been secretly buried. Many serious readers have tended to approach literature in a spirit something like that of the treasure-seekers who pored over *Masquerade*. If the mysteries of a given work were solved, then a treasure would indeed be found – not, of course, a physical treasure, but a mental or spiritual one – a message, a truth. Nabokov offers nothing like this. You need only look up 'Crown Jewels' in the index to *Pale Fire* to see how specifically he excludes easy solutions of this sort. The 'treasure' is not to be found as the result of the search but in the search itself. As you cross-relate and cross-relate the clues of *Pale Fire* you perceive, and indeed create, patterns. What we are offered is the inference that such patterning, and potentiality for patterning, could only exist in a patterned universe:

> A system of cells interlinked within
> Cells interlinked within cells interlinked
> Within one stem.

> ('Pale Fire', ll. 704–6)

As Shade moves towards the conclusion of his poem he expresses confidence in just such an idea:

> I feel I understand
> Existence, or at least a minute part
> Of my existence, only through my art,
> In terms of combinational delight;
> And if my private universe scans right,
> So does the verse of galaxies divine ...

> (ll. 970 ff.)

Nabokov doesn't permit the reader to share this confidence on easy terms. Within a few minutes of penning those lines Shade is shot dead, and his poem is left unfinished. But he dies (if he has ever 'lived') only within a fiction – perhaps a fiction which he himself has created. If we wish to judge the case more precisely we are obliged to seek the evidence, as Shade has suggested, 'in terms of combinational delight'. The game continues.

Chapter Three

Sociology

KRISHAN KUMAR

It is said that habit is Second Nature; but perhaps Nature is
only First Habit.

Pascal, *Pensées* (*c.* 1659)

Culture, A 'Second Nature'

Imagine a human baby, abandoned at birth alone on a desert
island. Suppose it doesn't immediately make a meal for a prow-
ling predator. What would its capacity for survival be? What
would it produce naturally, out of its biological make-up, that
would help it to cope with its environment? What is there,
biologically speaking, in the baby – in 'human nature'?

Very little, it appears. The baby would have a few physical
reflexes, such as a tendency to curl its toes around objects and to
suck anything that stroked its cheeks (on a desert island that is
more likely to be a poisonous weed than anything like a mother's
breast). These may or may not help it to survive. But it would not
be averse to drowning in a pool of warm water, sensing there only
a return to the warmth of the womb. Above all, even if it survived
for some time it would produce no *instincts* that would give it a
basic repertoire of responses with which to confront its environment. Faced with the sight of a particular plant, or the smell of a
particular animal, it would produce no automatic behaviour
governed by internal, unthinking, prompting. It would eat a

poisonous plant or stroke a dangerous animal as readily, and as randomly, as it sucked a cherry or cavorted with a koala. Even after many years, moreover, it probably would not walk; it certainly would not talk. In almost all the ways we think of someone as human, the baby would not grow up human. It would be a freak or a monster, neither man nor beast.

I may seem to have made this picture a little too harsh. I may have set unfair conditions. After all, most mammals, especially the higher mammals, develop their characteristic patterns of behaviour through early interaction with other members of their species. Very few develop instincts in total isolation. Most are also fairly plastic in infancy. A kitten, for instance, can experimentally be made to befriend, love and co-operate with a rat. The problem – for the kitten – is that once it has grown up it cannot change that pattern of behaviour. It will always and everywhere attempt to befriend rats, to its evident loss of esteem and friends among other cats. In the wild this pattern of behaviour would not normally be allowed to develop. It has no 'survival value' for cats. But the normal 'instinctive' animosity of cats to rats is an evolutionary heritage that has to be confirmed anew in every generation. Once learned, as in almost every case it speedily will be by the young, it sets up a chain of stimulus (rat) and response (attack) that is virtually unbreakable. This chain is what we call an instinct.

A rigid invariability of behaviour is at the heart of the instinct concept. An instinct is the response of a fully matured organism. As the animal develops physically into adulthood, the organic plasticity of early infancy gives way to a hardening of the neuro-chemical paths linking the organs and tissues. A particular stimulus increasingly gives rise to a particular, unvarying response – even when, as in the case of sheep following their leader over a precipice, the response is suicidal. Armed with a battery of such instincts, an adult organism, even in isolation, is able to respond adequately to most of the normal challenges of its environment. It is sensitized to friend and foe alike; it recognizes favourable feeding and breeding opportunities.

But by the same token it is incapable of changing its behaviour to meet changing circumstances. An instinct that is a blessing in one set of circumstances may be a curse in another. A mother robin will calmly watch her offspring die a few inches away from her because it has been displaced in the nest by a young cuckoo, to whose immediate presence and gaping mouth the mother instinctively responds (Russell, 1946, pp. 104–5). Too many instances of this kind and the robin species would die out. A dramatic or drastic change in the environment can mean that a species will find its instinctive equipment leading it along the path to extinction. This indeed is largely the story of evolution to date: a series of blind alleys, the result of specialized adaptation to an environment which has a deadly habit of shifting in unexpected ways.

The human species, alone, does not conform to this pattern (and therefore if it shares the common fate this will be entirely its own doing). The isolated human baby's predicament – that it exhibits no pattern of orderly growth and so is at the mercy of its environment – is the human species' salvation. As a result of an interruption and redirection of normal mammalian embryonic development – a mutation known as 'foetalization', specifically a form of embryonic regression – the human animal never fully matures. Compared with other mammals our organic growth rate is exceedingly slow; 'we rot before we ripen', as Julian Huxley cheerfully observes. 'Judged by the law (which applies to most other mammals) which regulates the amount of food consumed before the adult phase is reached, man's immaturity has been lengthened some sevenfold' (Huxley, 1955, p. 526).

This has been man's great opportunity. In wiping out the adult phase of normal mammalian growth, we have also wiped out instincts in man. The human organism does not harden into instincts. The learning period in humans continues – uniquely – throughout the life span. The fatal closure against a changing environment, which instincts impose in the case of all other species, is absent in us. We can in principle adapt to any environment, present or future. If survival consists in adaptability as well as adaptedness, then the human species alone is in a position to maintain the continuity of life.

J. B. S. Haldane's description of us as 'mad monkeys' vividly suggests the difficulties as well as the opportunities of this novel condition. We have no innate 'human nature', no given or fixed biological character. For us, as Pascal says, 'there is nothing that cannot be made natural; there is nothing natural that cannot be lost'. We make our own nature; we have no choice in this. But lacking instincts or drives, we also lack structure; and structure is necessary for survival. Here our unique plasticity and extended phase of learning have come to our rescue. They have provided a solution that, in principle at least, is among the most dazzling of nature's inventions. Instead of adapting to the environment by structural alterations in the physical organism, as do most other species, we adapt by creating and transforming structures external to our bodies. We have infinitely expanded our adaptive capacity by adding to our bodies 'extrasomatic organs' – tools, language, laws. We can discard, or change, or add to these without in any way modifying the physical structure of the human organism (although the shrinking size of the human toe, as we rely less and less on our feet, suggests at least some minor modifications). Instead of waiting upon the accident of genetic mutation to give us new structures and patterns of behaviour, we can constantly vary the type and amount of our 'extrasomatic organs' in response to changes in the environment. Instead of growing fur in a particularly cold climatic phase, we merely don thick clothes (often the fur of other species). Placed in a hot desert environment we change our clothes, or turn on the air-conditioning system. As a means of coping with the widest range of environments and of adapting to changes within them, no more powerful or flexible device can be imagined.

The sum of these extrasomatic organs we call culture. In losing the carapace of instincts we have donned the mantle of culture. Through culture we adapt to our natural environment. It is the means by which we satisfy our primary needs for food, clothing and shelter. But in satisfying those needs we create a new reality, a secondary or cultural reality. Increasingly the reality we have to adapt to is one of our own making. The tools, laws and language with which we confront the world themselves become a world within which we live, with its own pressures and demands. More than this, they become the means or the medium by and through which we relate to reality of any kind. 'Nature' for us is not something 'out there', a pure or pristine reality which we can directly perceive through our senses. Nature is for us 'human nature', a set of objects, and responses to them, which are our own cultural creation. Culture is our nature. We are cultural animals.

In throwing off the domination of instincts and replacing them with culture, we have become at once the freest and most dependent of all the species of creation. Cultural items are social, not individual, inventions. They are collectively maintained and, where necessary, collectively transformed. We are the most intensely social of all species. The human individual outside society is not only helpless, as in the case of our hypothetical baby on the island, but also meaningless. When Aristotle said that 'man is by nature a political animal [*zoon politikon*]' he did not mean that we live for parliamentary elections. *Zoon politikon* is better translated as 'social animal'. Aristotle meant that as creatures our whole meaning and existence are bound up with the life of the *polis*, the society. 'Man', he says, 'is a being whose nature it is to live with others.' A man outside a *polis* is not a man but 'either a beast or a god' (Aristotle, 1952, p. 5). In similar terms, a modern anthropologist has said that without culture man would be 'functionally incomplete, not merely a talented ape who had, like some underprivileged child, unfortunately been prevented from realizing his full potentialities, but a kind of formless monster with neither sense of direction nor power of self control, a chaos of spasmodic impulses and vague emotions' (Geertz, 1973, p. 99).

Our dependence on society is the primary fact of our existence. What is the nature of that social or cultural reality in which humans have their being – which is, indeed, the human essence?

Speech and Symbols

Our reality is, first and perhaps most of all, a linguistic reality. Or, since language is one kind of symbolic system, a set of conventionalized sounds and signs, we can say that our reality is primarily based on symbols.

The world 'out there' is for us a world clothed in symbols. These symbols identify or 'indicate' certain aspects of the environment to us and also structure our responses to them. When teaching a class once in Boulder, Colorado, I gestured at the mountains rising massively and magnificently from the edge of the Boulder campus. They are a part of the chain known as the Rocky Mountains. What, I asked the students, did the Rockies mean – 'symbolize' – to them? For many the Rockies were a place where they skied (Vail and Aspen are just down the road). For some the Rockies presented a mountaineering challenge: they saw them as rocks for climbing. Others saw them as a site of scenic beauty, or a 'wilderness' tract: they were a place for rambling or 'backpacking', for camping and sleeping out under the stars. For some, too, the Rockies in their majesty possessed a religious, mystical significance: they were a place for prayer, for religious 'feasts' and weddings in the woods. We thought of other meanings, not represented in the class. For the geologist the Rockies represent one of the most important areas of scientific research in the world (the Grand Canyon is part of the chain). Businessmen and prospectors, past and present, have looked at the Rockies with a different eye. For them, the Rockies are an Aladdin's cave rich in mineral resources – silver, gold, latterly shale for oil.

Different meanings, different objects. 'The Rockies', it turns out, is not one but many things – in some instances, incompatible things, as for the nature worshipper and the mineral prospector. We can, of course, attach several meanings to the same object. It can symbolize different things just as the same meaning can sometimes be attached to several apparently different objects. Freudianism is rampant with examples of the latter kind; take the case of sexual fetishism, where a parrot-handled umbrella may have the same meaning as the conventional erotogenic zones of the male or female anatomy.

But whether there is one thing with different meanings, or one meaning with different things, things and meanings remain inseparable. They are two parts of a bonded whole. Things only exist in so far as they have meaning – interest, value, purpose, function – for us. Without associating ourselves with the furthest reaches of philosophical idealism, we might say that the only way we recognize things in the world is by conferring meaning or value on them. We endow the world with symbols and respond to the meanings contained in them. So there are as many things in the world, and only such things, as we have meanings for at any given time.

Language and other symbolic systems codify these meanings. In using language, or other kinds of signs such as gestures, we impose a sort of grid on reality. Since language and other symbolic systems are social products, this is a socially constructed grid. So our reality is a social reality. There is not for us such a thing as 'pure' physical or natural reality – none, at any rate, that we can so recognize. A physical gesture such as a raised hand can be a threat or a greeting. We have no way of knowing which, unless we have learned to understand the place such a 'sign' has in the culture of the person or people concerned. Until we know that – and it could be fairly important that we know it fast – the gesture remains literally empty, devoid of all meaning or significance. Language places it and gives it meaning. Without a word to describe a thing, it remains unintelligible – to all intents and purposes, non-existent.

In line with this argument, Alasdair MacIntyre has said that 'the limits of action are the limits of description, [and] that the delineation of a society's concepts is therefore the crucial step in the delineation of its life' (MacIntyre, 1962, pp. 62–3). We can take an example from the history of social and political action. The concept of revolution, as a form of political action, acquired its modern meaning only in the eighteenth century, in the course of the French Revolution. Before that it was used largely as a scientific term in astronomy, to describe the cyclical motions of the stars and planets (as in Copernicus's *On the Revolutions of the Celestial Bodies*, 1543). If applied to politics, it echoed this derivation, denoting political upheavals that seemed to represent the turns of a political cycle. Eventually, by a series of 'revolutions', the cycle would return to its original starting-point, just as the heavenly bodies did. So Clarendon called the restoration of the Stuart monarchy in 1660 a revolution, while the events of 1640–60, which we often today call 'the English Revolution', he described as 'the Great Rebellion'. Nobody at the time called the Civil War of 1640–60 a revolution; that had to wait until the French historian Guizot designated it such in 1827, by analogy with the French Revolution.

Not only did the word revolution not mean the creation of something new, a new system of government or a new social order; political actors before the eighteenth century were entirely lacking in a term which allowed them to conceive of the making of a new order. When attempting change, they thought always of *restoring* an older order of things, of getting back to some 'purer' form of government or the 'original' state of society. This allowed them to do quite a bit: cutting off a king's head and abolishing the monarchy, in the case of the English Civil War. But it remained a fundamental barrier to political action before the eighteenth century that no concept existed which enabled societies to go beyond past forms. Revolutionary change, the total trans-formation of man and society, did not have a place in their poli-tical vocabulary. Lacking the word, they lacked the thing. All change had to be conceived and conducted under conservative auspices. Even the Levellers and Diggers, the most radical of the Civil War sects, remained imprisoned in their religious termino-logy. In picturing the good society they were forced to fall back on the practices of the primitive church; while as for the agency of change, nothing seemed to them more potent than the millennial Second Coming of Christ as prophesied in the Book of Revelation.

Language, as this example suggests, is a social fact. It exhibits an external, coercive and thing-like power – the characteristic attributed to all social facts by the French sociologist Émile Durkheim (Durkheim, 1964). It selects certain things for our attention and ignores or rejects others. If we can't say it, we can't think it; if we can't think it, we can't act on it. In inventing and enforcing *Newspeak*, a language of limited vocabulary and narrowly defined concepts, the totalitarian rulers of George Orwell's *Nineteen Eighty-Four* hoped to eliminate dangerous thoughts and rebellious actions. They had gradually removed old words such as 'honour', 'justice', 'morality', 'internationalism', 'democracy', 'science', 'freedom'. In their place were terms which evoked a quite different reality.

> A few blanket words covered them, and, in covering them, abolished them. All words grouping themselves around the concepts of liberty and equality, for instance, were contained in the single word *crimethink*, while all words grouping themselves around the concepts of objectivity and ration-alism were contained in the single word *oldthink*.
>
> (Orwell, 1954, p. 246)

44

But, as the example of revolution again shows, social facts are not set in concrete, for all time. They are social institutions and like all such institutions have a specific structure and a specific history, reflecting the life of the society in which they evolve. One way, in fact, of seeing the power of language to determine our reality is to consider the range and variety of languages in the world. Different languages define or discover different realities. The co-ordinates of the 'grid' they impose on reality differ with different societies. Different words, different grammars, different metaphors, these equal different ways of seeing, conceptualizing and acting in the world.

> No two languages are ever sufficiently similar to be considered as representing the same social reality. The worlds in which different societies live are distinct worlds, not merely the same world with different labels attached.
>
> (Sapir, 1956, p. 69)

The Aztecs have only one word for snow, frost, ice and cold. English has only one word for snow. The Eskimos have no general word for snow at all, but have over twenty words for different kinds of snow – snow on the ground, snow falling, snow drifting and so on. Their virtuosity is partly matched by the Koya of South India, whose language distinguishes among seven types of bamboo (Robertson, 1981, p. 73). It is surpassed by the gauchos of the Argentine, whose language gives them over a hundred terms by which to discriminate between the shadings of a horse's hide. All these differences can readily be traced back to the different ecologies and economies of the different societies; but George Steiner, who gives the example of the gauchos, raises the pertinent question: 'Do these terms in some manner precede the perception of the actual nuance of colour, or does that perception, sharpened by professional need, cause the invention of new words?' (Steiner, 1969, p. 87).

Differences of vocabulary are among the simplest ways in which language 'slices up' reality. Differences of grammar and metaphoric imagery make for more interesting and significant divisions within reality. The lack of a *tu* or *Du* form in modern English means that English speakers cannot immediately indicate the quality or type of social relationship between themselves and others. The Navajo Indian language contains no active verbs; in Navajo thought people do not so much act on the world as flow with it, participating in its varied phenomena as elements in a cosmic process. The language of the Hopi Indians lacks the equivalent of past, present and future tenses; the universe is organized into categories of 'manifest' (things that are or have been accessible to the physical senses) and 'manifesting' (things that are not accessible to the physical senses) (Robertson, 1981, p. 73). Another way of classifying the world is suggested by an interesting example of the use of metaphor, also from Latin America:

> There is a Latin-American Indian language, indeed there are a number, in which the future – the notion of that which is yet to happen – is set at the back of the speaker. The past which he can see, because it has already happened, lies all before him. He backs into the future unknown; memory moves forward, hope backwards. This is the exact reversal of the primary coordinates by which we organize our feelings in root metaphors.
>
> (Steiner, 1969, p. 87)

A language is a form of ideology. It selects, that is, from all theoretically possible descriptions of reality. But how can we know what is 'theoretically possible' if our consciousness is limited by our language? Is this not to smuggle in some concept of a non-social reality by the back door? Not necessarily. We can compare languages, which is a way of comparing cultures. The importance of this is suggested by Goethe's remark that 'the man who knows only one language does not even know that one properly'. Looking at other cultures is a way of looking at ourselves. Or we can look back into our own cultural past for alternative descriptions of reality. Used with caution, history is a cultural laboratory. Because human inventions, unlike the physical modifications of other species, are social not individual, they do not die with particular organisms. They accumulate in traditions. All cultures are storehouses of buried, discarded, or superseded meanings and interpretations of reality. These can, on occasion, be retrieved to act as a critical commentary on present beliefs and practices.

In these ways we can partly escape from a full-blooded linguistic or cultural determinism. Karl Marx suggested another way. Ideologies, he said, are never total, never completely closed off. They reflect the ideas and interests of the dominant social class: 'the ruling ideas of any age are the ideas of the ruling class' (Marx, 1963, p. 39). The reign of such a class is, however, only temporary. Its hold on society is progressively undermined by the contradiction between the legal and political framework of society and the new forces of production developing in the economic base. This contradiction leads to the rise to power of new classes, with alternative ideologies or 'world-views'. They in turn will, after a period of dominance, succumb to other classes. So in the Marxist schema the 'feudal' ideology of the medieval landowning aristocracy gave way to the 'bourgeois' ideology of the industrial capitalists and this in turn is destined to give way to the 'socialist' ideology of the industrial working class. The point is that these ideologies do not succeed each other in strict sequence, but overlap. In any society at any time, according to Marx, we are likely to see a struggle taking place between competing ideologies, based on competing classes. Such a conflict prevents the crystallization of one overall ideology which might shut out all alternative conceptions of reality.

With Marx, we enter upon a new kind of fracturing of social reality. The plurality of languages brings about one kind, that caused by divisions between cultures. For Marx the primary divisions are within cultures. How far do these subdivisions or 'sub-cultures' go? How does society, through its internal organization, seek to create a stable reality?

Small Worlds

No society is homogeneous. All, even the simplest, are differentiated in some way. Biology is used to underscore some of these differences but it is never the sufficient basis of them. So, for instance, all societies distinguish between the old and the young. But concepts of age and youth vary widely. In some societies the supposed wisdom and experience of the old enable them to control society to the very end of their days. In others they are treated as an inconvenience – tolerated, even cared for, but fundamentally a nuisance and in any case, by the obsolescence of their skills and knowledge, useless in the running of society.

Similarly with sex. There is no known society in which men are not considered the superior of women. But ideas of 'masculinity' and 'femininity' nevertheless seem to bear little relation to the relatively minor biological differences between the sexes. Not only do some societies, such as modern western ones, accentuate the division to the point of virtually creating two species, male and female. There seems, on a cross-cultural view, no general pattern or agreement about what is appropriately feminine or masculine behaviour. The modern western idea that women are fragile and delicate creatures – actually an invention of the upper classes of twelfth-century Europe – is belied both by the attitude of many non-western societies, where women do the bulk of the heavy agricultural work, and by the west's own pre-industrial pattern of equal work tasks for men and women.

Even more telling are Margaret Mead's examples from New Guinea. There she found one tribe, the Arapesh, where the outlook and behaviour of both sexes conformed to a type westerners would call 'feminine': gentle, passive, emotional, caring. Then there were the stormy Mundugumor, among whom both sexes exhibited decidedly 'masculine' characteristics: violent, aggressive, cannibalistic. The women dreaded pregnancy, hated nursing their children and were generally hostile towards them. A third tribe, the Tchambuli, stressed the differences between the sexes but reversed the normal western pattern. The women were domineering and energetic and scorned the wearing of ornaments. They did most of the work and made the largest economic contribution. The men did little work. They gossiped, engaged in endless petty quarrels, were expressive and artistic and were gentle and caring towards the children (and were thought superior to women in Tchambuli ideology (M. Mead, 1963).

The biological basis of racial divisions in society is equally unclear and equally reworked by society. Though by definition racial divisions fasten upon some physical characteristic – skin colour, height, hairiness – these are always the rather exiguous biological base for an immense cultural superstructure reared o them. Beliefs about and attitudes towards races are the result of cultural stereotypes. Sometimes these are simply an aspect of the usual in-group/out-group hostility between different societies: we yellow-skinned Chinese are superior to you white foreign devils. But where race is a principle of division internal to society, it is almost always the consequence not of spontaneously observed biological differences but of social and political processes: slavery, conquest, or colonization. The dark skin of an African or Asian in western society stands as the physical symbol, the easily identifiable badge, of peoples who have been enslaved or colonized. The biological inferiority attributed to them in racist ideology is a consequence, not a cause, of the social fact of white supremacy. Once firmly established, however, a racist ideology will operate with a built-in 'self-fulfilling prophecy'. People thought inferior will be consigned to the lowest levels of education and occupation in the society, thereby reinforcing the notion of their racial inferiority.

As is clear from the cases of age, sex and race, societies do not simply divide their members into groups, they also rank them. Man is, according to some thinkers, *homo hierarchicus* (Dumont, 1972). Social groups are ranked in a hierarchy of power, prestige, wealth and social worth. No absolutely egalitarian society has ever been found (which does not mean it could never be made). Hierarchy and inequality introduce another dimension of social reality. People of the same age, sex, race tend to consort together, setting up vertical lines of divisions within society. But these vertical lines are often cut across by a horizontal layering of group on group, in a system of ranks. One way of classifying societies is by the extent to which they stress the vertical principle of integration, as traditional, non-industrial societies tend to, or the horizontal principles, as is more commonly the case with modern industrial societies. In a traditional society, such as most peasant societies, landowner and peasant may be bound together by many kinds of reciprocal services in a relationship of patron and client. Here the vertical principle predominates. In a modern industrial society, on the other hand, a middle-class woman may feel that she has more in common with the men of her class than with the women of a lower class. The horizontal tie of class has cut across the vertical tie of sex. An ideally integrated society would balance vertical against horizontal divisions.

Age, sex, race can all be – and have been – categories of inequality as well as of differentiation. Old rule young, men women, white black. But two other kinds of horizontal grouping have been especially powerful: caste and class. The traditional Indian caste system combined in a spectacular way vertical and horizontal principles of integration. For over two and a half thousand years, the dominant Hindu religion divided all Hindus into four castes, hierarchically ranked. At the top were the Brahmans, the priests and scholars; next came the Kshatriyas, the nobles and warriors; below them were the Vaishyas, the farmers and merchants; and at the bottom the Shudras, the common labourers. (Not quite at the bottom: there was a vast mass of outcastes or 'untouchables' beyond and beneath the four main castes.) The hierarchy was in principle unshakeable and unchangeable, a reflection of the cosmic order itself. Castes were separated by an unbridgeable gulf. Diet, clothes, customs, occupation, all confirmed one's caste position. To move between castes was in theory impossible as well as blasphemous, though there were ways of doing it, painfully and slowly over generations.

But while this gave the strongest possible backing to the horizontal principle of inequality, it also provided for a high degree of vertical integration as well. For not only were economic differences within castes overridden; a poor Brahman was a Brahman still and shared more in common with a rich Brahman than a poor (or rich) member of another caste. The whole caste system was conceived as a mutually reinforcing system of reciprocal services – the *jajmani* system. A poor Brahman could provide a priestly service to a Kshatriya ruler in exchange for bodily keep, a Shudra washerman could wash the clothes of a Vaishya farmer in return for grain. Because occupations were largely caste-based such specialization and exchange of services were virtually forced on the system. While the hierarchical aspect of the caste system remained dominant, the *jajmani* relationship introduced a real degree of intercaste dependence to soften the horizontal lines of power and privilege (Dumont, 1972, pp. 133–50).

One was born into a caste in traditional India; one achieve

membership of a class in the modern industrial west. This is a real difference, certainly of principle. But as Marx insisted, perhaps too strongly, classes have a tendency to harden into castes. Classes like castes are largely self-recruiting – the amount of social mobility between classes over the past century has been remarkably low. Moreover, by knowing what class a person belongs to – however difficult it is to be precise about the boundaries of class – one knows practically all that needs to be known about a person's social condition and way of life. One knows, among other things, where he lives, what he eats, what kind of clothes he wears, how much formal education he has, what sort of person he marries, what his chances of divorce are, the kind of job he has, the kinds of games he plays, where (and when) he goes for his holiday, whether he makes love in the dark or with the light on (Reid, 1977; Marwick, 1981). If castes create separate universes, class often seems to draw the lines as tightly around its members.

Language, we might say, is the major determinant of reality for a culture. Age, sex, race, caste and class subdivide this reality into a series of smaller realities. All have a tendency to become closed off and mutually exclusive. But on an everyday basis, even these sub-cultural realities tend to be too large for most individuals. 'Working class' or 'middle class' may define one's reality for certain major issues, to do especially with work and politics. The 'working-class Tory' in Britain hence becomes something of a deviant, an anomaly to be explained. As a worker he 'should', in class terms, vote Labour, the party of the working man. He is more easily explained if we accept that most people do not consciously inhabit class realities for much of the time. Their attention is focused on the level of the job, the school, the home, the life lived with friends and neighbours. At this level they know the world largely as role-players.

Being old, or being a woman, is a particular social status. So too is being married or unmarried; being a teacher or a parent, a neighbour or a taxpayer, a prisoner or a mental patient. Each status carries a bundle of rights and obligations, the fulfilment of which constitutes the performance of a role. A role is the dynamic aspect of status (Linton, 1964, pp. 113–14). It tells us how to think, feel and behave in ways appropriate to a given status. A judge is stern, a mother caring, a doctor reassuring, a neighbour helpful, a soldier brave, a patient submissive. To occupy a particular status is to slip into a role as into a suit of clothes tailored for the occasion.

The role is binding on both actor and audience. It is a reciprocal relationship. It can constrain behaviour more directly and more forcibly than either language or class. A woman asked by her doctor to remove her clothes will do so without question. Asked to do the same by her solicitor her reaction can easily be imagined. The force of reaction in the latter case is the measure of the role's power in the former.

We do not invent our roles. We find them latent in the statuses we occupy, waiting to be actualized by our performance. Just as with the roles of a stage play, the script has already been written. Unlike the stage actor, however, we learn our parts largely unconsciously, unaware of the social script. The most apparently spontaneous and personal behaviour, when we feel most 'ourselves', often turns out to be a replaying of the lines of a tattered old script. Generations of American college students have gone through the elaborate courtship ritual known as the 'rating-dating' system, convinced that the form of the declarations they make to each other, the carefully timed moves in the growing intimacy and the playful revelations to friends, are all of their own making. The script is clear to everyone but themselves. More generally, the moves in that intensely personal game of romantic love, the tones and emotions of its expression, come from a script written by Provençal troubadours eight hundred years ago (Berger, 1966, pp. 101–3). And once we have taken the plunge and committed ourselves to that private, intimate association known as marriage, another well-worn social script takes over and stealthily but firmly guides our steps (Berger and Kellner 1974).

Individual and Society

Where, if anywhere, do we find our freedom in this world o determined realities? Our language, our class, our roles seen to condition our thoughts and behaviour so utterly that th

52

individual is reduced to a puppet, manipulated by society. Or he appears a prisoner, whose every attempt to break out of the prison-house of society drives him back behind its bars. Erving Goffman has shown that when we think we are disdaining our roles and expressing 'role distance', we are merely falling into other roles (Goffman, 1969, pp. 39–103). Our attempted escapes from social routines, through bizarre hobbies, foreign travel, drugs, divorce, are all themselves swiftly routinized (Cohen and Taylor, 1978). Society, moreover, encompasses us not just in space but in time. The 'dead hand of the past' lies heavily upon us; as Marx put it, 'the tradition of all the dead generations weighs like a nightmare on the brain of the living' (Marx, 1962, I, p. 247). It might appear, then, that 'society is the walls of our imprisonment in history' (Berger, 1966, p. 109).

This is to take too alarmist a view of our predicament. We are cultural and social animals. The 'touching tendency to keep a part of the world safe from sociology' (Goffman, 1969, p. 103), to reserve some 'free', 'private' and 'individual' space that is not invaded by society, is an unprofitable illusion. When Marx said 'it is society which thinks in me' he did not mean by this that the individual is a mere automaton. The opposition of 'individual' to 'society', as commonly expressed, is false. As Rousseau and Marx both suggested, the individual gains his freedom through society, not against or outside it. 'Individualism' as an ideal and a philosophy is a modern invention, the product of modern western society (Dumont, 1972, pp. 35–55). It sets up demands for individual freedom and autonomy which can only be realized through the organization or reorganization of society, not through its denial.

Society, as we have seen, is not homogeneous. Modern society in particular is plural to a degree never before encountered in world history. We may all have to be role-players, but there are also many roles to be played. We may choose to accentuate some and to play down others. If we do not like the latent identity offered to us in one role we may stress the identity offered in another. A waiter may dutifully perform his occupational role to his customers and his employers; but he may well attach greater value to, and invest more energy in, the performance of his role as the secretary of the local ecology party. In his mind, and in the manner in which he presents himself to the world, he is more seriously and wholeheartedly an ecologist than a waiter. The former is his life; the latter merely gives him a living.

A plurality of roles has a plurality of audiences. Any one of us inhabits a multiple 'role-set' which enables us to be different things to different people (Merton, 1964). As a mother I can be caring to my children; as a teacher severe with my pupils; as an animal rights activist inspiring to my fellow members. In this multiplicity of roles and in the segregation of audiences to which I play them, I find an area of choice and an increase of freedom.

But who is it who is doing the choosing? Who is the player who suppresses some roles and elevates others, who deliberately plays some well and some badly? The idea of a role presupposes an actor. An actor is nothing without his roles; but he is not simply a mechanical performer of them. Many roles are only loosely or generally specified. The role of Hamlet may be written into the script, but there are as many Hamlets as there are actors to play him. The way in which the role is performed, the particular nuances and emphases, in a word the particular interpretation of a role, leave a good deal to the creativity and imagination of the actor. As on the stage, so in life. We can creatively exploit the potentialities of our many roles and in doing so gain a further increase in individual freedom.

But this individual remains social through and through. Language needs users, class members, roles players; but users members and players are meaningless without language, class roles. Social institutions and processes are not the clothes but the substance of the self. There is, however, a dynamic interaction between self and society which prevents social closure and stagnation. In the conception of the American social psychologist George Herbert Mead, the individual can be thought of as containing both an 'I' and a 'me'. The 'me' is the fully socialized part of the self. It is the internalization of society, the part constructed through membership of it. But the 'I' remains the active, on-going, part of the self. It is the 'I' which indicates to its 'me' which roles to elevate as the most personal and 'characteristic' of the self, how best to perform them and so on. The 'I' is asocial. It has no material of its own, no instincts or drives. It is best conceived as a kind of impulsive energy, a property of the individual as a human organism. But it can live only through the 'me', the socialized self (G. H. Mead, 1967, pp. 135–226).

In many people, the 'me' seems to have overwhelmed the 'I' so completely that to all intents and purposes its creative and impulsive energy has been eliminated. These people, we may say, are not just socialized but 'oversocialized'. Aldous Huxley's *Brave New World* is a compelling portrait of such a condition. Here the players are simply the mechanical carriers, not the performers, of their roles. As social creatures this tendency is always present in us. It is what existentialists mean by 'bad faith'. But even in the most ritualized and bureaucratized society, the dynamic interaction between the 'I' and the 'me' remains, in however feeble a state. There is always some leeway, some indication that difference and diversity are a possibility in all human societies. The individual as an asocial being is indeed a myth. But it may be useful to think of the 'social individual'. Far from being a contradiction in terms, this would be the truest expression of the fact that human individuality is achieved only through the cultivation of our social nature.

Chapter Four

Biology

R. B. FREEDMAN

A Story

It is early summer in a monastery garden. The monk working in the bed planted with peas is a schoolteacher in his early thirties. He is examining the flowers on a row of standard tall pea plants; earlier he had removed the stamens from these flowers so that they could not self-fertilize. Now after a check that none has been missed, he is dusting each flower with pollen collected from flowers in another row of plants, all of which are unusually short, about one-fifth the height of a normal pea. After completing this fertilization of tall plants with pollen from dwarfs, Gregor Mendel moves on to another row, where dwarf plants have been emasculated, and does the reverse hybridization, dusting the flowers with pollen from tall plants. Next day, he is again in the garden, cross-fertilizing normal pink- and purple-flowered plants, with plants bearing white flowers. The 1850s are a peaceful time here in the Moravian provincial centre of Brünn, but inflation is bad and elsewhere in the Austro-Hungarian Empire troops are being recruited to fight in Italy. Mendel has just written reassuringly to his widowed mother enclosing the latest cereal market prices for his farmer brother-in-law.

Later in the summer there is more work to be done in the pea plot. Mendel collects the mature pea pods and shells the peas into cotton bags, one bag for each plant, and each labelled with its ancestry. Only one generation of peas can be produced per year.

56

so the experiments are slow, but Mendel is in no hurry. Next year all the peas are sown and Mendel records, without surprise, that all the plants grown from tall/dwarf hybrid seed are tall and all those grown from purple-flowered/white-flowered hybrids have purple flowers. Without surprise, because this has been reported before, in the scattered plant hybridization literature of the previous hundred years. But with puzzlement because Mendel knows that this uniformity in appearance of the first hybrid generation is deceptive. Whereas the tall peas with which he started the experiment are a true-breeding line and when allowed to self-fertilize produce only tall plants over many generations, the tall plants produced by tall/dwarf hybridization are different; the dwarf character is not apparent in the hybrid plants but will reappear in some of the next generation. So Mendel allows the tall hybrid plants to self-fertilize and allows the purple-flowered hybrids to self-fertilize, collects the seeds, one bag for each plant, and waits.

When spring comes, Mendel is out preparing his plots for the third successive year. He sows the seeds produced by self-fertilization of the hybrids, about a thousand seeds from each group. Most of the plants grown from the tall hybrids are tall, but each hybrid plant has produced some seeds which have grown into dwarf plants. In all, 277 out of a total of 1064 plants in this second hybrid generation are dwarf. Similarly, of the 929 plants grown from seed of the purple-flowered hybrid plants, 705 have purple flowers and 224 have white flowers. Mendel checks carefully because it is not clear from earlier work and finds that the character 'hidden' in the first hybrid generation reappears in the second generation no matter which way the original cross was made. Finally, Mendel looks again at the numbers and notices that in each case the 'hidden' character has reappeared in about a quarter of the plants; the ratio of tall to dwarf plants in the second hybrid generation is 2.84:1 and the ratio of purple- to white-flowered plants is 3.15:1.

This is new, intriguing and possibly a complete red herring. For the remainder of the year, between and during the normal round of school and monastery life, Mendel worries at three related questions. Are these ratios coincidental? If not, what is their significance? And anyway, what will happen next? The second question must be postponed, but the other two suggest experiments. Mendel has collected thirty-four varieties of garden pea, differing in simple discrete characteristics, and so he plans hybridization experiments with other pairs of characters for the next spring. And of course the second-generation hybrid plants which he counted were allowed to self-fertilize, so he has their seed to sow, which will allow him to study the third generation.

This experiment is completed the next year and the results are again clear-cut, although Mendel cannot explain them. A quarter of the second-generation hybrid plants were dwarf and *all* the seeds grown from these plants give dwarf plants in the third generation. But the seeds from the tall second-generation hybrids give a more complex picture. The seeds from one-third of these plants only give rise to tall plants, while those from the remainder give both tall and dwarf plants in the next generation, and if all the mixed offspring from these plants are counted, tall plants exceed dwarfs in the ratio 3:1. So Mendel restates to himself the result from the previous year. The ratio is not just 3 tall plants to 1 dwarf plant but 2 'hybrid-type' tall plants to 1 pure-breeding tall plant to 1 pure-breeding dwarf plant.

Although not yet ready with an explanation, Mendel is fairly confident of what he will find from the other hybridizations between plants with different-shaped pods or different positions of flowers. In every case all the hybrid plants in the first generation after cross-fertilization are identical and resemble only one of the parents; when these hybrid plants are allowed to self-fertilize, one-quarter of the second-generation plants resemble the other partner in the original cross, the one whose character was apparently 'hidden' in the first-generation hybrids. Seven different crosses produce the same result – a uniform first generation of hybrids and a 3:1 ratio in the second generation.

Mendel is writing in his notebook a protocol for some new experiments. Some time before this, an idea of what may be taking place has been hovering in his mind, first as an unfocused picture and later in words, but the idea has taken shape fully now that he can reformulate it practically as 'What if I cross the first-generation hybrids back with each of their parental varieties?' and 'What if I cross varieties differing in *two* characteristics?' The experiments take some time but the pattern of results is now not only clear but meaningful. Hybrid tall plants crossed with pure-breeding dwarfs produce a 1:1 ratio of tall and dwarf offspring; all the dwarf offspring breed true, while the tall offspring all behave as hybrids and produce the 3:1 ratio of tall: dwarf plants when allowed to self-fertilize. Likewise hybrid tall plants crossed with pure-breeding tall produce all tall plants, half of which breed true and half of which behave as hybrids. Finally Mendel crosses plants grown from yellow smooth seeds with plants grown from green wrinkled seeds and finds all the seeds produced are yellow and smooth. When he plants these and allows them to self-fertilize, all the plants produce mixed sets of seeds. Mendel counts carefully; three-quarters of the seeds are yellow and a quarter are green. Of the yellow seeds, three-quarters are smooth and a quarter are wrinkled; the same ratio of 3 smooth:1 wrinkled is found in the green seeds so that in all 9/16 are yellow and smooth, 3/16 are green and smooth, 3/16 are yellow and wrinkled and 1/16 are green and wrinkled.

It is now eight years since he began this series of hybridization experiments and Mendel is satisfied that he can explain all his results on peas. He is eager to continue recently begun experiments with hawkweed and to start work on stocks and snapdragon. But first he wants to present his pea results and he is writing a paper to read to his friends who attend the regular monthly meetings of the Brünn Society for the Study of Natural Sciences. He writes a modest title, 'Experiments in plant hybridization', and continues:

If no one has hitherto succeeded in establishing a generally valid law as to the formation and development of hybrids, who can wonder that knows the magnitude of the task ... Anyone who surveys the work done in this field will come to the conclusion that, among the numerous experiments, not one has been carried out comprehensively enough or in such a way as to make it possible to determine the number of different forms under which the offspring of hybrids appear, or to arrange these forms with certainty according to their separate generations, or definitely to ascertain their statistical relations ... In order to ascertain the relationships in which the hybrid forms stand to one another and to their

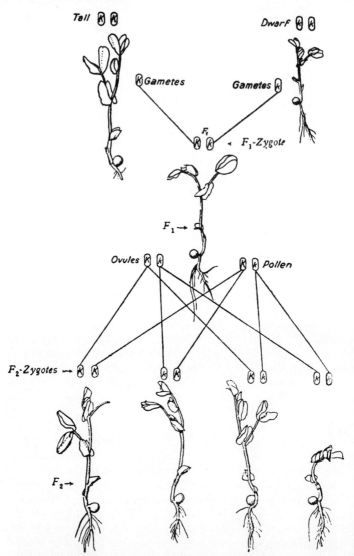

Figure 4.1   Crossing of a Tall with a Dwarf Pea
The F₁ generation consists exclusively of tall specimens.
The F₂ generation consists of talls and dwarfs in the ratio of 3:1.
(*After Morgan*) – (K denotes the heredity factor for tall, k the
heredity factor for dwarf.)
Source: Hugo Iltis, *The Life of Mendel*, Allen & Unwin, 1932.

progenitors, it would seem to be necessary that we observe the total number of the members of the developmental series in each successive generation.[1]

He goes on to report his results, but not only to record them but to express them in a notation where *KK* represents a true-breeding tall plant, *kk* a true-breeding dwarf and *Kk* a tall hybrid. Then by postulating that these tall and dwarf characters remain constant themselves but that they separate randomly in the formation of pollen cells and ovules and recombine on fertilization, Mendel is able to represent the results of his hybridizations and to explain the numbers of different types of offspring (Figure 4.1).

Mendel has read his paper to the society, to a polite but muted reception. Now, in 1866 he is distracted by the Prussian invasion and the consequent cholera epidemic. But at the same time he is pleased to see his paper collected with all the other proceedings of the society for 1865 and to see the volume printed and distributed to over a hundred corresponding societies across Europe. Forty copies of the paper are printed separately for the author and at the end of the year Mendel sends one of these with a polite letter to Nägeli, Professor of Botany at Munich. A correspondence follows on many details of experimental technique and on plans for future experiments on hawkweeds, but Mendel finds the professor unimpressed by his quantitative interpretations of the pea results. When, two years later, Mendel is elected abbot, he begins to wind up his experimental work and to concentrate on financial and political affairs, continuing with his bee-keeping and meteorological observations but only as recreations.

At the time of Mendel's death his paper, published eighteen years before, has been read by few and fully understood by none. But at least it has been referred to once, obscurely, in a comprehensive survey on plant breeding (Focke, 1881) where the author has noted Mendel as a 'trustworthy observer' and has recorded that 'Mendel believed he had found constant numerical ratios among the types produced by hybridization'. This reference takes on new significance in 1900 when Carl Correns, a former student of Nägeli, is in the library at Tübingen checking the literature before writing up his own experimental work on plant hybridization. The mention in Focke of constant numerical ratios leads Correns to Mendel's original paper. Soon after, Correns receives a brief paper[2] from Hugo de Vries, professor in Amsterdam. Now Correns cannot simply write up his own results and the brilliant model he has for explaining them. Instead he writes

> I have to thank Hugo de Vries for sending me his latest publication 'Sur la loi de disjonction des hybrides'. It came to hand yesterday and has induced me to write this paper. In my hybridization experiments on various strains of maize and peas, I have come to the same result as de Vries. In noting the regular succession of the phenomena and in finding an explanation for them I believed myself, as de Vries obviously believes himself, to be an innovator. Subsequently, however, I found that in Brünn, during the '60s, Abbot Gregor Mendel, devoting many years to the most extensive experiments on peas, had not only obtained the same results as de Vries and myself, but had actually given the very same explanation, so far as this was possible in 1866 ... This paper of Mendel's, to which Focke refers (though without doing full justice to its importance) ... is among the best works ever written upon the subject of hybrids.

Correns entitles his paper 'Gregor Mendel's rules on the behaviour of racial hybrids' and sends it to the German Botanical Society.[3]

It is 1910 and a decade of vigorous experiment has established a new scientific vocabulary of 'genes' and 'genetics' whose central principles are known as 'Mendel's laws'. The principles first deduced from studies on peas fifty years before have now been generalized, elaborated and extended; the verb 'to mendelize' has had a brief vogue but the adjective 'Mendelian' and the abstract noun 'Mendelism' are well established. A statue commemorating the late abbot is erected in Brünn.[4]

What Reality?

Where do we find 'reality' in the above account? Should we begin by distinguishing between the objects of study, the results and interpretations, and the consequences? We could claim that only one of these is real, or that they are all real in different ways. But if we think of all the human actions, thoughts and artefacts that contributed to it, our account of the 'reality' of genetics must be an inclusive one. It must include the earth and the plants and the buzzing insects in the garden at Brünn, the indescribable mental phenomena underlying the production of an original thought, the effort to express this thought most simply and clearly, the scraps of scribbled paper on which a notation is evolved and used to predict the results of new experiments, the disappointment of the correspondence with Nägeli, the copies of the paper uncut and unread in libraries across Europe. But it must also include the earth and plants and insects in the gardens of the many workers who did similar experiments without sufficient clarity of design or analysis to draw such productive conclusions, the daily laboratory life of the 'normal' scientists who, after the excitement of their rediscovery, extended the range of the general principles to new species and found explanations for apparent exceptions and anomalies, the textbooks and the lectures by which the science was propagated. It must include Vavilov and others dying in Stalin's labour camps as adherents of 'Mendelism'.[5] It must also include genes themselves, while acknowledging the changing meaning of the word 'gene' from an abstract heritable entity determining some observable character, to a definite physical entity, invisible but located somewhere along a visible chromosome, to a piece of DNA of defined nucleotide sequence. And in the 1980s the reality should include both the West Coast entrepreneurs with their ironic extension of the central dogma of molecular biology 'DNA makes RNA makes protein makes dollars', and the Greek-Cypriot expectant mothers in North London who, following examination of the DNA of foetal cells, can be assured that the child they are carrying will not be afflicted with inherited thalassaemia.[6]

Is Science Different?

If we want to talk with any conviction about how scientists see the reality of the natural world on which they work, or the reality of the direct products of their work, the theories, papers, patents, etc., or of the indirect products of their work such as drugs and machines, we cannot do it in the abstract. We must check our generalities against concrete examples. Hence the opening section. Furthermore, any account we give of the scientist's reality will be inadequate if it concentrates on the philosophical status of scientific theories and excludes the detailed human fabric of what scientists actually do. Hence the second section.

So let us start again and ask whether science is quite distinct from the topics dealt with in other chapters. Is it a superior intellectual construct whose impersonality, permanence and wealth-creating potential show works of art to be pleasant and diverting, perhaps, but limited, subjective and evanescent? Is it rather a cold destructive impersonal machine, a dark satanic mill grinding the human spirit and killing the imagination? Or does it have quite a lot in common with other incomplete and inadequate attempts to make sense of our messy experience? If we take this last view, we have to ask what – if any – are the distinctive features of a scientific approach and how much difference do these features make?

The starting-points of science, as exemplified in Mendel's work, are the common stuff of human experience, namely the use of observation and thought to make sense of the natural world. But it is clear that these common activities are constrained and refined in many ways during the design, performance, analysis and reporting of a piece of science. The aim is to describe phenomena accessible to any observer in terms valid for all such observers. This suggests that some kinds of experience may lie outside the realm of science. It also makes it clear that science is a social activity; neither experimental results nor theoretical models become part of science until they are communicated in terms comprehensible by others. But even when an appropriate question has been asked and a suitable language exists for communicating about it, there are problems at several levels about doing science at all. First the activity of observation necessarily perturbs the system under observation; Lewis Ryder discusses the most fundamental aspect of this problem in the chapter on physics. Secondly there are limitations arising from the inadequacies of the human intellect and imagination. The social structure of science involving communication and criticism within a community provides a powerful drive against these inadequacies, but finally we *are* constrained by language and imagination, so that in unfamiliar areas we do not have a truly 'open' mind but draw metaphorically on the familiar to provide models and versions of the unknown.

For most active scientists most of the time, these are marginal considerations. The natural world is out there, the tools are available. Are there really impediments to using one's senses and intellect to provide a satisfactory, self-consistent account of this world? If the enterprise is unsound, it will soon collapse. In the mean time let us get into the lab and make a start.

Choosing a System, Designing an Experiment

Making a start, of course, implies a starting-point. For a school textbook of biology,[7] discussion of heredity starts with Mendel and his account of independent particulate inheritance. But what was Mendel's starting-point? Just as the apocryphal little girl said 'How can I know what I think till I hear what I say?', so we can best discover what Mendel was thinking by looking at what he did.

First he was primarily interested in heredity and was looking at plant hybrids solely with this question in mind. At the time of his work, cross-breeding studies were also being used to examine the mechanism of fertilization and seed development and to throw light on the vexed question of the distinction between species and varieties within a species. Either of these questions, which we now blithely dismiss as not immediately relevant to the mechanism of heredity, might have been central to it. The structure of Mendel's experiments shows that he judged otherwise. Secondly he thought about heredity in terms of single observable characteristics; whereas his predecessors had chosen varieties differing in many characteristics for crossing experiments as likely to be the most informative, Mendel crossed varieties differing in only one or two quite specific ways. Whereas his predecessors had picked out for detailed study individual progeny which differed most extremely from the parental strains, Mendel grouped the progeny and counted them all. Did he think in this way as a result of his experiments, or did he do the experiments thus because of his ideas?

In Mendel's case it seems quite clear that he did the experiments reported in his classic paper with these first two ideas clearly in his mind.[8] But did the ideas come from earlier unreported experiments? And if so what ideas lay behind *them*? Historical scholarship can only take us so far; we cannot explain how and why an idea arrives in a particular form at a particular time.

We can obscure our inadequate psychology of creativity by saying that this innovator had a 'prepared mind'. That is necessary but not sufficient. He also chose an appropriate experimental system. The basic understanding of sexual reproduction in plants developed from the late seventeenth century onwards, but it was only a generation before Mendel that it was established that plant fertilization involved the combination of a single pollen grain with a single ovule. Peas were known to be normally self-fertilizing, so that uncontrolled cross-pollination by insects was not a serious problem. Hand-emasculation required some skill and had to be carried out before the flowers were fully open, to rule out self-fertilization, but in skilled hands it was reliable and allowed the experimenter total control of the cross-fertilization process. The plants are easy to grow and prolific. Finally, as well-established crops, a large number of consistent pea varieties had already been developed empirically, so that before beginning his experiments Mendel did not have to generate his thirty-four variant forms, only to collect them and check that they bred true.

Not only was the system tractable, but Mendel's experimental protocol was suitable. He kept the seeds from different plants and from different generations separate, so that he could always define an individual seed's or plant's ancestry precisely. He not only analysed results quantitatively by counting progeny and expressing the numbers as ratios, but he did the experiments on a sufficiently large scale for the ratios to be obvious and significant. He crossed several pairs of characters separately to establish the generality of results (Table 4.1). Having at some point developed a theoretical framework accounting for the results, he tested it

Table 4.1 *Mendel's Data on 'Single Character'*
Cross-Hybridization

Characters crossed	Character of F_1	Numbers in F_2		Ratio in F_2
Round/wrinkled seed	Round	Round	$= 5474$	2.96:1
		Wrinkled	$= 1850$	
Yellow/green cotyledon	Yellow	Yellow	$= 6022$	3.01:1
		Green	$= 2001$	
Coloured/white seed-coat and flower	Coloured	Coloured	$= 705$	3.15:1
		White	$= 224$	
Inflated/constricted pod	Inflated	Inflated	$= 882$	2.95:1
		Constricted	$= 299$	
Green/yellow pod	Green	Green	$= 428$	2.82:1
		Yellow	$= 152$	
Axial/terminal flower	Axial	Axial	$= 651$	3.14:1
		Terminal	$= 207$	
Tall/dwarf stem	Tall	Tall	$= 787$	2.84:1
		Dwarf	$= 277$	

F_1 = first hybrid generation produced by cross-fertilization
F_2 = second hybrid generation produced by self-fertilization of F_1
Source: adapted from Iltis, 1932

with back-crosses where the theory would make precise predictions.

In all these respects, the example we have chosen is characteristic of most kinds of natural science. Obviously it is exceptional in that the work was genuinely revolutionary. Mendel's work had a historical context, of course, but in terms of our present knowledge of genetics it still makes sense for school textbooks to start with Mendel. It is also exceptional in the extent to which Mendel was isolated and peripheral to the scientific community. He had had some education in botany and physics at the University of Vienna, the monastery library had a good collection of natural science books, and in Mendel's time Darwin's books were bought and Mendel certainly read them. But he was not a member of an 'invisible college'[9] of scientists, exchanging results and ideas and recognizing each other as leading figures in the field.

It is relevant, in thinking about the 'reality' of experimental

Table 4.2　*Reproducibility of Mendel's Data for the Crossing of Peas with Yellow and Green Cotyledons*

Source		Numbers in F_2		Ratio
		Yellow	Green	
Mendel	(1866)	6022	2001	3.01
Correns	(1900)	1394	453	3.08
Tschermak	(1900)	3580	1190	3.01
Hurst	(1904)	1310	445	2.94
Bateson	(1905)	11903	3903	3.05
Lock	(1905)	1438	514	2.80
Darbishire	(1909)	109060	36186	3.01
Winge	(1924)	19195	6553	2.93
TOTAL		153902	51245	3.00

Source: adapted from Sturtevant, 1965

results and of the theories constructed from them, to ask if these exceptional features made any significant difference in the long term. While it is interesting to attempt to trace the individual historical origins of Mendel's thinking, these personal factors cannot have significantly determined the shape of genetic theory, since subsequently three workers independently and simultaneously reached the same conclusions and many have since confirmed the results (Table 4.2). And although Mendel's comparative isolation must have contributed to the neglect of his work, it did not ultimately prevent its significance being acknowledged.

So while we have emphasized that science is not simply something out there, rather that it arises from the activities of scientists, we should not exaggerate the role of particular individuals. Mendel was the first modern geneticist, but if he had never lived, contemporary genetics would not be significantly different.

Science and Progress

It is characteristic of Science and of Progress that it constantly offers new vistas to our gaze. (Pasteur)

I have dwelt on Mendel and peas because it is an interesting story in itself and because his classic experiments are good examples of science at work. But it is quite misleading to illustrate science by single fundamental and revolutionary advances. Indeed, perhaps we should ask a few questions about what we mean by an 'advance' in science. Pasteur speaks of 'Science and Progress' with confident nineteenth-century capitals, but we may be more sceptical about this continuous process of change. University science textbooks go through many editions and are constantly under revision, while the Bible, *The Republic* and *The Prelude* are just reprinted, year after year. Do these works deal with a more permanent reality? Is there something wrong with scientists' account of reality which compels them constantly to tinker with it?

To answer this question, which is essentially about the status of scientific knowledge, I want to approach indirectly through thinking about how science operates in historical and social terms, rather than attempting a direct philosophical assault. By looking in detail at a science in the process of constant change, we may achieve a clearer view of the nature of scientific claims.

In the period from the publication of Mendel's paper to its 'rediscovery', two highly relevant lines of work were also in progress. Microscopists working on fertilization and embryogenesis recognized the important role of the nucleus. Subsequent technical advances led to the observation of chromosomes within the nucleus and of their division and segregation when cells divide; by 1883 Roux was proposing that chromosomes were somehow the bearers of the units of heredity. Over the same period, Darwin's *Origin of Species* had enormous impact, but while the process of evolution was widely accepted, it became clear to many that the proposed mechanism of natural selection was incomplete, since it included no satisfactory account of heredity or of how the variant forms (on which selection operated) arose. By 1900 it was abundantly clear that a theory of heredity was needed 'to place the keystone between the work of the evolutionists and that of the cytologists, and thus to bring the cell-theory and the evolution theory into organic connection' (Wilson, 1896).

The fact that Mendel's theory filled this gap and was immediately recognized as doing so by some people, did not mean that the arch was instantaneously completed. In fact evolutionists and Mendelian geneticists remained in conflict for many years and the ultimate grand synthesis, which gave an account of evolution arising from selection acting to change the frequencies of alternative genes in a population, was worked out twenty or thirty years later. But by 1903 it was possible to represent chromosomes as consisting of a row of genes, like beads on a string, and to account for Mendel's laws in terms of the known behaviour of chromosomes. By 1915 the work of Morgan and his students on the fruit-fly *Drosophila* had elaborated this interpretation in great detail. This completion of one-half of the arch covertly, but profoundly, changed the nature of talk about genes. The existence of genes, or heritable characters, was initially inferred from the results of cross-breeding experiments; the genes were abstract entities introduced to explain the results. The link to cytology redefined genes as concrete physical entities, as parts of chromosomes, things which could be seen without difficulty under a microscope.

One aspect of scientific advance can be seen here. A productive theory not only explains observations in its own field but makes useful connections with other fields. A second aspect is the gradual extension of a theory to cover a wider range of cases and examples. Thus by 1902 Mendelian heredity had been shown to apply to many diverse species of plants and also to some animals (mice and hens). Within the next few years many examples of apparent exceptions and of complex cases were worked on and shown to be explicable by elaborated versions of the basic principles. Such developments are often called 'normal' science.[10] No theoretical framework is overturned or established but a wide range of specific phenomena is brought within an existing framework and their relations to each other are established. By implication the framework is strengthened by this busy unspectacular activity.

In the process of 'normal' science, individual scientists have roles to play both as creators and as regulators. As teachers and as editors of journals, experienced scientists set standards for the conduct and the communication of experimental work. Are the methods used adequate to the demands made of them? Are the experiments described in sufficient detail to permit independent replication of them? Are the results communicated clearly? Are they internally consistent? Are the conclusions firmly grounded in the experiments? As organizers of scientific meetings and as members of funding bodies, scientists identify what they regard as important soluble problems and draw attention to work which they regard as promising or significant. As authors of reviews and textbooks, they summarize, organize and reformulate the growing body of knowledge. In this complex process it is wrong to focus on individuals; the scientific community as a whole is an active participant in the processes by which its knowledge grows and its views change.

From Classical to Molecular Genetics

By the early 1940s genetics had expanded in many directions but two key questions had still not been clearly answered. What are genes made of? And what is their mechanism of action: *how* do they specify hereditary characteristics? For both questions simpler systems than peas and flies were needed. By 1941 Beadle, a pupil of Morgan and a veteran of work on fruit-flies, had switched to the mould *Neurospora* and had shown that mutants which could not grow on a simple medium lacked identifiable enzymes each responsible for one of the steps in the many biochemical pathways by which the normal mould makes complex vitamins and amino acids from simple components. This was generalized to give the proposition that a gene specifies the production of a particular enzyme or other protein. But there was no direct evidence on what genes themselves were. Chromosomes were known to consist of protein and DNA; since DNA was (mistakenly) believed to be chemically simple and repetitive, while proteins performed nearly every important function in living cells, genes were generally assumed to be protein. This assumption was overturned by a sequence of three discoveries in quite disparate fields. First Avery, a bacteriologist working on *Pneumococcus*, the infectious agent of pneumonia, showed that mutant non-virulent bacteria could be transformed and became virulent when they took up DNA derived from virulent bacteria.

71

Secondly a classical organic chemist, Chargaff, showed that nucleic acids were more complex in chemical constitution than was previously realized, thus ruling out one possible objection to Avery's conclusion. Finally Hershey and Chase, working on bacteriophages, viruses which infect bacteria, showed that the genetic information for making new copies of the phage is carried into the infected bacterium by DNA from the phage, not by its protein coat.

When this last experiment was published in 1952, the work was already under way that would lead to the discovery of the three-dimensional molecular structure of DNA and hence show how it could act as a copiable carrier of genetic information. Wilkins and Franklin were already well advanced with X-ray diffraction studies on DNA fibres and Watson and Crick were already arguing about its structure. This development is the most documented episode in recent science[11] and a full account is beyond the scope of this chapter. But I want to draw attention to a number of features of the story.

First it should be stressed that the bulk of the genetics community in 1951–3 was *not* trying to solve the structure of DNA. Most geneticists were busy with the normal practice of science, accumulating and extending knowledge of particular genes in particular species, worrying at anomalies and applying known principles to problems in agriculture or medicine. Only a few people had responded to Avery's work and realized that DNA carried genetic information and fewer of these imagined that one could gain insight into how it did so by working out its three-dimensional structure by X-ray diffraction studies on pure DNA fibres. As is frequently the case, the striking advance in science is made when new people, new techniques, new ways of thinking are brought to bear on an old problem. In this case one of the major catalysts for establishing new connections was war. This provided new people, especially physicists, disenchanted with the destructive applications of physics in war and drawn to biology as a more constructive science. It also provided new tools; the radioactive isotopes of sulphur and phosphorus, used by Hershey and Chase to demonstrate the importance of DNA in phage replication, were available as a result of the construction of nuclear reactors in the Manhattan project to produce the atomic bomb.

One incoming physicist was Crick, who in wartime had worked on magnetic mines and by 1950 was doing a PhD. in Cambridge's Cavendish Laboratory. Here an innovative group was established, with support from the Rockefeller Foundation and the Medical Research Council, using the phenomenon of diffraction by X-rays (discovered by the Cavendish Professor, Sir Lawrence Bragg, many years before) to solve the detailed three-dimensional structure of proteins. The founders of this experimental approach, of applying physics to understand the structures of complex biological materials, were all British (by birth or adoption) and in 1950 this tradition was already strong in Britain and nowhere else.

In the USA a separate tradition, originally inspired by physicists such as Delbrück and Schrödinger (of the 'wave equation', see chapter 6) had led to a new way of talking about genes – as molecules conveying information – and to thoughts about what kinds of properties such self-copying informational molecules must have. From this arose an informal group of scientists, 'the Phage Group', who argued that the fundamental questions in biology, such as the nature of genes, could only be solved by studies on the simplest living things, namely bacteriophages. James Watson was a biologist from this strongly physics-influenced tradition, who in 1950 completed a PhD. in the laboratory of Salvador Luria, a founder member of the Phage Group. The conviction that DNA was important, the hunch that its structure would give insight into its function, the judgement that X-ray diffraction would reveal its structure and an instinct for quality that told him that the Cavendish was the place for X-ray diffraction, took Watson there in 1951. He also needed funds, of course, and through the patronage of senior members of the Phage Group he secured a fellowship from a medical charity.

Thus Watson and Crick brought together two rather different traditions, neither of which had much to do with classical genetics. Yet they were among the few people at the time who had the combination of access to information,[12] technical expertise and mental preparedness to define the problem in appropriate terms and to tackle it. Other things than readiness were necessary, of course. One can distinguish three crucial kinds of input. First they needed data on the X-ray diffraction properties of

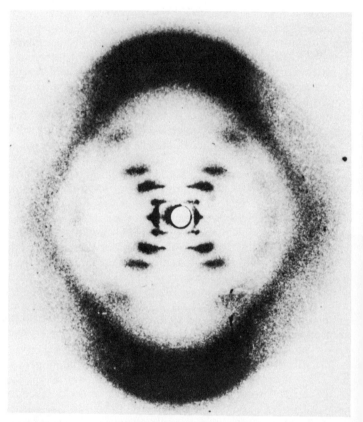

Plate 4.1   An X-ray photograph of DNA in the B form, taken by
Rosalind Franklin late in 1952

DNA. These came from Maurice Wilkins and Rosalind Franklin
at King's College London with whom they had informal but
prickly contact (Watson and Crick as members of the Cavendish
Laboratory were meant to be working on proteins, not on DNA).
Fortuitously, soon after Watson's arrival in Cambridge, Crick
had worked out theoretically the kind of diffraction pattern to be

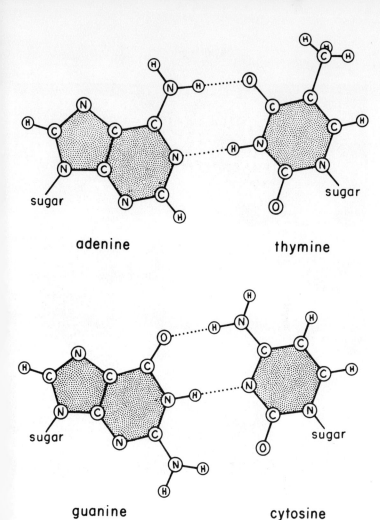

adenine   thymine

guanine   cytosine

Figure 4.2   The adenine-thymine and guanine-cytosine base pairs used to construct the double helix (hydrogen bonds are dotted). The formation of a third hydrogen bond between guanine and cytosine was considered, but rejected because a crystallographic study of guanine hinted that it would be very weak. Now this conjecture is known to be wrong. Three strong hydrogen bonds can be drawn between guanine and cytosine.

Source: James D. Watson, *Double Helix*, Weidenfeld & Nicholson, 1968.

75

Plate 4.2   Watson and Crick in front of the DNA model

expected from a helical molecule, so he and Watson were readily able to recognize this pattern in Wilkins's and Franklin's results (Plate 4.1) and to derive the overall dimensions of the helix. Secondly they took the view that they could solve the structure by trying to fit together models of the known structures of the components of DNA in such a way as to build a scale model helix of appropriate dimensions. This view followed from the success of the structural chemist Linus Pauling in identifying a major structural feature of proteins by the same approach. They also derived from Pauling ideas on the kinds of force which could give specificity in the internal structure of a complex molecule like a protein or DNA. Finally from the work of Chargaff they drew the information that in every kind of DNA the amount of the component adenine (A) was always equal to the amount of thymine (T) while the amount of guanine (G) was always equal to that of cytosine (C).

The essential creativity lay in seeing the relevance of these disparate pieces of information and bringing them together. Success came when Watson, juggling scale models[13] of A, C, G and T saw that A and T could be paired so that they interacted in a chemically plausible way, that C and G could be similarly paired and that the resulting pairs had identical overall dimensions (Figure 4.2), so that both types of pair could be accommodated within a regular double-stranded helix; wherever one strand of the helix contained A the other contained T and vice versa, and similarly with G and C. The double helical model so generated (Plate 4.2) obeyed all the appropriate chemical rules and had dimensions consistent with Wilkins's and Franklin's X-ray data. Not only that, but the molecule had exactly the properties which Delbrück and Schrödinger had argued a molecule must have in order to embody genetic information (Schrödinger, 1944). First it was 'self-complementary' so that it could be duplicated accurately; the two parts of the molecule (the two strands in this case) each fully specify the other part in the same way as do a mould and a plaster model cast in it.[14] Secondly it was informational; since there was no structural limitation on the order in which A, C, G, T, appeared along one of the strands, any sequence was permissible and hence the sequence could be used to convey a genetic message, just as a sequence of dots and dashes in Morse code conveys a literal message.

Conclusions

This chapter has been mainly a narrative with comments and explicit interpretations as asides. It is now necessary to come to some conclusions about what the practice of science (as exemplified

fied in this narrative) tells us about the reality which science seeks to describe and the reality of that description.[15]

(1) Science is a human activity carried out not by automata but by many individual diverse human beings. It is a basic human activity, not essentially different from a child's attempts to use observation, experience and reasoning to make sense of the world. In common with other such attempts, the results of science are human artefacts in the sense that they are devised by people.

(2) In practising science and in talking about it, scientists use mental techniques and language which have much in common with those of creative artists. They talk of doing a final experiment to 'complete the picture', they construct 'models' with predictable properties in order to explain observations and then 'demolish' them, they refer to a colleague who 'has a nice story to tell'. This emphasizes that scientific claims are representations and interpretations and to that extent they are as much fictions or metaphors as are other human productions.

(3) However, science is distinctive in a number of features. First in order to be useful and accepted into the body of current science, new scientific results or interpretations must meet certain criteria. They cannot be arbitrary or personal; they cannot simply claim validity 'in their own terms'. They must refer to aspects of the natural world to which anyone (in principle) could have access. They must be expressed in unambiguous, comprehensible terms. They must be supported by experimental evidence of a kind which could be repeated and alternative interpretations must have been considered and tested. They must be consistent with other empirical knowledge and they must be plausible in the sense of being capable of accommodation within broad encompassing theories.

(4) There is *no source of absolute judgement* as to whether a new scientific claim meets these criteria. Furthermore it could meet all of them at one time and cease to do so later when further experimental evidence had been gathered. In the absence of any such absolute judgement, scientific claims are

judged informally and continuously by communication between practitioners in the field in a complex process which usually leads to a consensus. This emphasizes a second distinctive feature. Science is a communal activity. Although it is easiest to convey the activity involved in doing science by reference to the internal logic of single influential experiments, science as an enterprise is not primarily carried out by isolated brilliant individuals making 'breakthroughs'. It is a communal enterprise taking place in a powerful institutional context and is steered, contained and partly propelled by that context. Conferences, grant-awarding bodies, editorial boards, laboratories with particular traditions, influential patrons, old boy networks, etc., all play a part in defining a consensus, i.e. what is generally accepted at a particular time. This social structure is inevitably fairly conservative. It is the guardian of the continuity and consistency of science, employing an organized scepticism to ensure that new ideas satisfy the criteria mentioned above before being generally accepted.

(5) This careful, thorough process of 'normal' science is not enough; it is hermetic and incomplete. Major advances within a field, and the great syntheses whereby distinct fields are shown to be fundamentally connected, often arise from the impact of new people, new ideas, new techniques, rather than from the steady progress of a single tradition. Such invasions of a field are partly determined by internal intellectual reasons, in the sense that advances in one field now provide insights applicable in another, and partly by external social or economic factors.

(6) Hence the final characteristic feature of scientific claims is their liability to change, to be modified or reformulated or pushed into the background. This crucial characteristic is related to the dependence of scientific claims on experimental evidence. As such the claims *must* be intrinsically testable, they must in some way offer themselves for falsification. A scientific account is therefore provisional rather than absolute. This does not mean that good, useful, well-supported scientific claims can pass abruptly from being true to being false. The whole of genetics has been rethought and rewritten

since 1953 in molecular terms, but that does not mean that classical genetics was wrong. In such a change of paradigm, a view which has been found to be inadequate or incomplete is usually subsumed into a more powerful and more embracing view.

(7) The provisional and consensual nature of science is a *strength* not a weakness. A secure scientific claim derives its power to persuade from the fact that it is consistent with all available knowledge and that no other interpretation is. This persuasiveness is *enhanced* by the fact that new experience and new observations *could* undermine it.

Notes

1 The original paper 'Versuche über Pflanzenhybriden' first appeared in the Society's *Proceedings* (*Verhandlungen des Naturforschenden Vereins in Brünn*), vol. 4, p. 3, in 1866. The first English translation appeared in the *Journal of the Royal Horticultural Society*, vol. 26 (1901). The most readily accessible versions are in Bateson (1913) and in Gabriel and Fogel (1955).

2 de Vries's short note appeared in *Contes rendues de l'académie des Sciences* (Paris), vol. 130, pp. 845–7 and a fuller account of his experiments was subsequently published in *Berichte der Deutsche botanische Gesellschaft* (1900), vol. 18, pp. 83–90.

3 Correns's paper, which introduced the term 'Mendel's rules', appeared in the same volume as de Vries's full paper, op. cit., pp. 158–68. A further report of the independent rediscovery of the phenomena, by Tschermak, appeared later in the volume, pp. 232–9 All three 'rediscovery' papers appear, in translation, in a special jubilee supplement of the journal *Genetics* entitled 'The birth of genetics' (1950).

4 The basic source for details on Mendel's life is the biography by his fellow townsman Iltis (1932). Not quite a work of hagiography, it is detailed and interesting as a source of insight into Mendel's social and intellectual circumstances. A brief and accessible modern account of the man and his work is given by Orel (1984). An account of Mendel's work in the context of the history of classical genetics to 1950 is given by Sturtevant (1965).

5 See, for example, Medvedev (1969) for an account of the career of T. D. Lysenko, the politicization of genetics and the consequent setbacks to genetic research in the USSR.

6 For a brief introduction to the commercial and medical potential of the latest developments in molecular genetics see Yanchinski (1985).

7 e.g. Birkett (1979).

8 The most thorough analysis of the experiments reported in Mendel's paper was carried out by the statistician and biometrician R. A. Fisher (1936) who on the basis of the space available and the number of years attempted to reconstruct the annual sequence of experiments. He concluded that they were carried out in the order described. He also concluded that Mendel's quantitative data consistently deviate less from exact ratios than would be expected at random. This conclusion is discussed critically by Sturtevant (1965).

9 This succinct term has been used to draw attention to the important informal social structures of science. Members of an 'invisible college' are an elite group defining a specific area of research who maintain contact through meetings, exchange of draft papers, swapping of students and other informal means. In this way new specializations are defined before they become 'visible' through the founding of journals, learnéd societies, etc. See Price (1963).

10 This definition of much of science was introduced by Kuhn (1962) as a contrast to what he terms 'revolutionary science'.

11 The original scholarly account and basic source is Olby (1974). An interesting and personal impression of the whole development of molecular biology, supported by interviews and pen-portraits of many of the protagonists, is by Judson (1979). To place the beginning of molecular biology in the context of other developments in biology in the last century, see Allen (1975). The most accessible and readable account, and yet one which should be treated with some caution, is Watson's own personal account (1968). This has now been reissued in a 'critical edition' (Stent, 1981) which provides the text of *The Double Helix*, a summary of the background science, an account of events surrounding its publication, a collection of some of the original reviews of the book, additional comments by several of the other participants and reprints of the key papers in which the solution of the structure and its implications were presented.

12 For example, Watson learned the results of the Hershey and Chase experiments on bacteriophage replication directly by letter from Hershey. Chargaff visited Cambridge and talked with Watson and Crick in mid-1952 although the meeting was not a great success. Watson attended informal seminars by members of the group at King's College London and he and Crick had access to a report of Wilkins's and Franklin's work written for the Medical Research Council.

3 A key factor in this success was that Watson shared an office with a

structural chemist, Donohue, who was in a position to correct the incorrect detailed structure of A, C, G and T given in textbooks at the time.

14 The original paper by Watson and Crick (1953) is dry and brief, but it ends, famously, with the self-conscious understatement: 'It has not escaped our notice that the specific pairing we have postulated immediately suggests a possible copying mechanism for the genetic material.'

15 For more systematic but highly readable accounts of the general position adopted here see Goldstein and Goldstein (1978) and Ziman (1978).

Chapter Five

Art

STEPHEN BANN

I should explain from the outset that this chapter does not attempt to deal with 'art' in the very general sense which the word has acquired. What I shall be discussing, essentially, is the tradition of paintings and drawings, most often portable and enclosed within a frame, which has persisted in Europe, and those areas under the cultural influence of Europe, since the fifteenth century. This is not simply for the negative reason that all the different forms of artefact classed as 'art' by past and present societies throughout the world would present a whole host of individual problems, intimately bound up with the different social, economic and cultural conditions obtaining in those societies. It is also for a very good positive reason. This is that for about four centuries following the so-called 'Renaissance' of the fifteenth century in Europe, the pictorial art of Europe observed the strict regime of what we have come to call 'perspective'. Treatises like Alberti's celebrated *On Painting* laid down the particular principles which painters were to follow in their representation of the visible world. Arguably, by their observance of these principles, they were enabled to 'capture' aspects of that world in a wholly unprecedented form of synthesis, which owed as much to science and mathematics as it did to the earlier practices of pictorial art. From the later part of the nineteenth century, as is well known, the regime of perspective ceased to have the binding force which it had exerted before. Painters felt free to experiment with different ways of representing the world and the possibility of an entirely 'abstract' art was eventually explored. But I shall suggest that we still need to know about the particular values invested in perspective, both theoretically and practically, before we can understand the pictorial art of the contemporary period.

The 'Essential Copy' and the 'Eye-Witness Principle'

Much has been written about the superior claim of paintings in 'correct' perspective to represent reality. Essentially the argument rages between those who claim that perspectivally based visual art is in some sense objectively true, since it reproduces the conditions of our normal vision, and those who claim that perspectivally based art is culturally bound and means nothing to those who have not learned the particular conventions which have developed within the European tradition since the Renaissance. I am not going to debate this question in general terms since I believe that both extreme positions in the debate are severely limiting. But I shall be using, in the course of my discussion of particular examples, some unifying concepts which relate to this argument about the nature of perspectival painting. These are Norman Bryson's concept of the 'essential copy' (1983) and E. H. Gombrich's concept of the 'eye-witness principle' (1980, p. 190).

Norman Bryson begins his study, *Vision and Painting*, with a quotation from the Roman author Pliny, who is discussing a competition between five legendary Greek painters. One of them, Zeuxis, 'produced a picture of grapes so dexterously represented that birds began to fly down to eat from the painted vine'. Thereupon his rival Parrhasius 'designed so life-like a picture of a curtain that Zeuxis, proud of the verdict of the birds, requested that the curtain should now be drawn back and the picture displayed'. Appropriately enough, Zeuxis conceded victory to Parrhasius on the grounds that he had only been able to deceive birds, whilst his rival had actually managed to deceive him' (Bryson, 1983, p. 1)

Like Ben Brewster in his chapter on film (p. 144), I am inclined to see a good deal of interest in this innocent little story. For one thing, it establishes deception, or at least 'illusion', as the necessary goal of painterly technique. The best painter is viewed here not as the person who is most capable of refining the conventions of representation but as the person who can create the illusion, however momentary, of presenting us with the 'real thing'. Of course, there is a paradox here. The birds are not going to be satisfied with the painted grapes and the painted curtain is not going to offer access to anything except its deceptive self. Why should we not admit that the painter can only give us what are necessarily mere substitutes for reality? This may seem an incontrovertible argument. But it does not diminish the effect which the myth of the 'essential copy' (to use Bryson's term) has exercised in the history of Western art. Perhaps we have to concede that we are adept in maintaining a kind of 'doublethink' in these matters. It is worth mentioning that we have a separate genre of painting called *trompe-l'oeil*, whose ostensible purpose is to achieve just the same feats of deception as the legendary Greek painters. But *trompe-l'oeil* paintings are also intensely problematic, in exactly the same way. If such works really 'deceived our eye', then we would not be aware that we were in fact in the presence of works of art. Clearly we enjoy being – as it were – *half*-convinced by the painter's illusionistic abilities.

Bryson's notion of the 'essential copy' implies that the artist is somehow enabled to transmute his medium into another substance. We think that it is a drawn curtain, or a violin hanging upon a cupboard door. But actually it is just a combination of glazed pigments, applied by a skilful artist. Yet the artists of the Renaissance and their successors were much more ambitious than Parrhasius and Zeuxis. They aspired to render in terms of paint not only objects in shallow space, but broad vistas of the visible world stretching away to far horizons which were marked, in pictorial terms, by the existence of a 'vanishing point'. How did they manage to do so and what unifying concept can we employ to make sense of the distinctive type of order which they succeeded in creating?

It is here that Gombrich's notion of the 'eye-witness principle' comes in useful. Gombrich rightly judges that 'complete mimesis', or the perfection of the 'essential copy', is bound to be 'a will-o'-the-wisp' and he suggests that it is more profitable to think in terms of a 'negative rule': 'the artist must not include in his image anything the eye-witness could not have seen from a particular point at a particular moment' (1980, p. 190). We should stop thinking of the painter as being caught up in the impossible task of reducing the astonishing complexity of the external world to a two-dimensional surface. Instead we should think of him as engaged in a kind of hypothesis from which certain consequences necessarily flow. Let us imagine the eye-witness at his particular vantage-point. He can only see the objects, or bodies, within his field of vision to the extent that they present a particular aspect to him – a profile, say, or a back view. He can only see them, moreover, if they do not stand in each other's way, and he may have to be content with an element that is only partially visible because another element is blocking it. And, no less important, he will have to reckon with the inevitable limitation placed upon human vision: that objects get smaller and more indistinct to the extent that they are further away from the eye of the beholder. Gombrich is right in stressing that this 'negative rule' helps us to conceive of the painter as engaged in certain specific technical tasks, all of them logically derived from the assumption that an eye-witness *could have seen* the vista in question.

Perspective, 'Istoria' and Cloud Formations in the Renaissance

Of course, Gombrich's 'eye-witness principle' does not solve all our problems for us. It could indeed be argued that the device of assuming a 'witness' to the scene represented is one that can be discussed on many levels and requires strict historical treatment if we are to extract any really precise meaning from it.[1] Nevertheless, it is worth adopting simply as a working hypothesis. The very fact that it does not fully account for all the features of correspondence between the visual image and the real world is an advantage since it will prompt us to a more complex and many-layered formulation of the problem.

Let us begin by looking at two Renaissance paintings in the

Plate 5.1   Follower of Fra Angelico, *The Rape of Helen by Paris*

light of the 'eye-witness principle'. The panel painting, *The Rape of Helen by Paris*, dated around 1450 and ascribed to a follower of Fra Angelico, is a delightful example of the fascination with perspective felt by the Florentine painters of the period (Plate 5.1). In all probability, it was originally part of the decoration of a wooden chest, which may account for the slight asymmetry in its overall octagonal form. But if the overall shape is predetermined by a decorative function, the image itself is organized according to clear geometrical principles. The world, or rather one selected vista, is laid out before us, as if we were observing the action from a central, raised position. To the right is a sumptuous palace, whose eaves, aligned windows and decorated colonnades recede sharply away from us. To the left is a more open prospect, with a ship standing at anchor and a series of other ships spread out along an estuary which stretches into the far distance. In the dead centre, or so it seems, stands a solitary tree. As we scan the picture, our gaze travels from left to right and back again, moving into the distance as the carefully contrived recession tempts us to do. Usually it comes to rest on the strong vertical accent of that solitary tree.

It will be evident from this brief description that this is not simply a scene as an 'eye-witness' might have observed it. Or to put it more clearly, this is not presented as being one of an infinite number of possible vistas which a witness of the Rape of Helen by Paris might have observed. Rather we might say that the scene itself is organized by the painter with regard to the optimum visibility – and also the optimum comprehensibility – of its different elements. The painting presents us with a kind of redundance, in that those elements which are most important to the story *are at the same time* most important to the construction of the space. Paris and Helen are dashing across from the palace to the waiting ship. But their movement has been arrested just at the point where Helen, or more exactly Helen's fashionable headgear, fits into the apex of a triangle extending from the implied lines of the palace architecture. The tree, slightly to the right of Helen, makes it all the more difficult *not* to pay attention to this central incident. And indeed there is another tree, of exactly the same form, on a far-distant bank of the estuary, which serves as a kind of target for our vision. This central area of the painting is not only where the main incident is taking place; it is also the area into which we can project the furthest distance.

I am not going to pretend that this little painting is 'correct' in its perspective down to the last detail. But I would claim that it shows up the high degree of empirical correlation between a painting constructed in this way – with linear emphases creating recession and repetition – and the visual world as we experience it. This does not, of course, mean that the painting exhibits an order which is, in some way, objectively true. In fact, we need our skills of interpretation to make sense of the schemata which are being put before us. Both the boatman to the left of the picture and the figurine, possibly of Apollo, in the palace to the right are reduced in size. But whereas we make the judgement that the boatman is reduced in size because of his notional distance from us, we are inclined to think that the figurine is simply smaller than life-size. This is not only because of the surrounding spatial clues – the dark space of the palace interior would allow us to read in a high degree of recession – but because of our prior knowledge. We know that there are such things as figurines of less than life-size.

Of course there are many more figures in the scene than Paris and Helen, Apollo and the boatman, just as there are fortified villages and clumps of trees extending over the far hillsides, and many other points of detail. What are they there for? Alberti provides the clue in his strong advocacy of the property of 'istoria', which is not so much 'history' or 'story' in our sense of the term, but might be described as the articulation of the story in such a way that a lively series of interrelated aspects may appear simultaneously to the spectator. To quote directly from Alberti, 'I say that *istoria* is most copious in which in their places are mixed old, young, maidens, women, youths, young boys, fowl, small dogs, birds, horses, sheep, buildings, landscapes and all similar things' (Alberti, 1977, p. 75). All these properties may not occur in *The Rape of Helen by Paris*, but there are quite a few of them and quite a number of others! Any reading of the perspectival system would be very limited if it did not pick up the point that such a constructed space is valuable to Alberti precisely because it facilitates the rich diversity of different elements, distributed throughout the deep, receding prospect.

There is a final point to be made about this work which raises a possible difficulty. Gombrich's 'eye-witness principle' is entirely compatible with the notion that the scene has been constructed, spatially, for the spectator's benefit; it is also compatible with the Albertian principle that it should exhibit 'istoria' – the interlocking of disparate elements in a putative 'story'. But is this painting actually showing a scene 'from a particular point' *and* 'at a particular moment'? It looks rather as if Paris and Helen are those two tiny heads peering out from the stern of the ship. In that case, the ship would be setting sail and maybe those other ships are in fact the same ship, picked up at successive points in the lovers' flight towards Troy. There would be nothing surprising if the painter had decided to give us a sequence of this kind, since the convention of showing different temporal stages of the same

Plate 5.2   School of Giovanni Bellini, *The Virgin and Child*

narrative within a single spatial continuum was, in fact, a familiar technique of the medieval artist which did not entirely disappear at the advent of the Renaissance. But if we were willing to admit this, we would have to say that, for this particular work at any rate, the simple operation of the 'eye-witness principle' could not be taken for granted. The painting would be a kind of hybrid, capable of being read in two rather different ways.

I will leave that possibility as unresolved, since there is no obvious way of resolving it, and pass on to our second painting from the Renaissance, *The Virgin and Child*, from the studio of the Venetian painter, Giovanni Bellini (Plate 5.2). Completed not long after *The Rape of Helen by Paris*, it represents, of course, a sacred rather than a secular scene; and in place of the variety of 'istoria' we have the concentration of the devotional image. The Christ child is placed upon a kind of ledge which tips slightly towards us. In fact, we could think of the picture as being organized in a series of parallel planes, with the Virgin at the rear, the Christ child in the middle (just behind the plane which is defined by the front of the window ledge) and the dangling tassel occupying the most frontal plane. Whereas the Florentine painting previously discussed employed pictorial devices in order to carve out a deep space, extending as far as the horizon, this Venetian work appears to be utilizing a directly opposite procedure. It deploys perspective in order to build out the elements of the picture, almost propelling the Christ child in our direction. This effect of immediacy is strengthened by the fact that we have no horizon line – simply the turbulent patterning of high cloud formations.

Although an argument based on single examples is bound to be tenuous, I would suggest that this contrast is an instructive one. For both these works the 'eye-witness principle' works perfectly well. Yet the ways in which we are induced to 'witness' are significantly different. It may be relevant to point out that the experimental panels of the Florentine architect, Brunelleschi, which have been widely credited as the first demonstrations of Renaissance perspective, opened up the possibility of a similar division. Brunelleschi constructed his panels – whether from optical or mathematical principles is not clear – by registering the perspectival recession of the surrounding buildings in two central squares in Florence. Yet the presence of the sky had to be indicated in his panels either by the mirror reflection of the real sky, or by leaving the top side of the panel open so that the real sky could be seen beyond.[2] In other words, the sky could not be constructed perspectivally; it remained as a kind of backdrop, to be filled in by a kind of 'cheating'. What I am going to suggest is that this significant exception to the rules of perspective is a pointer to the way in which the perspectival system will be overturned in the art of our own century. This Venetian *Virgin and Child* already suggests, perhaps, the problem posed for the perspectival system by an unorthodox pictorial organization: precisely because those clouds are so vividly evoked, with no stable horizon line to help in defining their distance, the whole composition is poised on the edge of a spatial vortex, disorientating but perhaps also delighting the spectator.

Perspective Improved: a Seventeenth-Century Dutch Interior and Two Modern Drawings

I have been suggesting that Gombrich's 'eye-witness principle' is a good guide to the general character of Renaissance painting but that it may not account for some of the most important aspects of these works. The notion of a 'negative rule' – that nothing must be included that could not have been seen from a particular point at a particular moment – is a useful one. But what about the convention of 'istoria', which means that the painting should tell a story and do so by incorporating the maximum variety of visual incident which is compatible with a clear articulation of what is going on? And what if we suspect that the painter is returning to medieval precedent and actually constructing successive moments within a given narrative? Passing from our Florentine to our Venetian example, what if the painter should deliberately disorientate us by giving prominence to the very element which cannot easily be accommodated within the conventional receding space of the perspectival construction?

The answers to these rhetorical questions can only be provided by looking at the course of Western art since the Renaissance. In a

92

Plate 5.3 Pieter Saenredam, *Interior of St Bavo's Church at Haarlem*

sense I am claiming that perspectival art, despite its unique claim
to reproduce the conditions of our natural vision, is a system
which possesses certain inbuilt inconsistencies and tensions; and
that we can understand its historical development in terms of the
ways in which these tensions have been alternately suppressed
and acknowledged. The 'reality' of such representations is strictly

93

dependent on the criteria which we use in evaluating not the system as a whole but its local and particular manifestations. In other words, it may not make much sense to say: does perspective adequately represent reality? It may be more relevant to ask the question: what role does perspective play in supporting or undercutting the *effect* of reality which is conveyed by this or that visual representation?

To underline this point I would like to turn to a painting from the seventeenth-century Dutch school, Pieter Saenredam's *Interior of St Bavo's Church at Haarlem* (1648) (Plate 5.3). If the Renaissance undoubtedly shows discordant features in the uses made of perspective, the Dutch painting of this period could be taken as the prime example of a practice which virtually elimi- nates such features. Svetlana Alpers has indeed written a sub- stantial study, entitled *The Art of Describing*, to sustain the argument that Dutch painters of the seventeenth century cannot be evaluated by the criteria which Alberti set up in his influential treatise. In particular, she claims, they have no interest in the complex narrative constructions recommended under the title of 'istoria'. Even when they use pictorial compositions which are reminiscent of the Italian school, their interest is really elsewhere. Indeed their true colleagues are not the Italian painters of the Renaissance tradition but the scientists and theorists of their own time and country, who were perfecting devices like the micro- scope in order to increase their detailed knowledge of the visible world (Alpers, 1983, pp. xxiv–vi).

This argument is a fascinating one from our point of view, since it suggests a crucial modification of the 'eye-witness principle'. If we imagine ourselves as eye-witnesses of the Rape of Helen by Paris, then we are essentially observing a dramatic action; the attendant ship and the crowded palace provide the theatre for this action, just as the perspectival space gives it an orderly medium in which to deploy its related sub-plots. But if, in Svetlana Alpers's terms, we are the eye-witnesses of a Dutch painting, we are noting the close correlation between what is represented in the painting and the intriguing variety of the phenomenal world. Indeed, we could almost be said to be using the painting as a kind of microscope, which offers up appearances in a quintessential, and therefore more intelligible, way. A painter who uses his skill to convey the amazingly varied surface textures of ivory and rose petals, pearls and clay pipes, is not interested in the superficial moral constructions that might be placed on his work but in the sheer success of his virtuoso rendering of the visible world.

It must be pointed out that Dutch painters of this period did in fact use technical devices such as reflecting lenses and the camera obscura to support their quasi-scientific efforts. They went much further than their Italian predecessors in experimenting with different forms of projection of the visible world on screens or other flat surfaces. But, of course, this does not mean that they were ready to eliminate the element of personal judgement in ensuring that the images which they produced were *perceptually* as well as mathematically accurate. Saenredam's great painting is a case in point. Martin Kemp's research enables us to trace the successive stages which led up to the achievement of the finished work. Saenredam began with a free-hand drawing which he dated 25 August 1635. Although he was not concerned with accurate perspective at this stage, he did mark the 'eye-point' – corresponding to his line of sight – on the drawing. Subsequently he produced an 'elaborate construction drawing', in which a geometrical framework of precise perspective was laid down, so that the architectural features could be mapped on to it. Finally he traced the main outline of the construction drawings on to a primed panel and painted this over to form the final composition. Yet even at this stage and after a considerable labour of measurement and geometrical reconstruction, Saenredam was concerned to modify elements of his scheme for perceptual reasons. A comparison with a mechanically produced perspective from the same viewpoint in the same church makes this point incontrovertible. Saenredam has increased the height of the main arch so that it extends to the top of the picture and he has also diminished the relative size of the figures in the left-hand aisle (M. Kemp, 1984, pp. 30–7).

This example suggests surely that the most painstaking and accurate use of perspective still leaves open the question: what is perspective to be used for? And the answer inevitably comes back: it is to be used to support and enhance the particular aesthetic effect which the painter desires to obtain. Saenredam is painting a type of picture in which all the ambiguities which we noted as being latent in the Renaissance practice are already eliminated; there is no story, and no landscape, let alone sky, to interfere with the strict recession of the architectural structure. He is painting in full knowledge of the recent sophisticated studies of perspective being made by his compatriots. He has not by any means excluded all literary or moralistic elements from his composition, as Svetlana Alpers's comments on the words inscribed on the organ loft make abundantly clear.[3] But at the same time, we can hardly doubt that his primary purpose was to record the awesome church interior with a degree of faithful precision which would captivate his audience. And yet in the final resort we find him slightly altering his laboriously obtained measurements and proportions in order to accentuate the awesomeness of effect. No one could possibly have detected the fact without the benefit of these exact reconstructions. The fact that it should be so indicates the narrow territory between objective record and subjective effect that Saenredam is conscious of having to occupy.

I doubt if anyone reading this will be surprised by the point which I am making here. After all, we are talking about the 'eye-witness principle', and eye-witnesses are obviously human beings, rather than detached retinas upon which a certain configuration of visual elements happens to be registered. Yet I think that it is also important to stress the fact that this conceptual distinction between what counts as objective and what counts as subjective in the representation of the external world is itself dependent on the historical development of forms of visual representation. To put it simply, there has to be an objective referent against which to measure the subjective vision, in order for us to be able to establish that it is, indeed, subjective. And that objective referent depends on the current spectrum of modes of representation. In the seventeenth century, no doubt, it could be found in the images produced by the camera obscura, or the armature of construction drawings as produced by Saenredam. In our own period it is to be found in the variety of different types of image which have derived from the invention of photography in the last century. Photography is indeed, on one level, the culmination of the 'eye-witness principle' in the sense that it involves both an objective record of the external world and the

Plate 5.4 John Tetley, *Banqueting House Interior, Hackfall*, 1986

participation of a human agent – whose hand has worked the shutter. Photography does not actually invalidate the point which I made previously – that eye-witnesses are human beings. But it allows us to conceive of the theoretical possibility that objective record and subjective judgement *could* be dissociated.

One consequence of the development of photography has therefore been that, from the nineteenth century onwards, visual artists have had to face a broad choice. Either they could insist that painting was devoted to achieving just the kind of correspondence with the real world that photography was unable to achieve, or they could concede that photography offered a particularly valuable kind of visual information which would enable them to develop and extend their own types of composition and construction. Of course, in a sense the most interesting painters were those who opted for both choices simultaneously. The Impressionists were, after all, accentuating the elements of vivid colour and lively handling of paint on the surface that photography, with its matt surfaces and early restriction to monochrome, most conspicuously lacked. But they were also using types of unorthodox composition, very far removed from Albertian space, which the unselective operation of the camera had thrown up.

In a sense the contemporary artist is still in the same position. He can react against photography, or make use of it, or indeed do both of these things simultaneously. And the undeniable fact of photography has to be taken for granted in any assessment of the part which perspectival projection plays in contemporary art. This point is confirmed by two drawings by two contemporary British artists, John Tetley and Stephen Farthing. John Tetley's work, *Banqueting House Interior, Hackfall*, belongs to the tradition of topographical art (Plate 5.4); it forms part of a series of works which document the decayed country estate of Hackfall in Yorkshire. Tetley's method of working has involved visits to the actual location and an extensive photographic documentation of the different buildings and garden features. Then the final works are elaborated in his studio. What we immediately sense when we see this particular drawing is its perspectival accuracy and its likely kinship with a photograph; but that impression is soon succeeded by an awareness of the dramatic

Plate 5.5 Stephen Farthing, *A Room from Balzac*, 'Monsieur Grandet's Room', 1982

compositional effect which the photograph has facilitated and a reaction to the interesting spatial ambiguity which the dark pencil strokes have created in following the surface of the projecting beam.

This drawing in fact trades on one of the most long-standing resources of perspectival art, which is the ability to convey the effect of a high, curved, receding vault. Saenredam's painting uses this effect too and an even more illustrious precedent would be Masaccio's great fresco of the Trinity, in the Duomo at Florence, which is usually taken as one of the most significant monuments in the developing art of perspective. By contrast, Stephen Farthing's *A Room from Balzac* draws its title from the dominant French realist novelist of the nineteenth century and uses perspective as a kind of bag of tricks whose exaggerated effects are satirically put on stage for our benefit (Plate 5.5). The room, actually 'Monsieur Grandet's Room', has to an accentuated degree the contrived recession which we notice in its unselfconscious form in *The Rape of Helen by Paris*. But the walls have been pierced and the whole contents are exposed in a kind of relentless visibility. If the Florentine painter peopled his composition according to the requirements of 'istoria', Farthing has set up a kind of parody of the visual field of the omniscient author, who must indeed pass through walls and eavesdrop on private thoughts to bring us our feast of knowledge. It is appropriate that, whereas Tetley used the finesses of lead pencil for his topographically faithful rendering, Farthing has used the soft effects of charcoal and conté to convey a world of sagging solidity. Tetley has a direct, uncomplicated relation to perspective, which serves as an aid to correct drawing, but Farthing offers us an ironic version of the eye-witness's all-conquering gaze.

Transformations of Perspective in the Modern Period

It will be obvious from the examination of these two drawings that the specific qualities of the medium have a distinct influence on the way in which we read such works and that considerations of the correctness or incorrectness of perspective cannot easily be disentangled from this aesthetic effect. Gombrich concedes that 'the standard of truth' is also related to the medium: 'the image cannot give us more information than the medium can carry' (Gombrich, 1980, p. 192). But he points out that the 'eye-witness principle' to a certain extent overrides this limitation. 'It was due to the eye-witness principle that standards of truthfulness or accuracy could be accepted by the artist irrespective of the medium.' What this implies, presumably, is that the objective mathematical basis of perspective is not dependent for its 'truthfulness' on the actual physical properties of varnished oil paint.[5] But, as Gombrich recognizes, this new 'standard of truth' is very much a product of the Renaissance. In the Middle Ages, artists thought differently about the truthfulness of their images. And surely the same can be said of the artists of today? At least, this is a hypothesis which can be pursued in this closing section.

One way of doing so is by reverting from Gombrich's 'eye-witness principle' to the other criterion which was discussed at the outset: Norman Bryson's 'essential copy'. That this notion is particularly important in the context of the Renaissance can be shown by referring once again to Alberti's treatise, *On Painting*. Alberti scorns the use of actual gold in paintings for the very reason that this prodigal employment of the precious metal is in no way a sign of the artist's skill; 'there is more admiration and praise for the painter who imitates rays of gold with colours' (Alberti, 1977, p. 85). That an artist is able to evoke the appearance of precious things through the use of pigments of minimal worth is a quintessential test of his new status at the time of the Renaissance. The difference in value between what the artist convincingly shows us and the intrinsic value of the object if it had indeed been real is a good measure of the value of genius. No doubt the artist of *The Rape of Helen by Paris* was particularly attentive to making his figurine of Apollo glow in the darkness with a silvery sheen! But what if the painter were to abandon the very test of skill which shows him creating value out of nothing? This would not necessarily be because he had lost the skill but because he had other intentions. What those intentions might be is cleverly hinted in a well-known passage by Guillaume Apollinaire on the late Cubist paintings of Picasso:

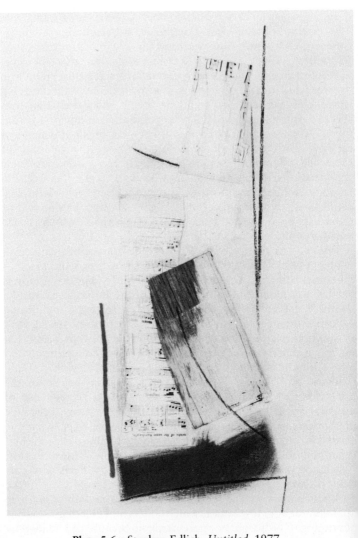

Plate 5.6 Stephen Edlich, *Untitled*, 1977

He has questioned the universe severely. He has grown accustomed to the immense light of unfathomable spaces. At times, he has not hesitated to entrust real objects to the light – a two-penny song, a real postage stamp, a piece of newspaper, a piece of oilcloth imprinted with chair caning. The art of the painter could not add any pictorial element to the truth of these objects.

(Apollinaire, 1972, p. 279)

This is the kind of passage which most people would no doubt take with a large pinch of salt, while accepting the point that Apollinaire was enthusiastic about Picasso's novel procedure of collage. Yet the terms in which the encomium is made are in fact very clear – particularly in the context of our own discussions. Picasso has rejected the 'essential copy' – and in so doing rejected that equation between artistic skill and illusionism which was consolidated by Alberti. He has done so not for capricious reasons but because of his new perception of 'unfathomable spaces' – presumably those spaces which cannot be enclosed within the mathematical parameters of perspective. His works display, not orderly groupings of objects governed by an 'eye-witness principle', but 'real objects' like a postage stamp and a piece of newspaper. Rather than being deployed in diminishing sizes along a receding prospect constructed by the painter, these 'real objects' are simply stuck to the surface of the canvas or paper.

More than half a century afterwards, the American painter Stephen Edlich is still working in the spirit of Picasso's innovation (Plate 5.6). 'Real objects' have been 'entrusted ... to the light' – two oblong pieces of printed music and two slices of the paper-thin wooden sheets that one finds in cigar-boxes. Of course they are not simply there in their own right, as indices of the different worlds of cigar-smoking and playing a Bach sarabande from the score. They are also there as part of a unified pictorial composition and it is worth seeing this aspect in the light of the particular tradition of perspectival art that we have been describing. Obviously there is no deep space here, methodically constructed so that it appears to reach away from the viewer towards a vanishing point on the horizon. The space is shallow, as it were

built out towards us, in a way that we might call reminiscent of the Venetian *Virgin and Child* discussed previously. Instead of the protruding ledge and its overlapping tassel, we have the inverted sheet of music (not to be *read* as music) and the overlapping slice of wood. Planes therefore overlap each other in shallow space and at the same time a thin layer of white pigment masks some of the sharp edges and obscures the detail of the printed music. This enveloping whiteness is perhaps an equivalent to the traditional function of the cloud in perspectival painting.

Stephen Edlich's *Untitled* (1977) suggests that neither the 'eye-witness principle' nor the notion of the 'essential copy' have been totally abandoned in contemporary art. They have simply undergone a transformation. The art of collage, by incorporating the 'real object', is the final, ironic stage in the game which fooled Zeuxis. The shallow, fluctuating space which we owe to the Cubist painters is a reversal of the deep, precisely bounded space in early Renaissance art. But the question remains. What does such a painting represent?

On the specific level there is little to be said in answer to this question. But let us probe somewhat more deeply into the issue. No doubt we can accept that the paintings of the Renaissance were not only representations of specific themes, like 'The Rape of Helen by Paris', but also, in some sense, of a new attitude to the visible world. Burckhardt called one of the chapters of his famous *Civilization of the Renaissance in Italy*, 'The discovery of the world and of man', indicating that in his view the humanist project of exploring man's mind went hand in hand with the vast expansion of knowledge about the far-away parts of the globe which took place in this period. Obviously the 'conquest of space' through the devices of perspective is not unrelated to this development, however much we would find it difficult to argue about the precise ways in which it was related. But if we concede this general point, we might also concede its corollary. Given that the Renaissance witnessed both the symbolic conquest of space through perspective and the actual conquest of space as a result of 'voyages of discovery', we might expect our own period, in which the era of Western expansion over the globe has ended but the colonization of the solar system has only just begun, to have seen an equally decisive mutation in the symbolic expression of space.

Such an argument may seem merely simplistic. Paintings change. Man's view of the world changes. But how can we expect to make a significant correlation? One of the ways, I would suggest, is to look at instances where a modern painter has specifically tried to give expression to a new vision of the universe. In *Equals Infinity* (1932), Paul Klee has lightly, but convincingly, employed his considerable knowledge of modern mathematics and cosmology for an artistic purpose (Plate 5.7). In his *Creative Confessions* of 1920, Klee is already seeking to express in language the infinite dimensions of the universe: 'Above our heads the stars shine (a seed-bed of points).' Hubert Damisch has deftly explained the exceedingly complex train of thought which led Klee to place the mathematical sign for infinity (somewhat metamorphosed into the sign for the sound-hole of a violin) in the midst of this 'seed-bed of points'. '*A seed-bed of points* where one could thus read (but in that case is it the right word?) the infinite just as Ruskin claimed to read it in a patch of Turner's *blue*' (Damisch, 1976, p. 58).

Damisch is here referring to a striking passage in *Modern Painters* when Ruskin celebrates Turner's ability to re-create the sense of infinity in landscape (Ruskin, 1903, p. 254). Klee's picture obviously does not evoke limitless space in the same fashion. For one thing, it incorporates *legible* signs – the 'equals' sign and the ambiguous symbol of infinity – in a composition which is otherwise a literal representation of Klee's 'seed-bed of points'. Damisch is right to ask if 'reading' is the right word for this apparently hybrid representation. Yet we should perhaps be chary of making too categorical a distinction between paintings which observe the conventions of perspective, like those of Turner, and contemporary paintings, like those of Klee. Once again, it may be a matter not of total rupture in the tradition but of transformation. A Turner painting is spatially organized according to a 'vanishing point' which is a purely theoretical construct. No such point exists, except in so far as the receding lines of the picture stretch towards it. Klee has made manifest his 'seed-bed of points', so that they are not the theoretical consequence of a system but the elements defining a fluctuating space. We can, if we choose, see his work as an attempt to visualize a universe which can no longer be plotted out in terms of the traditional linear co-ordinates.

Of course, the example of Klee cannot be taken as standing in for the whole of contemporary art. At the same time it would be wrong to take it as a completely isolated case. I have argued here that such concepts as the 'essential copy' and the 'eye-witness principle' may indeed help us to understand the particular correspondence to reality which Western art has traditionally sought to achieve. But these concepts should not be taken as transcending historical circumstances. Nor above all should they be taken to have relinquished their hold upon the artist in the modern period. What is made manifest by the development of Western art over the past five centuries is the founding, and subsequently the evolution, of a system. That is what we have to understand before we can appreciate the ways in which the system has been transformed.

Notes

1 It has been argued that the role of the 'witness' or 'beholder' of a perspectival painting is itself strictly dependent on the historical and cultural conditions in which it was produced and cannot be reduced to a merely mechanical relationship between a disembodied eye and a mathematical system. A recent article, for example, discusses Gérôme's nineteenth-century painting of *The Death of Marshal Ney* in the following terms: '[The beholder] is someone who comes upon the scene almost by accident and must first make sense of what he sees' (W. Kemp, 1985, p. 118). In the light of this kind of judgement, Gombrich's 'eye-witness principle' may seem a rather crude rule of thumb. But it is still valuable as a 'minimal' definition of what might be implied by a picture in correct perspective. Gombrich's require- ment that 'the artist must not include in his image anything the eye-witness could not have seen from a particular point at a particular moment' recalls the 'negative' principle that he uses in *Art and Illusion* to discuss two contemporary drawings of Tivoli: that 'those who understand the notation will derive *no false information* from the drawing'. The passage is quoted and discussed more extensively in the chapter on philosophy by Michael Leahy (pp. 167).
2 For a translation of the texts which describe Brunelleschi's experi- ments and a detailed commentary, see White (1972).

3 The words visible are extracted from a biblical text which exhorts us to 'teach and admonish one another in psalms and spiritual songs' (Alpers, 1983, p. 175).

4 This may well seem obvious. But Gombrich is probably concerned to disentangle this argument, about the 'truthfulness' of perspective, from the more general discussion of representation in which he has always tended to maintain that the 'medium' has no less an effect on the final form of the art-work than the representational purpose which it is intended to serve. In an early essay, he concluded neatly: 'The form of the key depends on the material out of which it is fashioned, and on the lock' (Gombrich, 1963, p. 8). In this more recent essay, he is more concerned to stress the 'negative' capability of perspectival pictures (and indeed photographs): 'The image cannot give us more information than the medium can carry. But this limitation does not lead to a denial of any standard [of truth]. On the contrary, while the principle may suggest that information of the visible world can rarely be completely matched in any medium, we also learn why it can still exclude false information' (Gombrich, 1980, p. 192).

Chapter Six

Physics

LEWIS RYDER

Introduction

One hundred years ago physical scientists (or natural philosophers, as they were called) considered that they had an almost
complete understanding of the physical world. Newton's laws
provided (it was thought) a faultless account of mechanics and
gravitation and Maxwell's equations did the same for electricity
and magnetism. The nature of heat, light and sound seemed to
hold no mysteries and it was felt that when a few problems
connected with atoms and radioactivity had been sorted out,
understanding of the physical world would be well-nigh complete. At that time there was boundless confidence in the efficacy
of science and this confidence is still felt in the public domain
today. Science is held in great esteem and is generally supposed to
provide irrefutably correct accounts of natural phenomena and to
offer an unambiguous world-view (a 'scientific' world-view).
Above all, scientific theories are supposed to be unchallengeable
and absolute, since they are founded on 'facts' – and who can
deny facts?

This view does not, however, correspond exactly with the way
present-day physicists understand their science. It is true that we
understand a great many things and our theories are, in almost all
spheres, well worked out and brilliantly successful. At a fundamental level, however, the simple world-view of the nineteenth-
century scientists has disappeared and this has happened because

of the great revolutions caused by Einstein's theories of relativity, particularly Special Relativity (1905) and the quantum theory (*c*. 1926). Einstein's theory, although it had its roots in Maxwell's equations of electromagnetism, came as a bolt out of the blue and proposed, amongst other things, that *time is relative*. There is no such thing as absolute time. Moving clocks go slower than stationary ones. Relativity poses a radical challenge to our everyday notions and assumptions but this is not the first time this has happened in science. Copernicus caused a similar revolution centuries ago. We shall in this chapter consider the Copernican revolution as well as the theory of relativity and examine what they have to teach us about science.

Even more disturbing than relativity, however, is the quantum theory. Relativity concerns the nature of space and time, quantum theory the nature of matter. It was found in the early years of this century that on the submicroscopic scale of the atom, matter does not behave the way it does on the 'everyday' scale. Atoms are not like tiny billiard balls. We may say of a billiard ball both where it is and how fast it is moving. But if we know where an atom is, we have no idea how fast it is moving; its speed is indeed intrinsically unknowable. We may on the other hand know how fast it is moving, but in this case we sacrifice all knowledge of its position; it then has no meaning to say 'it is here' since *in a sense* it is everywhere. These intrinsic limitations on knowledge at the atomic and subatomic level are summarized in Heisenberg's 'Uncertainty Principle' and of course pose another radical challenge to our understanding of the world. It is clear that the mechanics of the atom ('quantum mechanics') is completely different from Newtonian (or 'classical') mechanics, and the problem of *interpreting* quantum mechanics is still not solved to the satisfaction of most physicists.

Thus in the twentieth century the question of what is 'real' in science has become rather more than a trivial one. With this general question at the back of our minds, we shall in this chapter undertake a mini-tour of science, which begins with astronomy followed by Newtonian gravitation; these topics, as well as having a bearing on our theme, also stand as sound examples of classical physics. Next we consider relativity and then quantum theory, which in their differing ways have caused us to modify

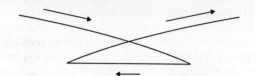

Figure 6.1 Path of Jupiter, as seen from Earth.

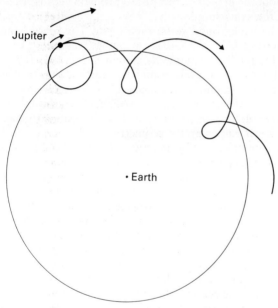

Figure 6.2 Path of Jupiter relative to Earth, according to Ptolemy.

our notions of the real in this century. We conclude with some general observations.

Astronomy: Ptolemy and Copernicus

We begin our tour with astronomy and ask the question: how do the sun, moon, stars and planets move? Everybody knows that the sun rises in the east and sets in the west. Stargazers also know that the moon and the stars do the same thing. Of course, the full picture is not quite as simple as this: the sun is lower in the winter than in the summer; the stars seen in the winter differ from those in the summer; and the moon has phases. But forgetting these details the *simplest* explanation is that the sun, moon and stars move round the earth in *circles* and the earth is regarded as fixed. It should be obvious that this theory explains the observed facts. What about the planets? They pose a problem because they don't move in the same simple way. They occupy different positions, against the background stars, each night. The word 'planet' in fact is derived from the Greek, meaning 'wandering star'. The path of Jupiter, for example, is shown in Figure 6.1. It clearly does not move in a circle round the earth. How then do the planets move? Claudius Ptolemaeus, a Greek astronomer living in Alexandria in the second century AD, answered this question by suggesting that the planets move in *epicycles* around the earth. An epicycle is the rather pretty geometrical figure shown in Figure 6.2. It is the path traced by an object, describing a circle, while at the same time the centre of the circle itself moves round a circular path. So an epicycle is a superposition of two circular motions. A moment's thought should convince you that if Jupiter does move in an epicycle, as observed, so to speak, from above, then as seen 'edge on' from the earth it will appear to move as in Figure 6.1, the reversals in direction corresponding to the loops in the epicycle. Ptolemy's theory accounted satisfactorily, in fact, *exactly* for the motion of all the planets, and the Greek 'geocentric' model of the cosmos, shown in Figure 6.3, was established. The earth is at the centre, while the sun, moon and stars move in circles around it, and the planets in epicycles. Ignoring, as mentioned above, the complications of the moon's phases and the difference between summer and winter, this model accounts well for the observed facts of astronomy. Note that in this system the stars (extremely distant) and the sun (very distant) take 24 hours to go round the earth, while the nearby moon takes 30 days.

This Greek model of the solar system is a scientific theory though the approach of the Greeks was somewhat different from our own. To appreciate the difference, let us codify our procedure and remark that a scientific theory is a mathematical model of

Physics

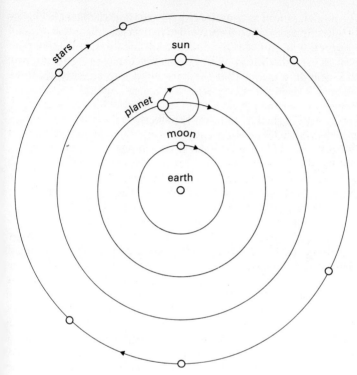

Figure 6.3 Motion of the sun, moon, planets and stars in the geocentric model.

construct which is in close correspondence with the observed facts, or empirical data.

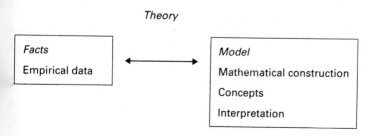

Theory

Facts		Model
Empirical data	⟷	Mathematical construction
		Concepts
		Interpretation

The model, as well as containing mathematical elements, will also introduce particular concepts and in many cases these will require *interpretation*, in order to 'understand' the facts. It is clear that even in everyday life facts by themselves cannot be understood; understanding means that they are fitted into some conceptual scheme. A scientific theory is such a scheme, with the additional feature that in the physical sciences, the model is mathematical. The Greeks argued as follows: (1) all celestial bodies must move in paths which are geometrically perfect, (2) circles are geometrically perfect, (3) hence celestial bodies move in circles. Ptolemy modified (2) by including epicycles. Agreement was then obtained between the observed facts and the mathematical model, and a theory of celestial motion was born. The Greek procedure, however, differs somewhat from the modern one; we would say that to state boldly that 'all celestial bodies must move in geometrically perfect paths' is an unjustified assumption. Who says they must? The way to find out how they move is to *look at them*! In other words, we place more emphasis than the Greeks did on observing the facts; the theory is then constructed to fit the facts. However, we do share with the Greeks the notion that the theory, or model, must be a 'neat' one, simple and appealing, or, as the mathematicians say, beautiful. I shall have more to say about this later, but let me just remark that if (say) after painstaking observations of some facts in a particular area of physics, the model constructed to 'explain' the facts was very complicated, unappealing and 'ad hoc', the theory would not be accepted as the last word. People would try to find a simpler theory, *even at the cost of ignoring one or two of the facts*; because some of the facts may be 'anomalous', due to other causes, irrelevant to the present concern. But this is jumping ahead; let us return to astronomy.

As everyone knows, the next great advance was due to Copernicus (1473–1543). He put the sun, and not the earth, at the centre of the 'world'. In more detail (see Figure 6.4), he suggested (1) that the earth *rotates* about its own axis and that the sun and stars are fixed: it is the rotation of the earth which makes the sun and stars rise and set in a 24-hour period; (2) that the earth and all the planets go round the sun in circles, the earth taking 1 year to complete a revolution; (3) that the moon circles the earth in 28

114

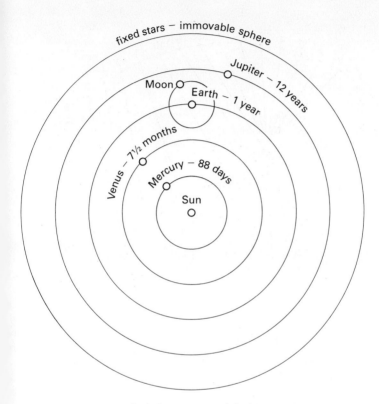

Figure 6.4 The heliocentric model of Copernicus.

days. The crucial and remarkable consequence of this model is that the motion of one of the other planets *as seen from the earth* is an *epicycle*. This is quite easy to see. Consider, for example, Jupiter, which goes round the sun once in about 12 years, so in one (earth) year it has moved about 1/12 of a complete revolution, that is through 30°. Figure 6.5 shows the movement of the earth during one year, with the months marked 1 to 12, and the motion of Jupiter over the same period. The question is, how will Jupiter appear to move relative to the background of the fixed stars? In January (month 1) Jupiter is seen in the direction of the

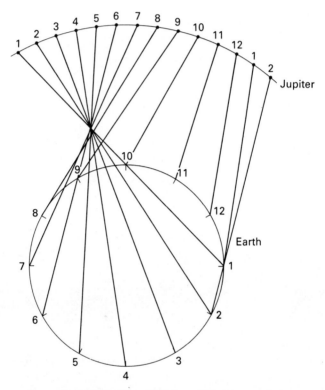

Figure 6.5 The paths of Earth and Jupiter round the sun.

line 1–1, in February along 2–2, in March along 3–3, and so on.
These lines are changing direction in the way shown in Figure 6.6
and Jupiter's path relative to the earth is seen to be an epicycle, as
promised. So Copernicus's model reproduces Ptolemy's epicycles, without having to include them explicitly; the only 'real'
orbits are circles.

It is worth quoting from a translation of Copernicus's 'De
revolutionibus orbium coelestium' (1543) (Sambursky, 1974
p. 184).

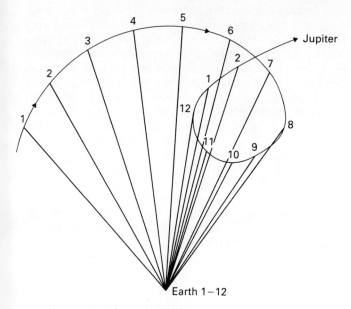

Figure 6.6   The path of Jupiter as seen from Earth.

Therefore, since nothing hinders the mobility of the Earth, I think we should now see whether more than one movement belongs to it, so that it can be regarded as one of the wandering stars. For the apparent irregular movement of the planets and their variable distances from the Earth – which cannot be understood as occurring in circles homocentric with the Earth – make it clear that the Earth is not the centre of their circular movements. Therefore, since there are many centres, it is not foolhardy to doubt whether the centre of gravity of the Earth rather than some other is the centre of the world. I myself think that gravity or heaviness is nothing except a certain natural appetency implanted in the parts by the divine providence of the universal Artisan, in order that they should unite with one another in their oneness and wholeness and come together in the form of a globe. It is

117

believable that this effect is present in the sun, moon, and the other bright planets and that through its efficacy they remain in the spherical figure in which they are visible, though they nevertheless accomplish their circular movements in many different ways. Therefore if the Earth too possesses movements different from the one around its centre, then they will necessarily be movements which similarly appear on the outside in the many bodies; and we find the yearly revolution among these movements. For if the annual revolution were changed from being solar to being terrestrial, and immobility were granted to the sun, the risings and settings of the signs and of the fixed stars – whereby they become morning or evening stars – will appear in the same way; and it will be seen that the stoppings, retrogressions, and progressions of the wandering stars are not their own, but are a movement of the Earth and that they borrow the appearances of this movement. Lastly, the sun will be regarded as occupying the centre of the world. And the ratio of order in which these bodies succeed one another and the harmony of the whole world teaches us their truth, if only as they say, we would look at the thing with both eyes.

The final sentence is particularly worthy of note: Copernicus's theory explains the same facts as Ptolemy's; it challenged the view of 'common sense', backed up by the authority of the church, but he regarded it as having the virtue of simplicity *and therefore of truth*. But to see this we must 'look at the thing with both eyes'. Theories are not derived from 'facts' alone. Creation of a theory involves the use of imagination and different imaginations will produce different theories accounting for the same phenomena. Copernicus claimed his theory was right because it was simple and this criterion is ultimately an aesthetic one, commonly invoked by mathematicians. The famous English mathematician G. H. Hardy wrote: 'Beauty is the first test: there is no permanent place in the world for ugly mathematics.' As for looking 'with both eyes', similar ideas have been expressed by well-known modern scientists: 'The important thing in science is not so much to obtain new facts as to discover new ways of thinking about them' (Sir William Bragg). 'Discovery consists in seeing what

118

everybody has seen and thinking what nobody has thought'
(Szent-Gyorgi).

Newton and Universal Gravitation

We resume our tour of physics, staying a moment longer with
Copernicus. As we saw, as far as the motions of the sun, stars and
planets are concerned, Copernicus's theory and Ptolemy's are
equivalent – they both explain the observed facts. This is not the
whole story, however. Following Copernicus, there was a good
deal of discussion about whether the planets went round the sun
or round the earth and whether the earth was really spinning;
wouldn't that cause it to break up and make constant breezes in
the air? A crucial step was taken in 1610 when Galileo (1564–
1642) saw through his telescope (1) that Venus and Mercury had
phases, like the moon, (2) that Jupiter had four satellites (moons).
First let us consider the significance of phases. The moon and the
planets do not themselves shine, it is only the sun that shines, so
we see the moon by light *reflected from the sun*. Look at Figure
6.4 and think about the sun shining on the moon, and us looking
at it from the earth. It is clear that if the earth is between the sun
and the moon we are able to see the moon in full, whereas if the
moon is between us and the sun we shall only be able to see part
of it, the part lit up by the sun. The rest of it that is lit up is not
facing in our direction. There will also be times when it will be
invisible (new moon), that is, when its lighted face is away from
us. So we have a simple explanation of the moon's phases. Now
consider a planet, say Mercury. In the Copernican model, it will
sometimes be on the same side of the sun as the earth and
sometimes on the opposite side, because the two planets go round
the sun at different rates. Hence we expect Mercury to have
phases. And this is what Galileo observed. These phases are
impossible to explain on the geocentric model of Figure 6.3.
There the earth is never between the sun and another planet, so
no planet would be seen in full phase (neither would the moon!).
The significance of Galileo's second discovery, that of Jupiter's
moons, was that this was evidence for a centre of rotation which
was not the earth. Galileo's findings therefore signalled the

beginning of the downfall of the geocentric theory and its replacement by the Copernican model.

These developments in astronomy, together with many penetrating observations on the nature of motion by Galileo, painstaking observations on the exact positions of planets over many years by Tycho Brahe and a brilliant mathematical summary of them by Johannes Kepler, formed the raw material for the formulation by Isaac Newton (1642–1727) of the laws of motion and the law of universal gravitation. These are so profound and far-reaching that for two centuries they were thought to be *absolutely true*; indeed they were always found to work to an uncanny degree of accuracy. Newtonian physics became the archetypal example of a perfect physical theory and its mechanistic spirit pervaded science until the nineteenth century.

Newton's first law of motion, well-known to thousands of people from their schooldays, states that bodies will remain at rest *or continue to move in a straight line with constant speed* unless acted on by a force. Boring as this law may appear at first, however, it is not obvious and in fact runs counter to common sense, at least the common sense of the Greeks and of Newton's contemporaries. (If it does not run counter to ours, this is a measure of how much Newtonian physics has influenced our everyday concepts. By a similar token, may it be that in a century or so our descendants may view Einsteinian physics and the relativity of time as more or less 'obvious'?) The Greeks regarded the state of rest as the 'natural' state for all bodies. If, for example, you push an object along the ground, or even kick a football, the object and the football will eventually come to rest, showing that rest is the natural state. Newton argued, however, that there is no essential distinction between being at rest and moving with constant speed. For the object that we push or the football that we kick come to rest because there are *frictional forces* acting on them – the friction of the ground and the air. Take away the frictional forces and the objects *never* come to rest. They continue moving in a straight line with constant speed. In practice we can never completely eliminate frictional forces, but we can almost do so. A glass marble rolling along a polished metal surface in a vacuum will barely slow down at all, since there is practically no friction. This shows the truth of Newton's law. It is also worth

120

remarking that the issue whether the state of rest is a natural state depends on what we regard as *significant facts*, or simply 'facts' (empirical data) in the scheme above (p. 112). 'Facts' really means facts which are relevant for the theory under consideration. It is a fact that objects pushed along will come to rest, but they come to rest at different rates. Newton regarded as *significant* the fact that sometimes objects take a long time to come to rest. This indicated to him that the 'natural' state of motion is to continue in a straight line with constant speed; the fact that objects do in fact slow down he regarded as irrelevant because it was due to *some other cause* (friction).

Now, turning to astronomy, the planets do not move in straight lines round the sun, neither does the moon round the earth; neither does an object thrown through the air. An object dropped vertically moves in a straight line, but not with constant speed since it accelerates towards the earth. In all of these cases, then, a force must be acting and Newton supposed that it was the same force, the *universal force of gravitation*. It has a mathematical expression: if two bodies (any two bodies) of masses m_1 and m_2 are a distance d apart, then they attract one another with a force F given by

$$F = \frac{Gm_1m_2}{d^2}$$

G is a number, called Newton's constant of gravitation. The remarkable thing is that using this formula one can indeed account for the motion of projectiles in the earth's gravitational field, as well as for the motion of all the planets round the sun. The formula works to an amazing degree of accuracy; in fact it appears almost perfect and for more than two centuries was thought to be perfect. It was used to calculate the positions of the planets in the night sky and in almost all cases gave exactly the right predictions. On a few occasions, however, the predictions were not quite right – a planet was not exactly where Newton's law said it should be. What was wrong? Was Newton's law only *approximately* true, or only true in certain circumstances? The answer was more subtle. It is true that the sun pulls on all the planets but the planets also pull on each other (since everything attracts everything else, according to Newton's law). The sun is

121

by far the biggest body in the solar system so its pull is much greater than the pull of the other planets. In certain cases, however, when two planets get fairly close together, they will affect each other's orbit and this has to be taken into account when predicting where the planets will be; this is in fact the way the predictions are made and it suggests the answer to the problem that sometimes a planet isn't where it should be. The answer is that there might be another, hitherto unknown, planet, pulling it off orbit. Newton's law can be used to calculate where this new planet should be. This is in fact how Neptune was discovered in 1846. The Frenchman Urbain Levenier analysed the observed perturbations in the orbit of Uranus and predicted a new planet, which was discovered by J. G. Galle at the Berlin Observatory. So what could have been a problem for Newton's law turned into a triumph; the law was preserved intact, a new planet was predicted and found.

Another profound consequence of Newton's laws, and one which was already foreseen by Galileo, is that in stating that a body subject to no force either stays at rest or moves uniformly in a straight line, it implies that there is no *essential* distinction between these cases. Being at rest is, from the point of view of the laws of physics, equivalent to moving with constant speed. In other words, there is no such thing as *absolute* rest or absolute motion. In the twentieth century this is easy to appreciate. Moving in a plane (or in a fast smooth train) gives no sensation of motion. They are moving fast, but only in a straight line with constant speed. All we can say is that they are moving *relative* to the earth. Not only is there no sensation of motion, there is actually no way of telling (barring looking outside!) what speed they are travelling at. An apple dropped in a plane falls vertically as seen *in the plane*, just as one dropped on earth falls vertically as seen by anyone at rest on the earth – though not, of course, by someone speeding by in a train! In fact there is no experiment that can be performed to detect absolute motion, so absolute motion is a meaningless concept. This is the *principle of relativity*. We shall meet it again when Einstein adds a new twist to it.

Newtonian physics is a superb example of a successful scientific theory. In one formula, quoted above, many diverse phenomena are embraced and countless single events 'explained'. W

122

may say, rather loosely, that when we throw a ball through the air it traces out a parabolic path 'because' Newton's law, which determines its motion, predicts this. The motion of projectiles, the motion of billiard balls in collision, the motion of the earth itself, the other planets and the moon, are all but instances of the application of one universal law. Perhaps it is better to say that the law tells *how* objects move rather than *why* they move, but in any case their motion is described, even determined, by Newton's laws. The motions of individual particles are 'nothing but' the working out of a universal law to which they are all subject. This is an example of reductionism; many thousands, even millions, of phenomena, are reduced to the application of a single law, a single equation, which explains them all.

This law, the equation above, is from the mathematical point of view very neat, even beautiful. What could be simpler than multiplying the masses and dividing by the square of the distance? How very remarkable, even wonderful, that this simple law explains so much! Even hymn-writers responded to the Newtonian vision. Joseph Addison (1672–1719) wrote

> The spacious firmament on high,
> With all the blue ethereal sky,
> And spangled heavens, a shining frame,
> Their great Original proclaim.
> The unwearied sun, from day to day,
> Does his Creator's power display,
> And publishes to every land
> The work of an almighty hand.
>
> What though in solemn silence all
> Move round the dark terrestrial ball?
> What though no real voice nor sound
> Amidst their radiant orbs be found?
> In reason's ear they all rejoice,
> And utter forth a glorious voice,
> For ever singing as they shine,
> 'The hand that made us is divine'.

This sense of wonder and beauty is akin to that of the mathematician who sees beauty in the elegant form of Newton's law. But Newton left another legacy, that of *determinism*. The planets, and other objects, are *forced* to move according to Newton's laws. If we know where a planet is at one time, we can predict exactly where it will be at all future times, because its motion is determined by mathematical laws. The French mathematician and physicist, the Marquis de Laplace, summarized this development of deterministic mechanics after Newton thus:

> We must envisage the present state of the universe as the effect of its previous state, and as the cause of that which will follow. An intelligence that could know, at a given instant, all the forces governing the natural world, and the respective positions of the entities which compose it, if in addition it was great enough to analyse all this information, would be able to embrace in a single formula the movement of the largest bodies in the universe and those of the lightest atom: nothing would be uncertain to it, and the future, like the past, would be directly present to its observation.

As Bernstein remarks (Bernstein, 1973), 'Considering the uncanny success of Newtonian mechanics in the description of the motions of objects from planets to cannon balls, it is little wonder that there was a tendency for scientists to accept this theory, somewhat uncritically, as the last word and ultimate standard in scientific explanation.' When we come to consider the quantum theory, however, we shall see that Newtonian mechanics is entirely inappropriate. It works well for planets and cannon balls but it fails completely for atoms.

Special Relativity

As the name implies, any theory of relativity is concerned with what is *relative*, as distinct from *absolute*. Let me give some examples. Left and right are relative terms. 'Albert's house is on the left side of the road' is a statement without meaning unless you also say which direction you are travelling along the road. Left and right by themselves are devoid of absolute meaning. Up and down are also relative terms, though this is not quite so obvious. We tend to think of 'up' as a unique direction in space but actually it is not. For one thing, the earth is round, so 'up' in

Paris is not the same direction as 'up' in Buenos Aires. For another thing, the earth rotates, so even if you stay in Paris, 'up' at 10 a.m. is a different direction from 'up' at 5 p.m. But for places close together, say Paris and Versailles, 'up' in both places at the same time is almost the same direction. Under these circumstances, 'up' (and 'down') may said to be 'almost' absolute, or, better, they *appear* to be absolute.

Our concern is with motion. As we saw above, speed is relative, not absolute. This is the principle of relativity. There is one exception to this rule, however, and that is light. It has been known for a long time that the speed of light is almost exactly 300,000 km/sec. That is very fast and corresponds roughly to going ten times round the earth in a second. In the nineteenth century it was realized that light consists of electromagnetic waves. Maxwell showed that his new theory of electromagnetism predicted electromagnetic *waves* and he was able to calculate their speed. It turned out to be precisely the speed of light. It was this fact which struck Einstein as being very strange and deeply significant. Maxwell's calculations, which were quite sophisticated and complex, nevertheless produced at the end a *speed* – the speed of electromagnetic waves. But *relative to what* was this speed to be measured? That was a good question! There is only one possible answer – relative to *anything*. The speed of light must be the same no matter what the state of motion of the observer is. This is extremely odd but is the only honest way of interpreting the theory. (It should perhaps also be mentioned that, besides Maxwell's theory, there was also direct experimental evidence that the speed of light had this universal property. This was obtained by looking for a change in the speed of light reaching the earth from stars, as the earth orbits the sun. Sometimes the earth is moving towards the star and sometimes away from it, but no variation in the speed was found. This confirmed Maxwell's theoretical prediction.) A moment's thought will show you how strange this is. If you are driving a car at 70 km/h and you are overtaken by a car travelling at 100 km/h, then, relative to you, that car is travelling at 30 km/h. That is the law of simple addition and subtraction that we are used to with speeds but it does *not* apply to light. Suppose you are in a spaceship and are sending a beam of light to someone in

125

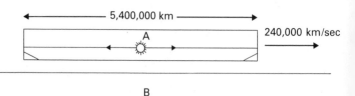

Figure 6.7 The Einstein train.

another spaceship, who has an apparatus for measuring its speed. If initially the spaceships are at rest relative to each other, the other person will measure the speed of light to be 300,000 km/sec. But now suppose you turn on your engines and move away from the other spaceship at a high speed, say at 100,000 km/sec, then what will the man in the other spaceship measure the speed of light to be? We would guess 200,000 km/sec, but we would be wrong; the answer is 300,000 km/sec. Even if your spaceship recedes at 299,999.9 km/sec, the speed of the light measured in the other ship will still be 300,000 km/sec. This result is extraordinary.

Einstein did not set himself the task of understanding it but simply of working out its consequences. Since the result is so bizarre, it is hardly surprising that the consequences are bizarre also. They are found by performing a *gedanken-Experiment* – a thought-experiment, which, though difficult to carry out in practice, is easy to think about. This *gedanken-Experiment* consists of a train travelling fast through a station, as shown in Figure 6.7. There is an observer A on the train and an observer B on the station, watching the train go through. The train is 5,400,000 km long and is travelling at 240,000 km/sec. (This enormous length and speed are necessary to make the constancy of the speed of light have a noticeable effect.) The train has a door at the front and one at the rear and these doors can be opened by A releasing a light signal. The light travels along the train in both directions and triggers devices at each end to open the doors. (There is nothing unrealistic here; such devices are common in everyday life – for example, to start escalators moving.) What will the observers A and B see? It is clear that, as far as A is concerned, it is irrelevant that the train is moving. It is, after all, only going in a straight line with constant speed. A presses the button. The light has 2,700,000 km to go to each door and travels at 300,000 km/sec, so by simple arithmetic the time it takes is the distance divided by the speed, 2,700,000/300,000 = 9 seconds. That is

A sees both doors open after $\dfrac{2,700,000}{300,000} = 9$ seconds.

The alert reader will realize that A does not actually *see* the doors open until another 9 seconds after they really do open, because the light has to travel back to A's eyes. But A is also alert and he realizes, when he sees the doors open, that they actually opened 9 seconds ago – they are 9 light-seconds distant from him. So the above statement is completely unambiguous. What does B see? The light is travelling up the train to the front door at 300,000 km/sec relative to the train, but also relative to B. B does not see the light moving faster simply because it's in a moving train – this is precisely light's strange property. So, as seen by B, in every second the light approaches the front door by 300,000 km, but the front door also moves away by 240,000 km. Hence the *overall* gain is only 60,000 km and

B sees the front door open after $\dfrac{2,700,000}{300,000 - 240,000}$

$= \dfrac{2,700,000}{60,000} = 45$ seconds.

For the rear doors the situation is the opposite. As seen by B, in every second the light travels towards the door 300,000 km, but also the door travels towards the light 240,000 km, so the door and the light pulse are actually 540,000 km nearer each other, and

B sees the rear door open after $\dfrac{2,700,000}{300,000 + 240,000}$

$= \dfrac{2,700,000}{540,000} = 5$ seconds.

B sees the rear door open and then sees the front door open *40 seconds later*. A sees both doors open *at the same time*. Two

Figure 6.8 Light bouncing between mirrors making a simple clock.

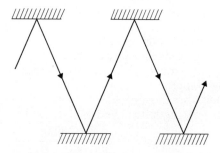

Figure 6.9 How B sees A's clock.

events which were simultaneous for A are not simultaneous for B. Hence simultaneity is a *relative term*. There is no such thing as absolute simultaneity. Further, a statement about simultaneity is really a statement about time. As Einstein states in his paper of 1905, 'If, for instance, I say "that train arrives here at 7 o'clock", I mean something like this: "The pointing of the little hand of my watch to 7 and the arrival of the train are *simultaneous events*".' So we may say that *time is relative*. This is Einstein's great discovery.

The reader will see that the above is very simple. There are no tricks. The reason for the strange answer is simply that the light has the strange property that its speed is always the same. That is all that is used in the above calculation, apart from the simple

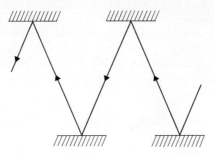

Figure 6.10   How A sees B's clock.

arithmetic with which everyone is familiar. There is another illustration of the relativity of time. Let us suppose that A and B both have clocks and that as the train rushes through the station each can see the other's clock as well as their own. Ordinary clocks are rather complicated affairs with springs or electronic circuitry to drive them, so we shall simplify matters by giving A and B very simple clocks, consisting of two mirrors facing each other, one vertically above the other, and light passes between them, bouncing off the top mirror, then off the bottom mirror, then back to the top, and so on (see Figure 6.8). This makes the tick-tock, tick-tock of the clock. Before A gets in the train, A and B synchronize their clocks so that they tick at the same rate. A then gets in the train and as it rushes through the station B looks at A's clock. What does she see? As shown in Figure 6.9, the light bounces between the top and bottom mirrors, but because the mirrors are in a moving train B sees them constantly moving to the right. The light clearly has further to go between the successive reflections than it has in the case of stationary mirrors. The light is (as seen by B) in a moving train but *this does not cause it to go any faster*. Hence it takes *longer* between successive reflections, so B sees A's clock as slowed down, or more precisely

B sees A's clock going slower than her own.

What does A see? The train is moving with constant speed, so he has no sensation of motion, and he simple sees the station rush by

129

and while it does so he watches B's clock. As shown in Figure 6.10, just as B saw A's clock moving to the right, A sees B's clock moving to the left. Again the mirrors move between successive reflections, so the light has further to go than if the clock were at rest (with respect to A), but also the light always travels with the same speed, so it takes longer between reflections and the clock ticks more slowly:

A sees B's clock going slower than his own.

A and B *both* see that the other clock goes slower than their own – 'moving clocks go slower'. This is very nice and symmetric. After all, there is no fundamental distinction between A and B; they are simply in relative uniform motion, so we expect them to see the same thing, and they do. We may be tempted to ask whose clock is *really* going slower? But that is like asking which side of the road is Albert's house *really* on – the right or the left? And the answer is it depends which way you are going. So in this case it depends who makes the measurement; if B does, then A's clock is going slower, and if A does, B's clock is going slower. Time is relative and so it has no meaning to say that one clock is *really* going slower than the other. For a question to have a real meaning it must be specified exactly how the measurement, which answers the question, is to be made. And in this case that means stating who is doing the measurement. It will be appreciated that this general stance towards the concept of meaning has a lot in common with logical positivism. In fact, the logical positivists were greatly influenced by these sorts of considerations in relativity and by similar ones in quantum theory.

From a fundamental point of view, it is obviously a revolutionary discovery that time is relative, but it has no practical consequences in our everyday life. There is no need to adjust our watches if we go on a plane journey, to take account of relativity. This is because even the fastest planes travel at only minute – even infinitesimal – speeds compared to the speed of light, so that although *in principle* the effects are there, *in practice* they are completely unobservable. In fact it is because this is the case that we have formed in our minds the idea that time is absolute; it *almost* is. It has some resemblance to the terms 'up' and 'down'.

We saw earlier that they are relative, but if we move only small distances over the earth, they may be considered as absolute.

On the other hand it must be said that Einstein's relativity has many profound consequences in physics. There are numerous examples of predictions made by the theory and they all turn out to be true. A very well-known prediction is the equivalence of mass and energy, by the equation $E = mc^2$. Here c is the speed of light – as we saw, an enormous number. It follows that even a tiny mass is equivalent to an enormous amount of energy. An example of the application of this equation is to nuclear fission and fusion. In nuclear fission a nucleus breaks up into two other nuclei but the combined mass of the product nuclei is less than the mass of the parent nucleus. The mass that has gone missing has been transformed into energy, by Einstein's relation. Another area where relativity has an application is in high energy physics. Subatomic particles are accelerated to enormous energies and travel at speeds very close to the speed of light. The successful design of accelerators depends crucially on taking relativity into account. In such ways Einstein's theory has been vindicated and is without doubt correct. High energy physicists, cosmologists and others use the theory of relativity all the time and for them it is simply one of the standard tools of physics. For people meeting it for the first time, however, it is very strange, even perturbing. Yet perhaps they can also see that it has a subtlety and a beauty all its own. As Einstein said, 'Raffiniert ist der Herr Gott, aber böshaft ist er nicht' – God is cunning, but he is not malicious.

The World of the Quantum

Quantum theory originated in 1900 with a paper by Max Planck. It developed slowly and at the hands of many physicists, reaching its present form in about 1925. It is a theory about the nature of matter on the tiniest scale of the atom; that is, at distances of about one hundred millionth of a centimetre. The theory was problematic in its development and despite the fact that, like relativity, it is an extremely successful theory, it still presents great problems of interpretation, which to this day lack a completely satisfactory resolution.

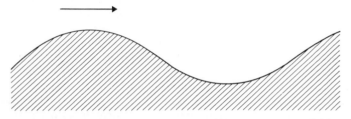

Figure 6.11 Profile of corn as the wind blows over a cornfield.

If we are asked to imagine or 'picture' an atom, or perhaps more simply a constituent of an atom, like an electron or a proton, we naturally think of something round and hard, like a midget billiard ball. If electrons are indeed like this, we should expect one to behave like a real billiard ball, obeying the same Newtonian laws of motion and collision. As we saw before, these laws are deterministic, so that if we knew the electron's state of motion at any one time we could predict its future motion. It was obvious from the early study of atoms, however, that they and their constituents do *not* behave in this way – or rather (and more bafflingly) do not always behave consistently in this way, though in some respects they do. Hence the Newtonian billiard ball model is not entirely satisfactory and the question arises, what other model has physics to offer?

Wave motion has been well understood for a long time. It is a collective motion commonly observed in nature and well described mathematically. When the wind blows across a field of ripe corn, the plants bend down and rise up in unison and we see a 'wave' spread across the field. We could, in describing the motion of the corn in the wind, detail the exact movement of each individual ear of corn, but this would be regarded as perverse. It is much more appropriate to say that a wave passes over the field, as shown in Figure 6.11. Another example is water waves. To describe what happens on the surface of the sea, it would be possible in principle to detail the individual motion of each particle (molecule) of water, but it is much simpler to say that a wave moves over the surface. In many areas of physics waves give an excellent account of what is observed, from waves in fluids to electromagnetic waves in radio and television transmission and reception. At the heart of the concept of a wave is that it is *spread out*; it is not localized at one point in space, like a miniature billiard ball. When we drop a stone into a pond, the water wave spreads out till it reaches the bank. It is obvious that the water is composed of countless millions of millions of molecules, but the motion of the wave is a collective motion and has a rigorous mathematical description – waves obey a (second order differential) wave equation, which can be solved.

The term 'quantum theory' derives from Planck's paper of 1900. Planck was addressing himself to solving what seemed to him a rather technical problem about the energy in the electromagnetic wave field. The problem was that this energy, using the conventional methods of calculation, had been shown to be infinite. Since this was obviously wrong (nothing in the real world is actually infinite), there must have been something wrong in the method of calculation, or in the basic assumptions behind the calculation. Planck showed that *if* it were assumed that the waves could *only* carry energy E equal to a basic unit (call it E_0), or twice this unit $2E_0$, or three times it, and so on (in equation form $E = nE_0$, $n = 1, 2, 3 \ldots$) then the problem of infinite energy disappeared. The energy in the wave field became finite and actually agreed exactly with observation. The theory was therefore, mathematically speaking, successful, but Planck was not at all happy about having to make the very odd assumption that the energy comes in 'lumps' E_0: you can have 1, 2 or any integral number of lumps, but not 2.5 lumps or 2.1 lumps. These lumps were called quanta. The quantum of energy E_0 was given by the formula $E_0 = hv$ where h is now called Planck's constant and v is the frequency of the wave. What Planck's hypothesis did was to suggest that the energy of electromagnetic radiation, previously thought to be entirely wave-like and therefore *continuous*, actually existed in discrete entities – and was therefore in some respects *particle-like*. Einstein showed in 1905 (that *annus mirabilis*) that Planck's quanta of radiation were not just a mathematical device: when interpreted literally, they explained a hitherto unexplained new physical phenomenon (the photoelectric effect). Much later the French physicist Prince Louis de Broglie suggested that if radiation was sometimes particle-like,

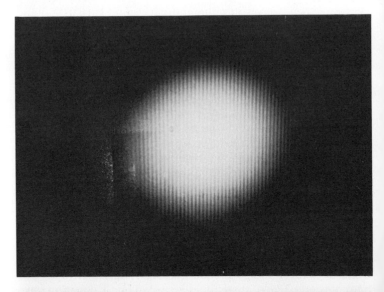

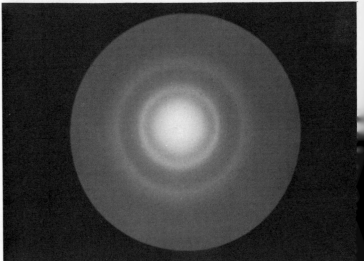

Figure 6.12 (a) light and (b) electron diffraction patterns.

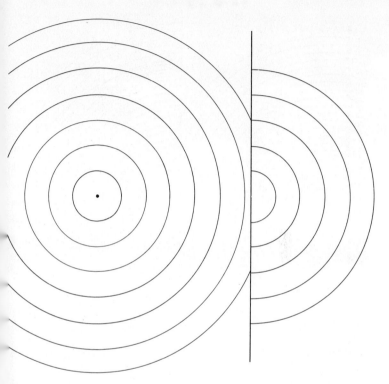

Figure 6.13 Wave pattern produced by a plane wave incident on a slit in a barrier. The slit acts as a source of semi-circular waves.

may it not be that what we think of as *particles* (such as electrons and protons) also possess *wave-like properties*? This led to the full-scale development of 'quantum mechanics' (to be contrasted with Newtonian or 'classical' mechanics). The wave-like behaviour of particles has been demonstrated in many experiments, but typical is the illustration of Figure 6.12. Figure 6.12(a) shows a photograph of a 'diffraction pattern' produced by light falling on a point target. The bright and dark circular fringes are characteristic of wave-like behaviour; on striking a point target, or a hole in a screen, the wave produces a diffraction pattern.

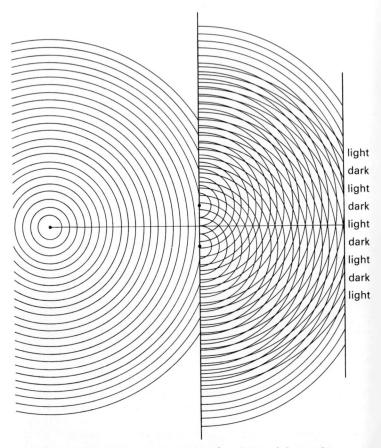

light
dark
light
dark
light
dark
light
dark
light

Figure 6.14 Waves impinging on two slits, and the resulting interference pattern.

Figure 6.12(b) shows the pattern produced by electrons impinging on a point target. It is seen that this is also a diffraction pattern. Hence electrons must, as de Broglie suggested, possess wave-like properties.

Following de Broglie's work, the Austrian physicist Erwin Schrödinger wrote down the equation, now named after him.

136

that the electron waves must obey. It is this Schrödinger equation which has been so spectacularly successful in describing the physics of the domain of the atom. It accounts exactly for the known properties of atoms and the light they emit. It laid the foundation for the prediction and subsequent development of transistors, which are now so much a part of our technological environment, from hearing-aids to computers. The success of quantum theory has been absolutely phenomenal. But what are we to make of its guiding premiss, that electrons have a wave-like character? How is that to be understood and interpreted? Actually, as we shall see below, the fact is that electrons *sometimes* behave like waves and *sometimes* like particles and it is this *dual nature* which makes the problem of interpretation so difficult. For the purpose of illustrating the problems involved, physicists commonly resort to a *gedanken-Experiment* which plays the same role in quantum theory that Einstein's train experiment plays in relativity and is known as the two-slit experiment.

Waves behave in an interesting way when they impinge on a barrier containing a slit. Suppose the waves are straight ('plane'), like waves in the sea. Figure 6.13 shows such waves hitting a barrier with a hole in it. The interesting thing is that the hole acts as a source for new circular waves, just as if a stone (in the case of water waves) had been dropped in the water at that point. What if the barrier contains two slits? They *both* act as sources of new waves but these waves interfere with one another. Figure 6.14 shows the resulting pattern. Let us take the semicircles radiating from each slit to represent the crests of the waves. In between two successive crests is a trough and the pattern is a 'photograph' of the waves at a particular time. In the region on the right there are crests and troughs emanating from the two slits. At points on the central line a crest from one slit will coincide with a crest from the other. This will make a 'double crest' – in the case of water waves the crests will be twice as high and the troughs twice as deep. The wave motion will therefore be more intense. In the case of light waves this means that the light will be bright along this line. Besides this line of light, there will be other lines where two crests from the two slits meet, and so the light will be bright. In between these regions, however, a crest from one slit coincides with a trough from the other and they *cancel each other out*; in the case

Figure 6.15 Photograph of the interference pattern produced by light in the two-slit experiment.

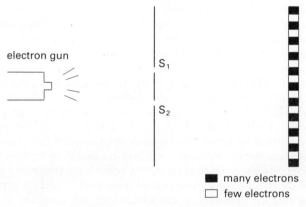

Figure 6.16 Two-slit experiment with electrons.

Figure 6.17 Photograph of the interference pattern produced by
electrons in the two-slit experiment.
Source: C. Jönsson, *Zeitschrift für Physik*, Springer-Verlag, Heidelberg, 1961,
vol. 161, p. 454.

of water waves, with one slit open the water would go up, with
the other it would go down, but with both open it does not move
at all. In the case of light, there is no wave motion and so *no light*.
Consequently if a screen is placed at the right, it will show a
succession of bright and dark fringes. This is precisely what is
observed – Figure 6.15 shows this characteristic 'interference
pattern' produced by laser light falling on two slits.

Now let us 'perform' the two-slit experiment with electrons.
The set-up is shown in Figure 6.16. Electrons are fired from the
electron gun and impinge on a screen containing two slits S_1 and
S_2. They are then detected at a bank of electronic counters. The
gun releases the electrons individually and they arrive individually, the arrival of each one being signalled by a click on a
counter. So the electrons are released as particles (miniature
billiard balls) and arrive like particles. If we run this experiment
for a long time, we may measure how many arrive at each
counter. This experiment has actually been performed and the
intensity distribution of electrons observed at the counters is
shown in Figure 6.17. It will be seen immediately that the pattern
is of precisely the same type as that obtained with light (Figure

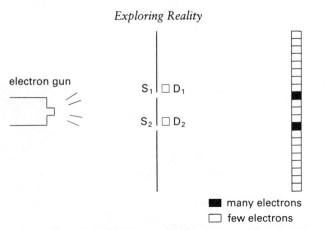

Figure 6.18 Two-slit experiments with electrons, and detectors D_1 and D_2 behind the slits S_1 and S_2.

6.15). The inference is that between the gun and the counter the electrons *travel like waves* and exhibit the interference pattern characteristic of waves. What is more, since the electrons are released and can be detected *individually*, we may say that each electron separately travels like a wave and interferes with itself. And for this to be true it necessarily passes through *both slits*. However, unlike a wave, when it arrives at the bank of counters, it does not arrive spread out over the whole array of them but registers itself *at one counter only*, as any well-behaved particle should. So the electron sets off as a particle and arrives as a particle, but travels in between as a wave: in particular, it is *not* true to say of the electron that 'it passes either through one slit or the other slit'. If that were true, then whichever slit it went through it would be irrelevant whether the other slit were open or closed, and the numbers registered in the detectors would be different – the detectors opposite each slit would register many electrons and the others very few (only stray ones caused by ricocheting off the sides of the slit).

To clarify this further, the intensity pattern in Figure 6.17 has also been drawn on the right of Figure 6.16. It clearly implies that we may not say 'the electron passes through either S_1 or S_2'. But you may say, this is ridiculous! Let us *measure* which slit each electron passes through; we can put a *detector* behind each slit and for each electron released at the gun, either detector D_1 or detector D_2 (see Figure 6.18) registers its passage, and then one of the final counters clicks registering its arrival. What do we then find? We find something remarkable: because we are *observing* which slit the electron passes through, it will pass through *one slit only*, so many electrons will arrive opposite S_1 and many opposite S_2, and not many elsewhere – as in Figure 6.18. This is, of course, exactly what we would expect if the electrons were miniature billiard balls, but it will be appreciated that the distribution of electrons over the counters here and in the first experiment (where there were no detectors behind the slits) is completely different. When the electrons are detected at the slits, their passage is completely deterministic – if an electron goes through S_1, it will register on the detector opposite S_1, and if it passes through S_2, on the detector opposite S_2. When the detectors D_1 and D_2 are removed, however, we revert to the original pattern of Figure 6.17. In that case, it is impossible to predict with certainty where an individual electron will go – only that it is very likely to reach some of the counters and very unlikely to reach others. Apart from that, we can only give a *probability* that it will arrive at a particular counter. And over a long time, the arrival pattern is that corresponding to the interference of waves.

We conclude that electrons travel like waves, each one spreading out and interfering with itself, as it were. If, however, we try to follow the path of an electron, it 'co-operates' and behaves like a particle – its wave character is destroyed. So the behaviour of electrons (and all atomic and subatomic particles) is intrinsically dependent on whether they are observed or not. It is impossible, in the nature of things, to make a measurement on an atomic system without changing it – and that in a completely unpredictable way. *Thus the notion of an outside world existing independently of the observer disappears.*

The unpredictability, or indeterminism, inherent in quantum theory was a feature Einstein could never accept; 'God does not play dice with the world' he proclaimed. However much we may share his unease, it seems that we just have to accept that God does indeed play dice; either that, or we must invent a better theory!

The succinct description of the indeterminacy arising from

wave-particle duality is Heisenberg's Uncertainty Principle. This states, as mentioned above, that simultaneous knowledge of an electron's position and speed is impossible. The reason for this is that there is a relation between the speed of an electron, denoted v, and the wavelength of the corresponding wave λ. If the mass of the electron is m, the relation is

$$mv = \frac{h}{\lambda}$$

where h is Planck's constant. This is called de Broglie's relation. (Hence the faster an electron is moving, the smaller its wavelength.) If we know an electron's speed v, we know λ, and so the electron is behaving like a *wave*. Since this (by definition) is spread out, we cannot say where the electron 'is' – in fact it has no meaning to say that. If on the other hand we want to specify exactly where it is, then the electron must have a particle-like nature, so its wave nature has gone and it is meaningless to talk of its wavelength λ and therefore of its speed v.

Quantum theory illustrates the radically different nature of the laws of physics on an atomic scale from those of the everyday world. On the atomic scale the simple notion of determinism disappears and the deterministic vision of the world offered by Laplace (see above) loses all its force; at the most elementary level, nature is not deterministic. And neither is it picturable; atoms and subatomic particles are not to be imagined as miniature billiard balls – indeed, they can hardly be pictured at all! Are they real? As stressed several times above, quantum theory is a very successful theory; that is, it enables us to *understand* the microworld, even though we have difficulty picturing it and interpreting it and even though it is a very strange theory. But its comprehensibility is the guarantor of its reality – there must be *something* there if we can describe it with a theory which works so remarkably well. The quantum world is real because it is comprehensible.

Conclusions

We have discussed several examples of physical theories, each applicable in certain domains of the physical world. We hav noted the importance of simplicity or mathematical elegance or beauty in the search for physical theories. Relativity has shown us how a logically consistent and indeed elegant theory can run counter to common sense. The theory is believed *both* because it makes many correct predictions *and* because it is elegant. Quantum theory does not possess the same elegance as relativity and the problems of interpretation lead some physicists to wonder whether it will one day be formulated in a more satisfactory and elegant way. But the theory as it stands is completely successful from the point of view of giving accurate predictions and results. Newton's laws, once thought to be absolutely true, no longer occupy such a pedestal; atoms do not obey them and also, when particles are moving very fast so that relativity becomes relevant, Newton's laws need modification. Schröd-inger's equation works for atoms but not for billiard balls. Atoms have a wave nature so billiard balls should too, but it turns out that the wave nature of large objects is almost impossible to detect (when m is very large in de Broglie's relation above, λ becomes vanishingly small), and indeed one of the achievements of quantum theory was to show that for very large collections of atoms (like billiard balls) Schrödinger's equation 'becomes' the ordinary Newtonian equations. These in turn are valid only if they are applied to objects not moving at speeds (relative to an observer) close to that of light. So the situation in modern physics is that we have different theories for different domains – quantum theory for the atomic domain, Newtonian mechanics for the dynamics of ordinary objects in motion, relativity for fast-moving particles, thermodynamics for gases and liquids (containing enormously large numbers of atoms) and so on. In each domain we have a perfectly good theory but the domains dictate the *limits* to each theory. Outside these limits the theory breaks down. Knowing where a theory's limits are, where it breaks down, as well as where it is right, surely gives us *more* reason to believe that we have a correct theory.

Scientific theories are creations of individuals, they are not God-given. In this sense they may be compared with artistic creations. They use the language of mathematics and strive for elegance and beauty. And yet they also describe the observed facts. Why is this? The answer must be that there is some deep correspondence between the world and the patterns by which we try to understand it. It is *not* simply that we *impose* patterns on the world. If we did that then *any* pattern would do, any theory would work. But the history of physics is littered with theories which have been proved wrong. It is (to put it mildly!) very difficult to find a correct theory, but when it is found it is usually very neat, and often neat in a way that could not have been predicted.

Finally, since physical theories are so fundamentally connected with mathematics, it should be asked, 'What is mathematics?' Is it a set of abstract relations derived ultimately from the outside world, or is it a creation of the human mind? Mathematicians are not agreed on this – and perhaps the fact that the question is so difficult to decide is not without interest! Even at this fundamental level there are no clear and obvious truths and we seem to be surrounded by mystery. As Einstein said, 'The most incomprehensible thing about the world is that it is comprehensible.'

Chapter Seven

Film

BEN BREWSTER

Replication versus Representation

Producing a perfect simulacrum of the world as it is seen is a
very ancient ambition of the visual arts. Ancient accounts of
painting by the elder Pliny and others have stories of paintings
of fruit which deceived birds into pecking at that fruit (see Pliny,
1896, Book XXXV, para. 65) and the ancient development of
perspective representation, linked as it seems to have been to the
painting of illusionistic decor for theatrical performances, was
part of this tendency. When these researches were renewed in
the Renaissance with the working out of the techniques of
monocular perspective painting, the system was praised for its
ability to reproduce on a flat board or canvas a three-dimensional space such that standing in front of the flat picture gave
exactly the same impression as standing in front of the three-
dimensional space depicted. The 'visual aids' to perspective
technique illustrated in Renaissance manuals emphasize this
effect: Brunelleschi's cut-out picture in which, if the spectator
was standing with his eye at the right point, a real cityscape
visible through a hole in the painting was perfectly aligned with
the drawing of that cityscape in the solid part; and Dürer's
foreshortened view of a lute produced by connecting threads
from points on the lute to a single point representing the eye and
marking where they passed through an intervening 'window'
(see White, 1957).

The prehistory of photography fits into this line of development. The camera obscura was another such visual aid for painters. Inside a dark room, a picture of the bright world outside could be focused via a pin-hole or, giving a brighter image without loss of definition, a lens, on to a flat surface. In the seventeenth century landscape painters could use a portable form of camera obscura, a tent replacing the fixed room, to produce perspectivally perfect sketches of landscapes they wanted to paint, simply focusing the view on to a sheet of paper or canvas and drawing in the outlines of the objects visible on the sheet. The camera in its modern sense is a direct development from this, replacing the artist's hand with a light-sensitive surface so the view is directly recorded. Various light-sensitive materials have been tried, but the one most important for modern still photography and cinematography in their early stages involved silver halide salts, which release black free silver when exposed to light; by the late nineteenth century microscopic crystals of silver bromide suspended in a thin layer of gelatine coated on to a flexible transparent base of celluloid made moving photography possible.

This brief and schematic history is a standard one for a technical device. An effect once achieved laboriously and by human skills that demanded years of practice and training is rationalized and then, step by step, mechanized and automated, increasing the ease and speed with which the desired effect can be obtained, but at the same time reducing the amount of skill deployed to do so. But where an aesthetic effect is at stake, such a development involves a paradox. What was held up for admiration by Pliny was not just the replication of reality, but the feat of skill that replication constituted. Once a machine can perform the replication as well as, or indeed better than, the most skilful draughtsman, the process of replication ceases to be aesthetically valuable, and in so far as art is also supposed to represent the world for us the replication begins to be seen as an inadequate representation, as in a sense even false.

And photography suffered from this paradox. When the Daguerreotype first appeared, its magical ability to reproduce the world as we see it made it immediately a metaphorical standard for realism in the other arts, particularly the non-visual ones; writers strove for 'photographic realism' in their descriptions o fact and fiction. But the high value set on photographic realism was soon infected by the photographic paradox, the way the very perfection of photographic reproduction undermined its value as representation, and a certain kind of superficial descriptive accuracy was labelled 'merely photographic'. In the visual arts proper, mere reproductive skill began to recede as an artistic qualification and is now hardly recognized as a desideratum at all (or if it is, the perfect reproduction conceals 'something else', as in Magic-Realist painting, and certain highly finished varieties of surrealism or pop art). It would be a mistake to see the rise of photography as solely or even principally responsible for this shift, but its existence certainly presented a foil to the less and less 'life-like' depictions that have become the norm in modern art. Still photography itself was, and still is, hard put to define itself as an art rather than a mere copying device like a xerox machine, as creative rather than merely reproductive.

In fact more had always been at stake in classical and neo-classical theories of representation than an illusionistic rep-lication of the world and the skill invested in producing it. In relation to drama, Aristotle had distinguished between the repre-sentation on the stage of things that had actually happened and that of those that were likely or probable (*eikos*), even if they had not happened, and had argued that the probable was preferable in drama to the true, or at any rate the latter had also to be endowed with probability to be as valuable. What was probable was more valuable in that its occurrence involved a generali-zation, whereas what had happened on one particular occasion was merely contingent. From a probable event the audience could learn about other events and link the event represented to events of their own experience, whereas the mere assertion that some-thing had occurred of itself had no implications that could be extended to any other event (Aristotle, 1965).

Neo-classical aesthetics, growing up contemporaneously with the rise of perspective painting, took the point further. 'Verisimi-litude' (a calque of the Latin translation of Aristotle's *eikos, verisimilitudo*) was preferable to the truth in so far as the presentation of an event or character in a work of art implied a judgement about that event or character. Corneille was criticized for having his heroine Chimène marry Rodrigue, the murderer of

147

her father, in *Le Cid*, even though this marriage was held to be a historical fact; it was immoral or at best inconsistent to make a character presented as a true aristocrat do something so contrary to the honour of her family and therefore it lacked verisimilitude. *La Princesse de Clèves* was criticized for showing the heroine confessing to her husband that she loved another man, on the grounds that such behaviour (the confession, not the love) was unwifely, and hence unverisimilitudinous in a character presented as a true wife. (The fact that both these actions do not strike many modern spectators or readers as unverisimilitudinous, that indeed the conflict between individual feeling and the demand to conform to social convention is what makes them seem life-like, shows that our notions of verisimilitude have shifted, in particular that we can bring to bear a valued model of the individual alongside those of aristocrat or wife, but not that we do not still apply a notion of verisimilitude sufficiently like the neo-classical one to serve my purposes here. See Genette, 1969.)

In painting, similarly, the purely illusionistic aspects of perspective representation were never enough to constitute paintings as works of art in the specially valued sense that became current in the Renaissance. As perspective technique was mastered, it began to be applied to a whole series of architectural, scenographic and novelty uses precisely to create illusions: false perspective to make a poky staircase seem grand, as in Bernini's *Scala Regia* at St Peter's in Rome, pure *trompe-l'oeil* for ceilings and walls representing the sky or completely unreal vistas, theatrical backdrops showing city- and seascapes, and anamorphoses, trick pictures that are uninterpretable until looked at from an unlikely and highly oblique angle, like the skull in Holbein's *The Ambassadors*. These devices belong in the lower domain of the applied arts, offering spectators no more than wonder and amusement; it is only when combined with other forms of representation (as in *The Ambassadors*) that they escape the pejorative implication of a mere exertion of decorative virtuosity.

In all these examples it is clear that what is at stake is a relation between contingency and necessity. Presenting a perfect simulacrum of something in the world (whether real, or fictional but indistinguishable from the real) is not enough to constitute a representation as truthful, as making valuable statements about

148

the world. On the other hand, artistic representation is a matter of depicting individuals, unique moments in time and space. Verisimilitude links the two, presenting the contingent individual and judging it as corresponding to some ideal necessity, offering a perspective on it, in a more metaphorical sense. *The Ambassadors* is an especially interesting example here in that it can be seen as anticipating a cinematic technique, producing a combined representation by showing two reproductions *in sequence*. A perspective depiction of its subjects surrounded by the signs of their glory[1] is interrupted by an illegible shape which a backward glance when passing under the picture would subsequently reveal as an emblem of death, the two images combined (and the impossibility of seeing them both together) providing the artist's judgement on his subject.

Thus, when photography emerged and became widely available in the nineteenth century, not only did it devalue the feat of producing a simulacrum of reality, it also produced a greater emphasis on verisimilitude as opposed to mere replication. Photography was a valuable scientific tool also useful for everyday recording purposes (the vast majority of early photographs were portraits), but if it aspired to the status of an art it had to find principles of verisimilitude beyond its mere ability to record the real world.

Film and Photography

Moving pictures are not, of course, necessarily moving *photographic* pictures. Most of the nineteenth-century optical toys that exploited the phenomenon of the persistence of vision to produce the illusion of movement by rapidly substituting for one another a series of slightly discrepant images used drawn and painted pictures rather than photographs (e.g. the Phenakistiscope), as did the earliest system of projecting a relatively long series of such images, Reynaud's Praxinoscope. However, the development of instantaneous photography, reducing exposure times well below the threshold of the persistence of vision, and the invention of apparatuses which could take series of instantaneous photographs at very short intervals in order to analyse the movements of animals, birds and human beings into a succession of phases lost on the naked eye, made photography the cheapest and easiest option when it came to providing the series of slightly discrepant images needed for moving picture devices, whether peep-shows like the Edison Kinetograph or projection systems (along the lines of the magic lantern) like the Lumière Cinématographe.

But although what the people who came to these machines were looking for was moving pictures, that is, not intrinsically photographic, what seems universally to have registered with them was an effect only achievable by photography. All the earliest audiences remarked that not only did the 'principals' in the pictures, the people and the vehicles, move, but so did the 'extras', the leaves on the trees, the steam rising from the kettle, and so on. It was this added reality that fascinated people and this was essentially an accidental by-product of photography. Although there are films made without photographing 'the real world' – animated films where what is photographed is series of drawn and painted pictures, and films made by directly drawing or scratching on celluloid, where the only photography involved is in the preparation of copies of the film for exhibition – photographic films in the strict sense have always predominated and are all that I shall consider in this essay.

Indeed, the photographic effect seems to have increased in importance since the early years of the cinema. Erik Barnouw (1981) has emphasized the important extent to which early film exhibition was handled by conjurers and how, for them, films replaced optically and mechanically complex disappearing tricks with simple cinematic tricks of the kind the French film-maker (and one-time conjurer) Georges Méliès specialized in. In this tradition the mobility of moving pictures is an illusion, what the pictures show no more really moves than the lady is really sawn in half: 'dot's nothun but a drick', as Momma Sieppe says in *McTeague*.[2] From this standpoint, the production of the illusion of movement is what is all-important in moving pictures; the authenticity or otherwise of the moving objects represented is secondary.

And indeed, although many early films are records of real events – the 1896 Derby, Queen Victoria's Jubilee Parade, the Tsar's official visit to Paris, President McKinley's inauguration etc. – less predictable newsworthy events were more difficult to film and film-makers generally had no compunction about re-creating them in a studio or on a suitable available location. Some spectators denounced this practice as 'fraud' and some exhibitors clearly thought their customers preferred to think they were seeing a record of 'the real thing' rather than a reconstruction and there-fore advertised what for the maker was patently a reconstruction as a real record. However, it seems that for many film-makers, exhibitors and spectators the distinction simply was not so clear. A moving picture of a newsworthy event was judged true to the extent that it accurately represented the facts concerned, that is, it was judged as a drawing of that event would be (and, of course, newspaper printing technology at the time meant that most illus-trations of the news took the form of engravings from drawings, even though some of these may have had photographs as their source); that it was an actual record made on the spot as the event depicted occurred was not a crucial consideration.

But this consideration has subsequently come to dominate the use of moving (and still) photographs for the presentation of real events in newsreels or documentaries. Moving photography, the creation of an illusion of movement, has become something much more passive, the recording of a moving event that unfolded in front of the camera, and the event recorded has become the focus of questions of truth and falsity. And this sense of moving pictures as a passive record of real events has affected our viewing of fiction films, too. These seem to be doubly fictional; not only is there a fictional world in which fictional events occur, but we are seeing a fictional recording of those events made by an invisible and ideally perceptive newsreel cameraman.

Thus the cinema became, if it was not so from the first, a medium conceived of as photographic; and as such it became subject to the photographic paradox: it only copied the world and could tell us nothing new about it.

Cinematic Verisimilitude

This objection, and the solution classical narrative film-making found for it, have been put perhaps most perspicuously by the

Hungarian critic György Lukács in his *Ästhetik*, the outline of a Marxist version of the neo-classical aesthetics I have been discussing. To qualify as 'realist' a work in any medium has to exhibit what Lukács calls 'double mimesis'. An immediate representation of the world (real and fictional) has to become the object of a second representation in the work; the first representation is of the 'merely photographic' kind, only in the light of the second can it offer genuine insight into reality. Different media use different devices for double mimesis. Where the cinema is concerned,[3] these devices are best illustrated by an example Lukács offers from Orson Welles's *Citizen Kane* (Lukács, 1963, p. 498).

The example occurs in the first of the two sequences showing Kane's second wife Susan making her debut in the opera *Salammbo*. We see and hear her on stage singing a grand-opera aria, then the camera moves bodily ('tracks' or 'cranes') upwards into the flies until it frames two stage hands looking down and listening; one of them turns to the other and holds his nose. The point for the story is that Susan's singing is bad; her voice and talent are suitable for musical comedy, not grand opera, and Kane is forcing her into the more prestigious art to get back at his first wife and her friends. We see a photographed record of the actress playing Susan (Dorothy Comingore) singing and hear a recording of a singer's voice singing (not the same actress's, in fact, but fictionally Susan's voice none the less). The singing is bad (according to the film's composer, Bernard Herrmann, the singer whose voice was dubbed for Susan's here was a good singer but singing above her range). However, it would be merely photographic (or rather 'merely phonographic', but the same set of arguments apply to the recording of sound as to that of light) to leave it at that. The film goes on to give us a second image with a judgement on the first; the stage hands – authoritative because they are anonymous professionals concealed in the dark and thus not open to Kane's influence, unlike the audience in the theatre whom we see feebly taking up his applause in the second sequence showing this episode – tell us that the singing is bad. Even if we thought the singing recorded was all right, we would either have to allow the film's judgement to override our own, or we would have to give up on the film. In Vincente Minnelli's *The Cobweb* it is an important point for the story that Stevie is a talented artist held back by neurotic inhibitions. We know this because Stevie's curtain designs are admired by everybody (including once again an otherwise uninvolved professional who appears in only one scene to screen-print them on to the curtain material). Considered as photographs of curtain designs (patterns I might be examining to choose curtains of my own), I think they are horrible, but for the sake of the fiction I can suspend this judgement and accept the one offered by the film (the suspension of disbelief central to all fiction is very often more a matter of suspension of judgement).[4]

Classical narrative film-making developed many ways of providing these judgements on the recorded material films contain. The simplest and commonest is verbal: in silent films narrative titles frequently offer judgements of characters' actions (for example, in D. W. Griffith's *True Heart Susie*, Bettina is seen off with the words 'And so she died as she had lived – slightly unfaithful') and in sound films character dialogue is used for the same purpose ('You be sure and cure this guy, eh doc?' from the screen-printer in *The Cobweb*). Lukács's example is deliberately chosen because it is a visual commentary that is offered – a second photograph, of a gesture, commenting on the first. Both of these are in the same shot, but judgemental commentary is more often provided by what had come to be regarded by most critics from the 1920s to the 1940s as the essential aesthetic means of cinema: editing.

Editing became highly valued by film critics because it seemed to be the aesthetic device most specific to cinema. In fact it has much in common with, and grew out of, the sequencing of views in lantern-slide shows, the division of stage plays into scenes and the organization of strip cartoons into temporally successive boxes. At its simplest, film editing (or cutting) is the gluing end to end of strips of film taken on different occasions and from different camera positions. Such lengths of film are called 'shots'.[5]

Editing serves a number of functions. The simplest, and the closest to the theatrical scene change, is to extend the range of time and space representable. If you want to show something happening somewhere else or at another time, change scene. (In the American cinema until the 1940s, what I am calling a shot was called a 'scene'.)

More complex is the use to show things that, from a theatrical point of view, are part of the immediate arena of action, but for one or other reason require a separate shot. This includes close-ups of details, showing things otherwise too small to be seen sufficiently clearly in a framing inclusive enough to represent a complex action, e.g. the text of a letter or newspaper that a character is reading, or a raised eyebrow. Then there are shots of things not immediately visible from the initial vantage point. These things may be in an adjoining space, for example, some-body observing the initial action through a doorway from the next room, and in that case shots of them are called 'cut-aways', or they may be in the space occupied by or behind the camera, in which case shots of them are called 'reverse shots'. In all these cases extension of the comprehensibility of what is shown is accompanied by a process of directing attention to what is significant, in other words a narrator's guiding hand judging the initial photographs, and in so far as character knowledge (the text of a letter being read, the fact that A sees B but B does not see A) and feeling (the close-up of the raised eyebrow) are also conveyed by these devices, a perspective on the action depicted is immediately introduced.

Another function is censorship, avoiding showing actions or things that are regarded as too offensive to an audience's suscepti-bilities to be shown directly. This too has a theatrical origin in the convention of classical and neo-classical drama that all violent action should take place off stage (because the direct represen-tation of something so shocking would be unseemly – unverisimi-litudinous – in the civilized space of a theatre), news of it arriving by messenger, or, at the limit, by sound off (Agamemnon's cries for help from the bathhouse in the first play of Aechylus's *Oresteia*). Once cutting within a scene became normal, for the other reasons suggested above, it could also be used to avoid direct representation of unseemly things and events within the scene itself, thus increasing the flexibility of the device, cutting away from the action to the face of a horrified witness at the crucial moment, and so on.

Finally, editing is used to establish a normal shot length which acts as a standard in relation to which shots markedly longer or shorter acquire, simply from their deviant length, interpretive power in respect to their photographed content; long-held shots imply there is more in what can be seen than meets the eye (this apparently innocent passer-by is in fact a detective trailing the hero), short shots a character's reaction of surprise at a sudden occurrence (the brief glimpse of the gull in the sky as it attacks Melanie in *The Birds*). This can be generalized to provide overall commentary, fast cutting implying urgency, slow, calm. Cutting rates or average shot lengths change from year to year in mainstream narrative cinema as a whole, at any one time there is a range of variation from film to film, and there is some variation from reel to reel of a single film, but these ranges are relatively small, so there are strong expectations as to the appropriate rate at which new information will be delivered to the spectator (for detailed discussion of average shot lengths, see Salt, 1984).

Before the First World War, average shot lengths were generally high, with the result that film shots functioned very like stage scenes. But by the end of the war some American films had average shot lengths of as little as four and a half seconds (more than 1000 shots in a ninety-minute feature), and given that this number can be supplemented, as in Lukács's example, by camera movements within a shot that reveal new elements of a scene, it is clear that very subtle patterns of constantly revised judgement of what is shown can be developed over the length of a feature film. A classical film in effect presents moving photographs (and recorded sounds), then by editing (supplemented by camera movement, dialogue and other means) perspectives on those photographs (and recorded sounds), then perspectives on those perspectives, and so on, generally resolving these multiple perspectives into one authoritative judgement on most of what has been seen and heard by the end of the film (see Heath, 1976, and MacCabe, 1974).

These editing devices were developed slowly and, in America at least, where editing developed more quickly than in Europe in the 1910s, in a fairly *ad hoc* way: editing was often seen as no more than a way of saving money or circumventing having to stage censorable, illegal or supernatural actions and film them directly in long-held, long-distance shots. Shooting a sequence set in Venice by cutting between three fairly close-in framings of small sets representing three different fragments of Venice was cheaper than building a vast set representing a major part of the city and filming all the actions in a single shot in different parts of that set; and if a Persian soldier had to be thrown from the hundred-foot-high battlements of the walls of Babylon (as in Griffith's *Intolerance*), his body was seen landing in a second, closer shot, because you cannot kill extras to get the action in one shot. Cuts of this latter type came to be known as 'cheats'.

However, in the 1920s a group of young Soviet film-makers who were admirers of American editing nevertheless attacked this pragmatic attitude, arguing that 'cheating' was the central cinematic device and that rather than thinking of the whole scene in long shot and then 'cutting in' to closer shots for the details of the action, film-makers should realize that the whole is a purely fictional construction out of a series of detail shots which may be filmed, indeed should be filmed, from realities which do not have the spatio-temporal and other relationships in reality that they will have in the fictional world represented in the film (Pudovkin, 1929). The director Lev Kuleshov carried out a series of famous experiments demonstrating that spectators will accept a series of shots of parts (head, hands, feet, etc.) of different people as representing one person, a series of shots taken in different cities as representing one city, and reaction shots of an actor expressing some emotion as representing completely different emotions when inserted into different series of surrounding shots providing a different narrative context (Kuleshov, 1974). The last example is particularly important because it demonstrates the extent to which the reality depicted by a film has shifted away from the reality photographed (an actor pretending to express, or perhaps a real person really expressing, emotion x) into the editing context in which we know by narrative conventions that the expected cutaway to the close-up of a face must depict a character expressing emotion y.

This group of Soviet directors deliberately flaunted their editing, making the cuts as visible as possible and creating a style now known as 'montage' cinema (from the French-derived Russian term for editing). American film-makers, on the contrary, led in the development of a series of conventions for 'matching' one shot with its surrounding shots, minimizing the spectators' need to re-orient themselves with each cut, reducing the proportion of new information to old in a new shot and cutting at highly predictable moments, so that spectators are hardly aware of the cuts and can rarely remember having seen them after the screening. This system came to be known as 'invisible editing'. However, despite the pragmatic origins and 'invisibility' of this editing, it is just as dependent on the Kuleshov effect; we know more about the meaning of a shot from its place in an editing context than we do from what we actually see and hear in the shot. The more complex editing becomes, the less contribution to the depicted world is made by the initial photographs and recorded sounds, until they are providing hardly more than an alibi that *qua* photographable, the world represented is real, even though almost all that is known about it derives from editorial judgement and from narrative expectations, that is, from a series of conventions. The drive to deepen the superficial reality of the photographs in fact came to undermine that reality, replacing it by conventional wisdom. Thus much of the best screen acting consists of an ability to express absolutely nothing. A close-up of a blank face in a narrative and editing context that tells us (i.e. we already know it before we see the shot) that the character is suffering deeply, is all the more moving for the inscrutability of that face. We think we see someone suffering, but that knowledge comes not from what we see but from its availability to a conventional interpretive schema.

This did not worry critics in the 1920s and 1930s, who generally insisted that film was artistically valuable in so far as it did not record reality, that its aesthetic strengths were its reproductive weaknesses (thus the veteran film critic and theorist Rudolf Arnheim argued and still argues that the introduction of sound and colour, which increased the reproductive power of the cinema, were aesthetic disasters, forcing film-makers to abandon the highly artificial conventions of late silent cinema and become mere duplicators of stage plays – see Arnheim, 1933 and 1975). But in the 1940s one critic emerged who attacked both of the highly edited film-making traditions of the 1930s, the American cinema of 'invisible editing' and the Russian cinema of 'montage', for their artificiality, and demanded a return to a realism based on the recording powers of photography. This was the French critic André Bazin.

Recording Re-evaluated

Bazin championed three recent developments in film-making against these traditions: first the films of the French film-maker Jean Renoir, which used relatively long-held shots, a camera moving relatively independently of the making of a narrative 'point' (i.e. in-the-shot editing effects) and a system of deep staging combining many planes of action in a single shot; second the deep-focus cinematography introduced into American cinema by the photographer Gregg Toland in films directed by Orson Welles and William Wyler, employing long-held and often relatively static shots staged in depth in a more extreme manner than in Renoir's films and with sharp focus maintained from close to the camera to the rear of the sets; and third the largely location-shot films of the postwar wave of Italian directors known as 'Neo-Realists'. In the first two cases what Bazin praised is continuity of space and time against editing fragment-ation. The last case is more complex, as in the 1940s the films of De Sica, Rossellini and Visconti were quite highly edited (though later Rossellini in particular began to use longer and longer takes, so his last films contain very few shots); here Bazin emphasized the unconventional character of the content and set-tings, but also an editing which was rapid because it was ellipti-cal, because conventionally expected parts of the narrative or reaction shots were missing (Bazin, 1967 and 1971).

Bazin's position is often misrepresented as purely a demand for more continuity and less film-maker's intervention. The example of Neo-Realism shows, however, that what was at stake for him was not the lack of continuity as such but the highly conventionalized character of edited realism in films and the need to re-emphasize the recording moment of cinematogra-phy in order to restore to the cinema a sense of reality that it had lost. Photography and sound recording provide a direct contact with reality, bypassing any human intervention, but this does not give a convention-free access to reality to the spectator. The renewal produced by a re-emphasis on that contact rather temporarily disrupts the smooth incorporation of reality into conventionalized systems of representation which cloak it in seemly verisimilitude. It is reality's resistance to representation rather than its availability to it that constitutes the realist effect for Bazin.

To express this he used the metaphor (from physical geography) of the equilibrium profile of a river: in a stable landscape a river wears down its bed until it reaches not a completely flat trajectory but a completely smooth curve (a cycloid curve if the bedrock is homogeneous throughout its course). Once this trajectory has been reached the river ceases to engage with its bed, until the configuration of the landscape changes, the river bed is raised and the river starts cutting into the bedrock again. For Bazin the invention or development of a recording technology is such an upheaval if the flow of film production is the river. The renewed contact with reality forces the conventions of representation embodied in film-making processes to struggle to adapt to the new reality, and it is in the struggle rather than the eventual successful adaptation that the sense of reality is felt. Once a new arrangement of the system of conventions adapted to the new technology has been achieved, the sense of reality is lost. In the 1930s, Bazin thought, existing film-making practices had reached such an equilibrium profile, but this was disturbed by the emergence of the technological preconditions for deep-focus cinematography in the USA and a radical shift in subject matter (for political reasons) requiring an application of existing technology under quite new conditions in the Italy of the period of postwar reconstruction.

This relativistic conception of realism brings Bazin surprisingly close to the account of realism in art offered by the Russian linguist and poetician Roman Jakobson in an article originally published in Czech in 1921 entitled 'On realism in art' (Jakobson, 1971). In this article, Jakobson argued that artists and their audiences could have two diametrically opposed criteria for realism in a work of art. Either works could be held to be realist because they conformed to an existing set of canons of realism, a system of verisimilitude, or on the contrary they could be regarded as realist because they broke away from those existing canons, seen as conventionalized and stereotyped. The transgressive realism of today will, however, become the canonic realism of tomorrow. In the same way, for Bazin a new use of the recording machinery of the cinema breaks away from a conventionalized, stereotyped realism, but is itself doomed to become tomorrow's stereotype. The difference between Bazin and Jakobson is, of course, that for Jakobson, as a Russian Formalist, the devices of art are all-important and aesthetic effects are produced by 'making strange' any existing canons of representation; that these canons are called 'realist' is only incidental. For Bazin on the other hand it is the possibility of direct contact with the real world offered by the recording apparatuses of cinematography that has to be constantly asserted against the dead hand of stereotype, with the result that a realist vocation is intrinsic to the cinema for him.

The Neo-Realist example also shows that, although Bazin thinks in terms of technological advances that make a more integral recording of reality possible, it is often the difficulties and even failures of such new means applied to reality that produce the effects he desired as much as their successes. To take an extreme instance, he praised the documentary *Annapurna* because the film totally fails to present any images or sounds of a catastrophic accident while the mountain was being climbed; an avalanche swept away and destroyed the camera recording the expedition that day. The accident is represented in the film by a gap, but this gap registers a very extreme contact between reality and the recording apparatus and produces a far greater reality effect than a standard documentary shot of an avalanche from a safe distance would have.

A less extreme example (my own rather than Bazin's) of the same kind occurs in Renoir's film *Toni*. Directed for the Marseilles film producer Marcel Pagnol in the south of France, it was the first film made in France using almost entirely direct sound on location (as opposed to the controlled environment of a studio). The technology for directly recording sound was still very much cruder than it has since become and the possibility of re-recording sound to make mixed tracks after the event may not have been available to the film-makers. As a result there are a lot of sounds that a modern sound crew would reject as extraneous, poorly balanced, distorted, etc., but in the evidence these failures present of the difficulties of recording the sound, the reality effect produced is striking.

In one scene the hero Toni and his friend Fernand light the

160

fuses for a blast in a quarry where they work and wait the other side of the quarry for the explosion. The scene is filmed in a long shot with Fernand and Toni in the foreground, the rock wall a considerable distance beyond them. We see the wall explode, then after a second we hear on the sound track not a loud bang but a feeble splutter and crackle. The microphones have not been able to cope with the shock wave and have given up on the sound. This differs from what would have happened in a mainstream American film of the same date (or indeed from then to now) in two ways. First there would have been a verisimilitudinous bang. This would probably have been made in the time-honoured theatrical way by shaking a metal sheet, the sound would have been recorded and then dubbed on to the sound track. Second the bang would have occurred simultaneously with the image of the exploding rock wall, allowing no interval for the passage of the sound from the explosion, its speed slower than that of the light.

The first point is a clear instance of verisimilitude overriding the truth of the recording – the sound should meet our expectations of a quarry-blasting rather than be a direct effect of the blasting itself on the recording apparatus. The second is more complex. It is of a piece with two other characteristics of classical narrative film's representation of space. First, although at the beginnings of the use of synchronized sound there was a lot of discussion in the technical press about how to achieve 'sound perspective', that is, effects of depth in the sound track, and it was generally agreed that long shots should have softer and more reverberant sounds than close-ups, in practice in shooting a scene a single level of volume and reverberation was used for all the shots in the scene unless an extreme effect of distance was required (e.g. a cut from a close-up of a speaker in Congress to an extreme long shot of him from the gallery emphasizing his isolation) (see Wood, 1984). Second, although the image obtained from a film camera automatically reproduces the spatial dispositions of objects in depth on the picture plane characteristic of the ideal of Renaissance perspective painting, film sets and camera angles were generally designed to avoid the things that specialists in *perspectiva artificialis* flaunted, like chequerboard marble pavements and receding colonnades, and oblique angles were generally preferred to frontal ones. All these studiously avoided properties of image and sound – the time-lag between seeing the source of a sound and hearing it, the variation of volume and reverberation of sound with distance, the geometry of a rectilinear display in perspective representation – provide means whereby the distance of the object or sound source from the observer can be more or less precisely *calculated*. Classical cinema rejects this precision in favour of a general sense of depth which can then be calibrated according to conventional models rather than precise geometry – for the purposes of the story people have to be such and such a distance from each other or their surroundings, so they are seen to be so, and anything that might too clearly indicate how far apart the objects in front of the camera and the microphone really were is suppressed. A conventionalized depth is preferred over a real one (for a slightly different account, see Bordwell, 1985).

Record and Representation

Bazin drew his examples from mainstream narrative film-making in the USA and Europe (plus a few equally mainstream documentaries) and in this essay so far I have assumed that films are the fictional feature films normally shown at circuit cinemas, art houses and on television. But there are film-makers and film-making traditions outside these institutional parameters with quite different approaches to the photographic character of cinematic means of representation and the consequences to be drawn from that character for the possible relations between film and reality. These solutions are diverse, but to be alarmingly schematic, three tendencies, singly or in combination, can be distinguished: a greater emphasis on the use of the film camera as a means of pure record, both in the sense of the home movie and in that of the film's ability to record traces of light, even when these form no recognizable picture; a greater willingness to assemble film material in ways which are individual to the film-maker or entirely arbitrary (determined by some numerical scheme, by random processes, or by changing shot whenever some event – a character entering shot, the sun coming out – occurs in the image or sound track, say); and a flaunting of the

162

paradoxes of photography and sound recording I have been discussing in this essay. The first of these tendencies is illustrated by much of the work of Stan Brakhage, the second by that of landscape film-makers such as Chris Welsby, the third by work in the structural film-making tradition by Hollis Frampton and Michael Snow. However, rather than discussing these experimental film-makers' work, I prefer to take my last examples from that of two film-makers with much closer connections to traditional narrative film-making, though only marginally involved in its institutions. These film-makers are Jean-Marie Straub and Danièle Huillet.

In their films Bazin's emphasis on cinema as involving the recording of sounds and images occurring at a particular point in space and time is taken much further. Their best-known film, *Chronicle of Anna Magdalena Bach*, tells the story of Johann Sebastian Bach's life from his marriage to his second wife to his death, using a voice-over commentary from a (fictional) diary of that wife. The rest of the film's material is provided by shots of a variety of documents from Bach's day including his manuscripts and printed works; filmings of performances of Bach's works by musicians in eighteenth-century costume in the settings where Bach's music was performed in his lifetime; brief representations by the same musicians and other actors of incidents from Bach's life ranging from minor domestic events to conflicts with the Leipzig city authorities over his conduct of the choir school and a visit to his son Carl Phillip Emmanuel at Potsdam; and a few shots of landscapes empty of people.

This material is conventional enough for a dramatized documentary or biopic but it is handled much less conventionally. Straub and Huillet exploit the fact that music has an identity that is re-created again and again in performance, whereas the film camera records one moment in time. Despite differences in interpretation, Bach's Brandenburg concerto no. 5 is that concerto whenever it is played, whereas each rescreening of a film points back to the never-returning moment when the camera was set up before the scene to be recorded. Bach in the film is played by Gustav Leonhardt, in both senses, so what we see and hear is a filming of Leonhardt playing the fifth Brandenburg concerto in 1967, but also Bach playing that concerto in the eighteenth century, and Leonhardt is not 'pretending' to play the concerto in the sense that he is 'pretending' to be Bach, he *is* playing it. The film-makers are helped in this by the artificiality of eighteenth-century dress: eighteenth-century musicians, like modern actors playing eighteenth-century characters, wore wigs.

This strategy is assisted by never cutting within a scene of musical performance and always using the sound take recorded with the picture footage seen, even if the performers make a mistake. Some shots use a fixed camera, others a slowly panning or tracking one. As long passages of music are filmed, the result is, of course, very long-held shots and no editing effects, even of the 'in-the-shot-by-camera-movement' kind. Despite the unconventional dress of some of the musicians (choirboys, of course, still often dress today as they did in the eighteenth century), it is constantly borne in on us that we are watching and listening to a modern performance of a Bach work. The representations of Bach's extra-musical life, though mostly much more edited, are similarly not subject to editing interpretation. They are far too brief and 'insignificant' in content and do not carry forward a narrative line; the sound and image tracks in succeeding shots are not 'graded' to make them blend smoothly into one another (as they would be in a mainstream fiction or documentary film); the acting, mostly by professional musicians rather than actors, is deliberately flattened, again emphasizing an action recorded rather than interpreted, and there is no editing to supply the missing expressiveness; the verbal delivery of the actors and of the voice-over, and the eighteenth-century German of both, makes listening to them more like listening to verse than to the kind of speech that can be immediately assimilated to the surrounding action as participating in it; and the editing rhythms, shifting abruptly from short to long-held shots, refuse the 'dosed' delivery of new information typical of classical editing. Thus, image and sound, image and voice, shot and shot, never fuse together into a homogeneous verisimilitudinous representation but remain a set of articulated recordings.

Finally, the empty landscape shots are placed in the film at the ends of the reels (in 35mm prints, the gauge on which the film was shot and should be seen and heard). In a projector a film is under more strain at the beginnings and ends of reels, and as a print ages, breaks and scratches accumulate there more than elsewhere. Putting empty shots at the reel ends protects Bach's cadences from disruption by such print damage. But these shots also accumulate visible wear unique to this print and some of it unique to this screening. Thus the moment in time when this projection is taking place (now) and the age of the print are drawn to our attention. Shots whose content is timeless – views of sea-shore and trees without human figures, indeed without any signs of human existence at all – emphasize a temporality we only usually become aware of at the expense of our investment in the film, the age and wear of the print itself.

In other words, the film refuses to fuse the time represented fictionally (the eighteenth century), the time of its visual and auditory recording (August–September 1967) and the time of the screening (now). Straub in an interview (Straub, 1970) once cited a remark of Cocteau's to the effect that 'the cinema is death at work' and a concern with the mortal implications of the passing of time is found at all levels in *Chronicle of Anna Magdalena Bach*, most obviously in the similar emphasis in the texts of Bach's cantatas sung during the film, but also in the frequency with which death appears, almost incidentally, in the biographical fragments. Moving photography with its ability to re-create the most obvious sign of life, movement, in a portrait, was often seen by its first viewers as a way to conjure death. *Chronicle of Anna Magdalena Bach* undermines this illusion, though no more gloomily than Bach's music. In the last shot, the voice-over describes Bach's death, but what we see is Leonhardt/Bach standing looking out of a window at the light. The voice-over tells us that just before he died, the sight he had almost completely lost was briefly restored, so the image is directly appropriate; it is also metaphorically appropriate given all the film has told us about Bach's expectations of his own death. But it is also a picture of Gustav Leonhardt, who is still alive although he will die, and he does not pretend to be dead any more than he pretends to play the Brandenburg concerto. The film thus demonstrates that it is not only by rejecting or transcending the technological basis of the cinema in machinery for making records of the real world that the cinema can deal more than superficially with reality.

Notes

1 The utensils and instruments on the stand between the two subjects include a large number which Renaissance iconography, the system that associated depictions of everyday objects with symbolic meanings, classified as emblems of vanity. Iconography here is functioning in the same way as the system of verisimilitude I have been discussing does: it derives a generalized meaning from the depiction of a set of individual things.

2 Trina thought the moving pictures wonderful and Mac was awe-struck, but this simply suggests they disapproved of tricks less than Mrs Sieppe (see Norris, 1899, ch. VI). In the American vaudeville – and it was at a vaudeville house that Norris had the Sieppes and McTeague see a projecting version of the Kinetoscope, Edison's system of moving pictures – conjuring took a particularly rationalistic form, casting off, even denouncing, the appeal to the supernatural that had often been an integral part of it in the past. The tricks were very explicitly presented as illusions depending on the skills of the conjurer and the scientific effectivity of his machines. This allowed audiences to enjoy the wonder of the trick while protecting the religious susceptibilities of their older members, often educated in a strict Puritan tradition. Moving photography, an invention of the 'Wizard of Menlo Park', Thomas Alva Edison, was in just this way a scientifically guaranteed producer of a wonderful illusion. See McLean, 1965, and Burch, forthcoming.

3 It should perhaps be said that the cinema is only of secondary interest to Lukács and most of his ideas about it derive from his compatriot, the film-maker and theorist Béla Balász. I have modified Lukács's example slightly, but the argument is his.

4 I should cite a counter-example here, lest I be accused of oversimplifying classical film conventions; there are very few of these that cannot be transgressed in a classical fiction film, precisely because (relatively) surprising the audience is one of the aims of such film-making. Moreover, classical films are open to other approaches than ones which emphasize the predictable and familiar aspects of their functioning and my concentration on these aspects should not be taken as a dismissal of classical cinema, far from it. In Fritz Lang's *Scarlet Street*, the action turns around the artistic and monetary value of the pictures Chris Cross, the hero (or anti-hero) paints in his spare time and which eventually obtain fame under the false attribution to his mistress Kitty Marsh. However, the film never provides a trustworthy evaluation of these paintings – is their success the result of mere media hype, or a genuine naive talent? And in a way not untypical of Lang'

films this uncertainty infects other judgements in the film. Kitty and her boyfriend Johnny are judged naive by the film, because they think the pictures must be valuable (monetarily). But if we are not sure of the value of the pictures either, how can we be confident of this judgement of Kitty and Johnny? And so on. That is why it is difficult to decide whether Chris Cross is a hero or an anti-hero.

5 Strictly speaking a shot is what *purports to be* a length of film taken on one occasion from one position or a continuously moving position. · Trick effects often depend on presenting material filmed on several occasions, that is, several 'takes', as if it were a single 'take' – a shot is a fictional take. The track into the flies in *Citizen Kane* is one shot, but almost certainly consists of two takes, a track up from Susan and a second track up on to the stage hands, probably filmed on the same level. Indeed, so pervasive is process work in this film, that it is conceivable that there never was any camera movement in the shots, the effect of movement being produced by scrolling in a printer.

Chapter Eight

Philosophy

MICHAEL LEAHY

In the introduction to this book I presented an outline theory of reality. The account emerged as an alternative to the fourfold theory of positivism and was fairly abstract in nature. In this chapter I shall begin with an approach from another direction, that of demonstration rather than abstract description, much as a hopeful car salesman eventually discards brochures in favour of taking you for a spin. Some aspects of Michael Irwin's treatment of poetry and the novel in chapter 2 will be developed. The implications will rapidly extend beyond literature to history and science. I will then focus upon three recurrent concepts of the whole book: subjectivity, selectivity and convention. In the process the lack of a theory of error in my outline theory will be remedied. I will conclude with a discussion of explanations in theology. Whether or not these explanations fit the theory of error will be left to readers to decide for themselves.

Is the 'Pathetic Fallacy' a Fallacy?

In chapter 2 it was argued that the poetry of John Clare and William Wordsworth presents the poet and his subject matter in complex interaction. The subject matter is nature: animals, the countryside, simple unreflective rustics. The style of the lyric poet, typifying what the Romantics saw as the revolution o imagination over reason, presented nature transformed by the feelings of the poet. A contrast was drawn with the style of the natural historian, Gilbert White (1788), where the effect is cooler because the author seems less involved. Clare and Wordsworth depict nature variously as being in sympathy with our feelings, soothing and reassuring, a model of human fortitude betraying its origins as a divine creation. Wordsworth, more given to generalization than Clare, presents a pantheistic vision of nature[1] as a religious experience, presumably surpassing the traditional pantheon of gods, virgins, prophets and saints,

> In which the heavy and the weary weight
> Of all this unintelligible world,
> Is lightened ...
> While with an eye made quiet by the power
> Of harmony, and the deep power of joy,
> We see into the life of things.

> ([1798] 1944, p. 260)

But disillusion, so it seems, is close to the surface. Clare, in old age, laments the doubtful provenance of his 'summer thrills', and Wordsworth, probably most explicitly in 'Lines composed a few miles above Tintern Abbey' (1944, pp. 259–63), fears that the qualities he attributes to nature are simply the additions of an extravagant and enthusiastic imagination. The sublimity of the pastoral idyll is allegedly revealed as a pretty trick where fantasies of the poet masquerade as facts of nature. He is unmasked as a purveyor of illusion, guilty of Ruskin's 'pathetic fallacy'.

I hope to show that the basis for Wordsworth's misgivings is mistaken. It clearly depends upon assumptions of a positivistic kind to be persuasive: specifically the claim that only the wholly neutral observer can give us facts and, in consequence, depict reality. Any quality in which the beholder has an active part to play is thus illusory; the catch-all 'subjective' often crops up here. So 'sad', 'design' and even 'beauty' will be subjective. But which qualities will *not* be so and therefore qualify as real or objective? 'Shape' and 'colour' are possible candidates. But shape is a product of design and I have already, in the introduction, remarked upon the elusiveness of colour judgements in satisfying the positivistic criteria. It is important to notice that the allegedly contrasting and factual descriptions of Gilbert White are also prone to the pathetic fallacy, if it *is* a fallacy. The sympathy and delight of the writer are encapsulated in his descriptions: 'wonderful', 'elegant', 'perfectly round', and so on (see pp. 17–18). It should be clear that I am objecting only to the argument, which supports a wholesale use of the pathetic fallacy, that any factual attribution of a quality which can be traced to a contribution of the observer or author is automatically undermined and unreal. It does not follow that *every* attribution will be factual;[2] indeed much of Clare and Wordsworth might be suspect. The point is that they cannot be ruled out simply because of their origin in the poet's psyche. How we settle upon properly factual judgements will emerge later.

The Novel, Autobiography and Science

The fantasies of the poet have their counterparts in the selectivity of the novelist. However rigorous the insistence of a George Eliot or Henry James that their novels were faithful to life they also admitted, albeit somewhat reluctantly, that their descriptions were a selection of the multitude of facts available. George Eliot in *Adam Bede* writes:

> My strongest effort is to ... give a faithful account of men and things as they have mirrored themselves in my mind. The mirror is doubtless defective; the outlines will sometimes be disturbed, the reflection faint or confused; but I feel bound to tell you as precisely as I can what that reflection is, as if I were in the witness-box narrating my experience on oath.
>
> (Eliot, [1859] 1961, p. 174)

This reluctance originated, as before, from the assumption that i authors are active in manipulating their material they therefor transgress the requirement of passivity and consequently th reality of their depiction is at risk. Where George Eliot and Henr James ([1884] 1968, pp. 399–400) merely avert their eyes fror this dilemma, James Joyce challenges it. *Ulysses* (Joyce, [1922 1986) is an extravaganza confined to the events of a single day. *Portrait of the Artist as a Young Man* (Joyce, [1916] 1977) is a explicit attempt to re-create the author's childhood experience untainted by the intrusions of the later Joyce, the writer.[3] Not surprisingly, as Michael Irwin shows (in chapter 2), Joyce's experiment is doomed to failure. The author's attempt to describe the child's consciousness betrays a mature and sophisticated linguistic style. This is a studied choice by the Joyce of 1914 who also invents the various contingencies (it being a fictional narra- tive) within which the youth acts. This failure, the 'dilemma of modernism' and in like manner the embarrassment and break- down of romantic realism,[4] was thought to lead to the constric- ting conclusion that all novels were unintentional autobiography, revealing not reality but the author.

   The arguments giving substance to this dilemma of modernism, implicit in Wordsworth, Clare and Coleridge and explicit in George Eliot and Irwin's reconstruction of the position of the modernist novelists, are a mess of half-truths and confusions engendered, again, by our unreliable *alter ego* positivism. For a start, the novel could not possibly be autobiography intentional or otherwise. Were the arguments correct, autobiography would itself be problematical. If the fatal flaw in Joyce's theory justifying *Portrait of the Artist* is the covert selectivity, interpretation and choice of language of the later, authorial, Joyce then surely the same faults are present in any *non*-fictional autobiography. Here the selection is guided by what someone, not always the author, remembers; *how* it is remembered, its implications, point often to contemporary ends; the style is mature. So, in an odd sense, autobiography is itself doomed to failure. (We are assuming, temporarily, the implications of the argument I regard as falla- cious.) But now we are well and truly upon a slippery slope. If autobiography is itself bogus then clearly biography must be as well since the writer is describing someone else, perhaps long dead, whom presumably he knows less well than he knows himself.[5] Furthermore what do we say of a writer claiming to give us a realistic account of events occurring hundreds or even thousands of years ago, about people culturally remote, from sources often suspect? Clearly selection, interpretation and anachronism will be the order of the day. But we are talking of history, one of the most respected of non-fictional disciplines. The argument we are pursuing is all-consuming (this itself is grounds for suspicion) since common sense and science will not escape either. The most detailed account of the doings of the day will not avoid the objection that it is selective. Lengthy minutes of a committee meeting are, in part, the creation of attentive secretaries and exclude what is thought to be irrelevant material. Nor is the methodology of science that of the omniverous beachcomber gathering in whatever comes to hand and classifying it. Indeed even beachcombers show selectivity. Theorists such as Thomas Kuhn (Hacking, 1981) and Karl Popper ([1934] 1959) have made it something of a commonplace that scientists begin not by random casting about, but with a *problem*. For its solution they propose an hypothesis. This hypothesis is then tested for its *dis*confirmation by experiments with the possible outcome of refuting the original hypothesis. In the event of refutation alternative hypotheses become necessary. Inventing hypotheses and devising the necessary 'crucial' experiments involve intense ingenuity, painstaking trial and error, great selectivity. Clearly the positivist's emphasis upon lack of selectivity destroys any attempt to distinguish between fact and fiction and undermines the pre-eminence accorded to science. This outcome was anticipated in the Introduction.

So let us return to the poets and novelists in the spirit of the alternative view of reality. It is wrong to accuse Clare and Wordsworth of simply reading-in their emotions and values in describing nature and *thereby* distorting its reality. (Indeed Irwin in chapter 2, page 22, interestingly points to what he describes as a fall-back position in 'Tintern Abbey' and 'The Excursion' where Wordsworth himself seems to acknowledge this.) The observer is equally active in far less contentious areas than those of lyric poetry. Take the description of a hostess as *intimidating* This might well refer to the lady's overbearing personality; to a positive desire to dominate. But it might not; there are people who frighten us without any intention of so doing and are disagreeably surprised to learn of the fact. But the description would in either case be in order and not to mention that she was intimidating might well be regarded as a serious omission. This is what in part she is, *really*. Yet what is here at issue is the effect upon an impressed observer, not unlike the effect of nature upon Clare or Wordsworth. Here is another, equally pregnant

172

example: the possession of a banknote, a $10 bill. It is of some, perhaps ever decreasing, value: acceptable for services rendered, exchangeable for goods, reassuring in one's pocket and not to be used for lighting fires. These manifestations of value would be vital to any account of what it was to be a note of currency.[6] Yet it would need no change in the outward appearance of the $10 bill for this value to diminish to nothing, as Confederate money became worthless after the American Civil War or stocks and bonds after the Wall Street Crash. The UK half-crown was consigned to a similar fate from 1 January 1970, this time by Act of Parliament. The state of affairs which maintains the value of currency is the operations of a set of *conventions*, cultural and legal, which are subject to change. The banknote is at the mercy of such fluctuations and we sometimes mark this fragility by the observation that cash is 'only bits of metal and paper'. But cash is *not* only bits of metal and paper, despite the possibility of its becoming so, and it is the prevailing conventions which promote it. What the conventions enshrine is a complicated value system of a society at a given time. To ignore these conventions is to ignore the reality of a $10 bill. There is little temptation to pursue what a dedicated positivist ought to want to pursue, namely, the argument that the $10 bill was *really* only a scrap of paper; or should it be atoms and molecules; or micro-particles? But if financial conventions bestow reality to a banknote then why should we ignore the power of other sets of conventions, for example, those of lyric poetry, to be equally demonstrative in other areas? I will return to this.

Views of the Self

The dilemma of post-modernism was, in part, that descriptions of reality seem to collapse into partial autobiography. We might well now wonder why this is so dreadful. The objection will be made that selves are isolated phenomena; isolated from other selves, from earlier manifestations of the same self (as in *Portrait of the Artist* or any straightforward autobiography) and from reality. So to aim at reality or at other or earlier selves and to reveal only one's present self points to a colossal failure.[7] Now the objection would indeed have a point if the nature of a self, of what it was to be a conscious *person*, was as described. But attempts to pin down an elusive and constantly changing self-consciousness are self-defeating and far removed from the *reality* of relations between ourselves and others. This reality is illuminated by the analogy of an animal body. The body is an organism composed of many parts: brain, internal organs, limbs, and so on. Let us, rather loosely, call all these parts organs. Now any organ, say a toe, gains its individuality as a toe, rather than as an ear or an eye, from the role or roles it plays in the functioning of the organism. The organism, as a result of the concerted and harmonious action of its component organs, has a complexity of operation far beyond them. The organs are here analogous to individual selves and the organism, which is really a collection of less complicated organisms as well as organs, is analogous to the groups to which individuals belong: the family, tribe, local community, nation and others. The analogy simplifies the very complicated nexus of social relations. Its value is that it does seem to do justice to the attempts we frequently make to give substance to persons; ourselves and others. We describe persons as fitting into various roles in society; for example, her parents are teachers, she's married with two children, her interests are playing chess and working for an Open University degree, and so on. Now it is an implicit feature of the analogy that the organism and organs reflect mutually. The purposes and activity of the organism establish the nature of the organs and vice versa Likewise, an anthropologist studies a society and its individuals to understand both; they are interdependent, in reciprocity. The important conclusion is that in learning about persons we learn about other persons including ourselves. An understanding of the individual self makes reference to a *collective* unity. Usually this is implicit but where it is not, for example, where we are attempting to get to know someone from a relatively remote culture through an interpreter, then some preliminary social research might be required.

Let us now apply our analysis to the novelist, and perhaps the historian, accused of unintentional autobiography. The mature James Joyce, the author, forms part of that collective unity which includes not just his childhood self, the subject of *Portrait of the*

Artist, and his friends and relations but also the collective experience of the literary figures, from Aristotle to Henry James, of which Joyce's novel is an instance. This is another way of saying that Joyce's main role is that of novel writer; a role which has a labyrinthine history and the aims and methods of which intelligent readers of novels appreciate. Thus Joyce can give us a realistic account of Stephen, not in spite of the intrusion of the later self, but *because of it*. Likewise the historian betrays his self in his writings and, if he is an unbiased and well-versed writer, what will be revealed will be an instance of the collective genre of history-writing at a particular time. The aims and methods involved will be similar to but different from those of the contemporary novelist but, again, intelligent readers will understand them.[8] In each case what I have described as the aims and methods of the discipline in question are akin to the conventions which gave reality to the $10 bill. What is important is that the conventions are shared; they define important aspects of society and are not the values of an isolated 'subjective' self. In like fashion the roles of novelist and historian are collective; they share a tradition and it is within this tradition, this set of conventions, that they gain their reality. It is now relatively easy to give the lyric poets their proper place. They are not tricksters but neither are they historians. Lyric poetry has its conventions which concentrate the descriptions of nature in terms of effects upon a sensitive observer. Remember the example of the intimidating hostess; such descriptions are not confined to lyric poetry.[9] But the sophisticated reader will appreciate the emphases upon such descriptions and not misunderstand. Thus a tree described as sad will not be expected to shed tears, despite what the poet writes, nor 'the tell-tale flowers'[10] to which Clare has 'talked ... with childish pride' be hoped to answer back *in the same vein*. In like fashion, our understanding of novels is implicitly conventional. We ought to find no oddity in the fact that although a story ends without the death of everybody in it there is no justification in speculating about 'what happened next'. The temptation, when it exists, is a sign of confusion in a reader between the conventions of fiction and those of other types of account, for example, those in a newspaper or history book, where it is quite in order to wonder what the characters are now doing or if they are even still alive. It is a feature of many traditional novels to cater to this confusion by closing with potted 'histories' covering the remaining years of the main characters.[11] Another convention is that of the omniscient narrator whose psychological probings of character cannot be questioned for their accuracy. These conventions enable fiction to interpenetrate other conventions to considerable effect. Perhaps its most important role is in the provision of models of explanation which can be used in other contexts. John Fowles writes of his heroine, Sarah Woodruff: 'Without realising it she judged people as much by the standards of Walter Scott and Jane Austen as by any empirically arrived at' ([1969] 1977, p. 50). I am giving this observation much wider application. How we characterize other people might well be affected by the novels we read and, depending upon which they are, guide common sense usefully or otherwise. This is to describe what happens; not to attempt a *justification* of literature, although it might well constitute one. Literature, like chess and pure mathematics, is not desperately in need of purposes beyond those it creates for itself.

Subjectivity

Wordsworth's own misgivings in 'Tintern Abbey' led him to question the origin of the qualities attributed to nature in his poems; were they truly in nature or simply the inventions of a fevered mind? The self-accusation here, with which critics often join, was that the lyric poet is a spinner of illusions; the qualities he attributes to nature are not real but *subjective*.

On the uninformed fringes of intellectual debate 'subjective' is too frequently and notoriously abused. It implies much more than that the viewpoint so labelled has its origins in the subject for it also disparages that viewpoint as having little or no validity for others. It is a standard cliché of youthful rebels, to confound their critics, that strongly held convictions about the evils of child abuse or the superiority of a singer like Billie Holliday to the latest manifestation of the pop scene are 'just subjective'. The slogan provides such people with a comfortable refuge from change, self-analysis and self-improvement.[12]

The argument in earlier sections pointed to the inadequacy of the straightforward identification of a judgement which originates in an observer with one that is false, illusory or unreal. We saw that such judgements might well be satisfactory representations of reality, although some might not; we contrast the work of the disinterested historian with that of the biased. The description of something as a $10 bill was another example of the active involvement of participants; and colour judgements, despite being dependent upon anatomically similar eye states which might well show cultural variation, were, it was argued in the Introduction, almost always factual. Now although all of these candidates fail to satisfy the *positivistic* criteria, and reasons have been given for rejecting these criteria, it is a mistake to describe them as 'subjective' with all its implications of individual whim and fallibility. For all our candidates are dependent upon *conventions*. Conventions are like the rules of chess,[13] although not always as strictly codified, and are held collectively. It is probably correct to describe them as *relative*, but this is a far cry from 'subjective'. This is a distinction of first importance. A preference for mint-flavoured ice cream would probably qualify as subjective, properly used (McGinn, 1983, *passim*), for although you might prefer strawberry it would be something of a joke to insist that you were right and the other wrong. But an eccentric who breaks the rules of chess to enhance their chances, or insists that a $1 bill is more valuable than a $50 bill because George Washington was a more admirable man than Ulysses Grant, has deliberately flouted conventions and made a *mistake*, a factual error.[14] This is notwithstanding that the conventions are relative; they might have been different and could well change. This conclusion, the distinction between the subjective and the relative, is reinforced by our analysis of the *self*. That persons can be understood as collective unities with shared identities (as different organs share the functions of the organism which gives them their identity) makes the omnipresence of shared conventions that much more plausible.

Conventions and Naturalistic Drama

Let us now focus attention upon conventions. Although they are a feature of all acts of description, as we shall see, they are most obviously to the fore in certain art forms which paradoxically strike many people as the most artificial and unnatural; opera is a prime example. Auguste Strindberg, previously mentioned in connection with the nineteenth-century school of realist or naturalist writers, was obsessed with the problem of ridding another art form, namely drama, of conventions. In a famous preface to his play, *Miss Julie*, Strindberg ([1888] 1976, pp. 91–103) not only criticizes the extravagant styles of acting then prevailing and instructs his actors and actresses to the contrary but he objects also to footlights, intervals, make-up and unrealistic décor. He even praises improvisatory acting. Now what Strindberg thought these recommendations would achieve was a drama free of artificial conventions and that much closer to reality. But in paving the way for Stanislavski and many innovations of the twentieth-century theatre Strindberg was inadvertently achieving something quite different. He was not freeing drama of conventions; he was replacing old ones and inventing new. This created a variant language of theatre (more than a mere metaphor) and revealed fresh dimensions of dramatic representation. For Strindberg, these were the displacement of myths about human nature by scientific understanding, the presence of the unconscious and the therapy of hypnosis.[15] He was successful in his manipulation of a rejuvenated realism but mainly because of his theatrical flair rather than any theoretical insights on reality and its relation to science.

Just as we cannot begin to understand the world as it is revealed upon the stage without conventions, which is the reverse of Strindberg's own position, they are of equal importance in other manifestations of reality.[16] I have hinted at what might seem an extreme view: that conventions are a necessary condition of *any* reality. Yet it is difficult to generalize about them in straightforward terms; it is misleading, for example, to say that they are all artificial or man-made. Those of drama, let us say, are in *some* cases mannered and perhaps in need of updating whilst others seem perfectly natural. Does this make the first group

178

artificial? Does the fact that the clutch of conventions that we call modern drama has its origins in the *Poetics* of Aristotle[17] and the tragedies of Aeschylus and Sophocles, whilst these in turn emerged from folk ritual and priestly ceremony scarcely guessed at, make them all man-made? It seems trite to say so. But what is true is that conventions constantly change and adapt to the circumstances dictated by other conventions. Those of drama and literature, as we have seen, were penetrated by those of a rapidly advancing scientific consciousness in the nineteenth century. They are not independent of human experience. That a theory of reality is grounded in conventions should shock us only when we lapse into traditional intuitions.

Dress, the Visual Arts and Language

To appreciate the diversity and proliferation of conventional practices let us examine three more examples to demonstrate the theory.

(1) Virginia State troopers dress identically, as do London policemen and the Canadian Air Force. Clearly this is not accidental; it is required. If a state trooper appeared on duty in grubby jeans or dressed as a Canadian pilot disciplinary proceedings would be inevitable. Identity of outfit is implicit in the word 'uniform'.[18] Much the same occurs in the world of professional sport although it is now seldom a matter of explicit regulation. Certain players gain 'old-fashioned' or 'oddball' reputations by slight deviations from the norm: eccentric headgear or ankle-length boots rather than shoes. There are parallels in the charismatic sartorial flamboyance of some military leaders, particularly in combat. In all these situations dress is far more than a twentieth-century update of the hides and furs with which our ancestors vainly attempted to keep the later ice age at bay. The uniformity advertises membership of an often exclusive group and one's status within it. The deviations are even more interesting in creating possibilities for group members to trade upon this uniformity for the ends of individual self-expression. The norms and the departures from them create the reciprocal

conditions for people to be individuals because they are members of the group.

The keen student of fashion will know that similar practices, for they are what these behaviour patterns constitute, govern not just the world of *haute couture* but our more mundane habits as well. The Wall Street financier would not dream of attending the office in the previous evening's softball equipment unless it were to reinforce a contemptuous resignation. Note how the norms give reality to this *particular* expression of contempt. The financier's disaffected children rebel against middle-class affluence by, among other things,[19] donning garb better suited to Mexican peasants. As in the Strindberg case, the expression of rebellion is an exchange of one set of conventions for another. To be a middle-class American walking about like a Mexican peasant *means something*; a Mexican peasant similarly attired means something quite different. The conventions of dress create the realities of a vast variety of human behaviour. It must be obvious that without an understanding of the nuances of implication in certain attire, for example, a precisely striped tie or an earring in one ear rather than the other, such realities pass us by.[20]

(2)   As E. H. Gombrich has shown, most notably in *Art and Illusion* ([1960] 1977), the visual arts of sculpture, drawing, painting and photography relate to reality far more comprehensively than was traditionally thought. That they aspire to *mirror* the world has already been seen to be a misleading metaphor since mirrors themselves are not inert reproducers of what is seen in them. We learn to use mirrors in a variety of remarkable ways and mark their use by talking of their images as exemplars of the real.[21] Yet we only rarely mistake them for what we *see* otherwise we would be tempted to touch the images, or like Alice to join them in the other world beyond the glass.[22] Photographs require an even greater adaptability. There can be unending debate over the denial that a likeness has been adequately caught or whether a black-and-white print might not be more satisfactory than one in colour. The well-attested stories of pigmies unwilling to accept that photographs were of themselves on the interesting grounds that they are 'not that small', bear this out. The viewing of mirrors and photographs is nearer to a *reading* the account that Ben Brewster, in chapter 7, gives of ou

understanding of the reality of film. In no case is there a straightforward replication of what we see.[23]

It is not surprising that the various styles of drawing and painting that claim to be realistic in what they depict is very varied. The explanation of this is not that at best the claims of only one style can be correct and that at worst none are. Take the caricature of an American President or a prominent member of the British royal family by an artist whose style typically involves the highlighting of one feature, for example, the nose or lips, at the expense of the rest. Compare it with a so-called official portrait of the same person. Might it not be claimed that they are both equally realistic or even that the cartoon is more so in that it gives us more information about how the person looks? 'But', you reply, 'the cartoon is distorted!' Yet this apparently obvious observation is misleading. It would only be correct to describe the drawing as distorted if a sophisticated audience understood the artist to be depicting a person whose face was truly a disaster area, with outlandish nose or grotesque lips. But we get no such impression. The conventions of the cartoonist require that we approach his images with different expectations than those involved in the appreciation of the official portrait. Indeed it is a frequent criticism of the latter genre, as it is of out-of-date photographs in newspapers, that they miss the mobility of expression which only an economy of line can capture.

Gombrich's most well-known example is of two competing groups of art students sketching Tivoli, a beauty spot in nineteenth-century Rome. The Germans with sharpened pencils lovingly and meticulously rendered the detail of every leaf, whereas the French group, working directly with paint upon canvas, astounded the others by appearing contented with what they (the Germans) saw as a series of heavy lines and daubs. Which style was the more realistic? In declaring the contest a tie Gombrich is laying possible foundations for a theory of reality:

This difference in styles or languages need not stand in the way of correct answers and descriptions. The world may be approached from a different angle and the information given may yet be the same.

From the point of view of information there is surely no

181

difficulty in discussing portrayal. To say of a drawing that it is a correct view of Tivoli does not mean, of course, that Tivoli is bounded by wiry lines. It means that those who understand the notation will derive *no false information* from the drawing – whether it gives the contour in a few lines or picks out 'every blade of grass' as Richter's friends wanted to do. The complete portrayal might be the one which gives as much correct information about the spot as we would obtain if we looked at it from the very spot where the artist stood...

But what matters to us is that the correct portrait, like the useful map, is an end product on a long road through schema and correction. It is not a faithful record of a visual experience but the faithful construction of a relational model.

Neither the subjectivity of vision nor the sway of conventions need lead us to deny that such a model can be constructed to any required degree of accuracy. What is decisive here is clearly the word 'required'. The form of a representation cannot be divorced from its purpose and the requirements of the society in which the given visual language gains currency.

(Gombrich, 1977, p. 78. Italics in original)

Successful artists are those sufficiently skilled at their craft to provide their audience with the means of demonstrating to everyone what artist and audience see. But for this to happen all parties to the contract must understand the *meaning* of the images involved. Gombrich puts this succinctly if paradoxically 'the artist will therefore tend to see what he paints rather than paint what he sees' (1977, p. 73). He is, at this point, discussing the interrelation of the two plates reproduced in my introduction (page xviii).

(3) The most ambitious example of a series of conventional practices is language itself. This conclusion is both implicit and sometimes explicit in my argument up to this point. Many of the practices discussed, history, the novel, lyric poetry and much science, for example, are linguistic; others such as dress, currency and the visual arts are not. But language is none the less pre-eminent in creating understanding as the main medium of s

many practices and serves as a paradigm of all. Such phrases as 'the language of painting', 'the language of dress', 'musical language', 'the language of colour', are more than metaphors. They mark the fact that what is at issue is a structure with the capability of bestowing significance as language does.

My main conclusion should by now be obvious although I have also stressed that it is not uncontentious. Language and its cognate practices do not have the task of somehow reflecting or re-creating reality, the world, which lies beyond them. They create the real in creating *understanding*. A young infant, for example, does not begin by grasping the world incoherently in thought and sense and later learn to give voice to these inchoate intuitions in language. It begins to learn language much as it learns to play with toys or control its own body and, *in so doing*, is beginning to understand that it has a body and beginning to think real thoughts. This way of looking at things, so I am told, is supported by a great deal of work in recent child psychology. My route to the conclusion has of course been quite different.

A Theory of Error

Gombrich's conclusions can be put to more general use in elaborating the theory of error and forestall the objection that any explanation is, given the alternative to positivism, as reliable a guide to reality as any other. There are basically three requirements that need to be satisfied.

First: the explanation must be in accordance with a recognized set of conventions. In some cases, for example, with games or the law, there will be explicit rules; in other cases, such as the writing of history, there will be more or less general agreement at a given time but with a considerable periphery of grey areas. These conventions will settle what is expected of the different explanations in general. Thus a cartoonist balances features differently from other artists, natural scientists are normally expected to offer experimental evidence and the characters of a novelist are not born and do not die as do those of an historian.

Secondly: an account might fail to satisfy criteria internal to the practice itself. These fall roughly into two groups and are often matters of great dispute. One can give some examples. There are requirements of *competence*: drawing is a skill, for example, which some master only imperfectly and others not at all; or in science, let us say, some allegedly crucial experiments are seen by other scientists to be indecisive. There are also requirements of *intention*. We have already seen that the selectivity which is a feature of all explanations and judgements is guided by the aims of the practitioner in question. But these aims must be pursued, in most cases, with *impartiality*. Achieving this, however, is frequently a tight rope act since some aims will be difficult to realize without a form of selection which other investigators would deplore. Let us say that a well-known politician had been arrested for importuning in a public place but no charges were laid for lack of evidence and the event was not reported. Now a biographer finds out about this occurrence, the sole blot in the copybook, but decides to suppress it on the reasonable grounds that it is bound to be misunderstood by a sceptical public. The fact that no charges were laid would cut no ice with those, perhaps a majority, who would assume that pressure 'from high places' had been brought to bear because of the political implications. It might well be argued that this biographer had been swayed by sympathetic *bias* and the book discounted. Is this dismissal justified? There is no simple answer here. Any process of selection requires that only relevant evidence will be considered. But what guides relevance? The answer lies in what is expected of the practice involved, here biography. What is expected of a biographer is that the book will give an accurate account of the life and character of the subject. This information might well justify the excision of what, in the author's professional judgement, is dangerously misleading information. This example presents a typical problem-case for the biographer, historian and scientist but carries fewer lessons for the novelist or popular journalist who frequently sell copy on the *strength* of the bees in their bonnets.

Thirdly: there will be explanations which satisfy the internal criteria of a well-known practice but are nevertheless unsatisfactory. This will be because the validity of the *practice as a whole* is questionable; a matter of external, rather than internal criteria. Most people would place astrological predictions palmistry or the diagnoses of a voodoo doctor in this category. Now the vast variety of conventional systems giving meaning to the world frequently coexist peacefully; for example, the alternative descriptions of a table by a micro-physicist in his scholarly papers and with his family at breakfast ought not to upset anyone. Any conflict is only apparent. Descriptions of this sort are often compared to *tools*, like hammer, chisel, spirit-level and so on, which perform quite different tasks.[24] But serious problems arise when the conflict is real. A product of the Cornell Medical School tempted by voodoo, for example, could not possibly reconcile the two treatments. A choice would need to be made; to choose one would be to reject the other.

The plot thickens, however, since practices which would compete if in coexistence might cohere satisfactorily with the practices of a different culture. Voodoo might be an example. Another might be the case, already mentioned, of alternative colour vocabularies. Our theory supports the view that it is a fact that healthy grass is green; the proposition describes *reality* despite the necessity for an active observer whose eyes respond to light similarly to those of the vast majority of other people. Someone else now insists that the grass is *red*. He is not joking and is discovered to have a retinal deformity known to have been the *norm* in ancient Greece. We call him colour-blind; he is wrong! But why are we so emphatic if he is, as he might protest, correctly describing how the grass looks to *him*? The answer lies in the fact that such a person would perpetually be at odds with the rest of society, making potentially fatal mistakes when driving or going wrong when following other colour codes. He would thus be seriously disadvantaged and full of uncertainty. Being right or wrong, realistic or fanciful, relates in part to how our judgements lead to behaviour which fails to cohere with that of others. The technical term frequently used here is 'convergence'. True beliefs converge with those of other practices, other people, and hang together with other beliefs of the same person in a way that false ones do not. Central to the argument is that the charge of colour-blindness would *not* extend to the ancient Greeks. The anatomical variation, described as a deformity in *our* culture, would have been normal in Greece. So ancient Greek culture would have reflected this in quite different convergences. Colour codes, for example, which require the ability to discriminate between red and green are common in the present-day Western world. Such codes would be pointless if this ability were not widespread and if their purposes would be served more appropriately by ones which required, let us say, the ability of Eskimos to differentiate twenty different shades of white; one of several such examples cited in the chapter on sociology. The inescapable conclusion is that reality, fact and even truth are affected by temporal and cultural location. To what extent would the prediction of an astrophysicist of genius that educated people in two hundred years' time would have evolved a quite different way of describing shapes affect the validity of our late twentieth-century certainty that the earth is roughly spherical? I am suggesting that the answer would be: 'Slightly, if at all!'

Theology at Bay

Of the subjects which contribute to this book, theology is the one which seems to betray the greatest lack of convergence. Here are some samples: the virgin birth, the view that Mary conceived by the Holy Ghost, is contradicted by medical science; that God created the world fails to square with the theories of astrophysics; the efficacy of prayer flies in the face of common-sense experience of cause and effect; God's omniscience turns free will into an illusion bred of ignorance and his omnipotence is self-contradictory.[25] Most notably, perhaps, the popular proofs for God's existence are mere travesties of those of science, as David Hume ([1779] 1947) amply demonstrated two hundred years ago, and are found persuasive only by those predisposed to believe anyway.

These problems are not exactly original; some have been debated for a thousand years or more. Believers tend to react in one of two ways. The first is simply to refuse to face up to these discrepancies or to acquiesce in perplexity or even to delight in contradiction: 'I believe *because* it is absurd' was something of a Christian rallying cry in the eighteenth century. Many people do seem to limp along in this way and whether we regard it as a sign of courage or blinkered myopia will depend partly upon our

186

temperamental reaction to self-examination. The alternative is to attempt to argue that the lack of convergence is only apparent. An argument to this end is often thought to be adaptable from the defence of lyric poetry and the novel earlier in this chapter. It was concluded that it is a naive misunderstanding of the conventions to expect that a tree, properly described as sad, would shed tears or that flowers answer back. In like fashion the religious apologist will argue that critics are misusing the conventions which give meaning to talk about God. The reconciliation with the sciences and common sense is ensured by stressing the metaphorical nature of religious redescription.[26] In the process the appeal to pseudo-scientific proofs becomes no longer necessary. It is in this spirit that John Wisdom begins his much-quoted essay 'Gods' (1953, p. 149): *The existence of God is not an experimental issue in the way it was.* (Italics in original.)

Wisdom's arguments are discussed at some length by Dan Cohn-Sherbok in chapter 9 and so I will merely hint at a problem in adapting the defence of fiction to religious apologetics. Redescriptions can rob religion of the meanings that, for many believers, are its main appeal. If the virgin birth is seen to be really a charismatic way of pointing to a required purity of mind, or prayers to God an expression of human solidarity, or God himself not a kindly father, not even a person, but the *mysterium tremendum* of the Quakers, then some might think wryly that the operation to achieve convergence can only be successful if the patient dies. A later resurrection will invariably be in a quite different form, as humanism perhaps or a Wordsworthian pantheism. But on the other hand any alternative to accepting the metamorphosis will mean a relapse into the myopia and insularity previously described. There is a dilemma here. It casts equally dark shadows both upon traditional belief and the 'new' theology.

Notes

1 Pantheism (literally 'the all-god') is the view that the Divine Being is identical with the totality of the natural universe.
2 Because it is false that all unemployed youngsters are football hooligans it is quite wrong to argue that none are. So because it is

false that all authorial reading-in must be illusory it is wrong to claim that none can be.

3 I was tempted to describe the attempt as 'herculean' rather than merely 'explicit', but it is quite clear that Joyce knew that he was asking for the moon in both novels, hence the frequency of tongue-in-cheek.

4 Particularly the French realists: Balzac, Zola, Flaubert *et al.* Strindberg is also an important figure. Anthony Trollope, on the other hand, making a virtue of necessity, cheerfully admits to his authorial autonomy, or freedom, thus looking forward to the post-modernism of, for example, Nabokov and Fowles, and backward to Sterne. See Zola ([1868] 1981), Strindberg ([1888] 1976) and Fowles (1977, esp. pp. 85–8).

5 This is not as obvious as it seems. *Do* we know ourselves better than others know us? Why then seek advice in distress and often take it? Why the lure of psychiatrists and other 'experts'?

6 We have here to adopt a stance frequently required in such discussions and one that requires imaginative effort. We must suppose that we are describing something familiar to us, in this case the cut and thrust of the world of money, to someone quite ignorant of it; a child perhaps or a Brazilian bushman. Such efforts bring to light our tacit assumptions.

7 We find ourselves involved in a discussion of the philosophical problem of the self. It is a notoriously difficult arena. B. Williams (1973, pp. 1–81) offers some clarification. Kafka's short novel *Metamorphosis* ([1916] 1961) and J.-P. Sartre's *Nausea* ([1938] 1965) illustrate the profundities of the issues. The notion of the self as an isolated phenomenon has much in common with post-Reformation ideas of the Christian soul and is particularly associated with the important philosopher René Descartes (1596–1650). See Descartes ([1641] 1960). The alternative view originates with the equally famous Georg Hegel (1770–1831) and F.H. Bradley (1846–1924). Gilbert Ryle (1949) is an important contemporary source.

8 This understanding is again usually tacit. We approach the daily newspaper in a quite different frame of mind from that adopted for a scholarly account of the 1914–18 war but are rarely conscious of the shift. Young children, however, get very confused in the process.

9 It is also a feature of much novel writing, an outstanding example being a passage in Sartre's *Nausea* ([1938] 1965, pp. 182–93).

10 The title of a less known poem by Clare (1954, pp. 121–2), another product of aged disillusion. There is a section in Lewis Carroll' *Through the Looking-Glass* where the point appears to b

contradicted ([1872] 1962, pp. 205–18). There are more complex conventions interleaved here; those of the dream.

11 Bernard Shaw was quite explicit, when providing the epilogues to his plays, about the naivety of readers on this point.

12 There are, of course, proper limits for the use of 'subjective'. See Williams (1973, 1985) and Colin McGinn (1983). A classic earlier treatment, of importance in aesthetics, is David Hume's essay 'Of the Standard of Taste' ([1741/2] 1963).

13 The rules and practices of games are seminal examples of conventional systems.

14 The non-American reader might not know that the different denominations of dollar bill bear the portraits of different presidents. Washington is on the $1 bill and Grant on the $50 bill.

15 We have seen how the defences of the realist novel by George Eliot and Henry James failed to satisfy their own positivistic criteria of truth. The Continental realists were bolder in their theories. They argued, equally in positivistic vein, that the art form will only be true by becoming more scientific. So Zola ([1868] 1981, pp. 21–7) compares the insight of a novelist to that of a scientist testing under laboratory conditions. Another example is that of impressionist paintings. Apologists claimed that they exemplified the truths of optics in reproducing the play of light and colour on the retina.

16 They are sometimes called *institutions*, also *practices*. The former points to the rule-governed nature of the systems but 'practices' is more apropos in stressing the fluidity and dynamism involved. Even games, in both cultural ethos and rule-book, evolve constantly.

17 Aristotle (384–322 BC). His *Poetics* is still a basic source of philosophical speculation about the arts ([*c*. 324 BC] 1965).

18 There are, of course, variations in uniform depending upon role and rank within the same forces. The point is that they are all matters of regulation extending in most cases even to the amount and style of hair on the face and head.

19 They will, of course, say and write things. Dress is only one form of self-expression, albeit an important one.

20 It is no wonder that anthropologists encounter problems in understanding other cultures. Peter Winch's *The Idea of a Social Science and its Relation to Philosophy* (1958) is compulsory reading on this topic.

21 Is this perhaps why the reactions of animals and birds to mirrors is, in general, so low-key?

22 *Through the Looking-Glass* (Carroll, [1872] 1962).

23 This could be misunderstood. What we see is itself capable of

ambiguity and depends upon the conventions we bring to that activity; for example, those of colour vision.

24 The analysis in these terms was made famous by Ludwig Wittgenstein in his *Philosophical Investigations* (1958) and other late works. He is often regarded as the most important philosopher of the century. Wittgenstein also coined the influential phrase 'language game'. It describes roughly what I have called a conventional system or practice.

25 Omnipotence gives rise to famous paradoxes: could God create a stone too heavy for him to lift? If 'Yes' then there is something he cannot do, viz. *lift* the stone. If 'No' then there is also something he cannot do, viz. *create* the stone. In either case he lacks omnipotence; the notion is self-defeating.

26 Wittgenstein's *Lectures and Conversations on Aesthetics, Psychology and Religious Belief* are a successful demonstration of such redescription, all the more so for extending the analysis to Freud and aesthetics (Wittgenstein, 1966). They are quoted from, at some length, in the chapter on theology.

Chapter Nine

Theology

DAN COHN-SHERBOK

As we have seen in the introduction, when people speak of reality in an ordinary, everyday context, a picture of the physical features of the world is normally evoked. Reality thus consists of such objects as tables, chairs, books, stones, etc., as well as animals and people. Reality embraces the whole of what is perceived by the senses – seen, heard, felt, smelt, tasted. This is what is meant by the empirical world. In other words, 'to be real' means 'to be perceived' – two sides of the same coin – and those things we perceive we call 'facts'. 'My cat has a long tail' – a fact. 'The White House is located in Washington' – a fact. 'Prince Charles married Lady Diana Spencer' – a fact. The world we inhabit is therefore composed of facts; this is what people normally mean when they say that the world is real, and this position is identified with the positivistic view of reality.

Turning to religious experience, however, we find that most religious believers, though accepting the world we inhabit as real, extend the notion of reality beyond the boundary of human perception. For the religiously devout the invisible world of God, or the gods, of heaven and hell, and so forth are conceived as real, indeed more real than the world we perceive empirically. Thus, reality for the non-believer is narrower than for the believer; for the believer it extends to a transcendent world lying beyond ordinary perception. There he finds the ultimate – the really real.

A serious problem with this religious understanding of reality is that it seems to be entirely subjective. That is, since beliefs about an invisible world are not empirically grounded – and indeed never could be – they appear to be simply the product of very vivid imaginations. For this reason both ancient and modern critics have ridiculed religious beliefs, arguing that rather than representing 'true reality' as their defenders claim, they are nothing more than illusions.

One such criticism was launched some time ago by philosophers called 'logical positivists'. Presupposing that all knowledge originates in sense perception, they asked how it could be possible to obtain a conception of reality other than the reality presented through the senses. From empirical observations, they argued, no inference can be made to matters which transcend the empirical domain. Thus when Christians, Jews, Muslims, Hindus, Buddhists, etc., make claims about the nature and activity of God or the gods, such claims are meaningless. Logical positivists were careful to distinguish their view from atheism and agnosticism: the atheist holds that religious statements are false; the agnostic sees no evidence to support either the truth or falsity of such statements. But both these positions imply that religious statements are meaningful assertions. This, however, is exactly what logical positivists deny.

Is there any way to salvage the reality of the invisible world of religion? In this chapter I will sketch a possible line of defence. As we shall see, there are good reasons for thinking that statements about a reality which transcends empirical experience are meaningful claims. Religious perception should not be understood simply as a peculiar and mistaken form of perception, analogous to sense perception. Rather it should be viewed as an interpretive mode of seeing.

The Challenge to Religious Belief

All faiths maintain that religious beliefs are factual – they are understood as true assertions about ultimate reality. Logical positivists, however, have strenuously argued that this religious assumption is a mistake. The only true propositions, they maintain, are those which can be verified by experience; factual significance is defined in terms of empirical testing. According to logical positivists, ordinary statements about the everyday world are meaningful assertions – they can be shown to be true or false on the basis of observation. But this is not true of religious claims since they are not amenable to the same process of verification. Thus they lack meaning. They are neither true nor false – instead they are nonsensical utterances. A. J. Ayer claimed (1952, p. 115) in a classic explication of logical positivism,

> to say that God exists is to make a metaphysical utterance which cannot be either true or false. And by the same criteria, no sentence which purports to describe the nature of a transcendent god can possess any literal significance.

What Ayer is saying is that religious statements (like 'God exists') look like ordinary language; they have the same grammatical structure in that they are meant to be factual claims. But in fact they are not; they possess no literal significance because they cannot be verified by any normal means. Thus Ayer concludes that religious beliefs whether they are Western or Eastern are non-sense statements.

A similar point was made by Antony Flew, in a famous symposium about the nature of religious language. According to Flew (Flew and MacIntyre, 1964) not only are religious statements unverifiable, they are unfalsifiable as well. As Flew states:

> Take such utterances as 'God has a plan', 'God created the world', 'God loves us as a father loves his children'. They look at first sight very much like assertions, vast cosmological assertions ... it often seems to people who are not religious as if there was no conceivable event or series of events the occurrence of which would be admitted by sophisticated religious people to be a sufficient reason for conceding 'There wasn't a God after all' or 'God does not really love us then' ... Just what would have to happen ... to entitle us to say that 'God does not love us' or even 'God does not exist'?
>
> (Flew in Flew and MacIntyre, 1964, pp. 97–9)

Flew's question is rhetorical; for the believer there appears to be nothing which could demonstrate the falsity of his beliefs. This is so because religious claims are inherently unfalsifiable. For

Flew the difficulty with religious discourse is its compatibility with every state of affairs – whenever a fact is used as evidence against a religious claim, the religious statement is modified so as to accommodate this information. If, for example, we are told that God loves us as a father loves his children, this statement is qualified in some way – God's love is not merely a human love or it is an inscrutable love. Even in the face of insuperably difficult counter-evidence – such as the death of a child from inoperable cancer – the believer holds fast to his belief in the fatherhood of God. This means, for Flew, that religious language is doomed since its compatibility with all events deprives it of any factual content.

An Existential Understanding of
Religious Belief

Is there any way to defend religious beliefs from this attack? Ayer and Flew maintain that religious utterances are nonsensical because they are neither verifiable or falsifiable. For them this means that religious discourse – and indeed the entire enterprise of religion – is a misguided activity practised by those who have mistaken illusion for reality. Yet recently a number of writers have attempted to rescue religious belief from this onslaught. These thinkers have emphasized that Ayer, Flew and others like them have failed to appreciate the true function of theological discourse. In particular they stress the existential use of religious language. All human beings, they contend, are aware of the inevitability of death and it is against this background that theological affirmations should be analysed. Donald MacKinnon, for example, stresses that religious claims about an afterlife should be understood more in terms of the existential discontent which evokes this sort of language than in terms of any alleged descriptive content. Language about immortality, he argues, stems from a deep disquiet about the human predicament.

> To put it very crudely, just what is it that is at stake for a person in this matter of immortality? What is it that is bothering him? Of course, you can show the queerness, the

194

confusedness of the way in which the bother is expressing itself, when it does so by means of the traditional language of survival, and so on. You can discredit this means of expression by showing the logical confusions into which it plunges: but does that settle the perplexity, the issue in the mind of the bewildered person?

(MacKinnon in Flew and McIntyre, 1964, p. 263)

For MacKinnon, the purpose of language about life after death is not to offer any kind of scientific description of the hereafter, but to underscore the fact that human existence is significant. Claims about a future life allow people to affirm the significance of life itself in the face of death. Philip Leon makes a similar point (1955, p. 151). Theological discourse, he maintains, is not the same as the language of science. Scientific statements derive their meaning by referring to things and events, but theological language is embedded in the life of the believer. Religious statements, he writes, are 'not logical but existential, revelational, or inspirational'.

A similar point was made by Ludwig Wittgenstein in a well-known discussion of the function of religious claims about the Last Judgement. According to Wittgenstein, such assertions should not be seen as straightforward assertions of facts, but as expressions of deeply held assumptions about human existence. Thus statements like 'There will be a world to come' are not like ordinary, everyday statements, such as 'There will be an exam this week', or 'A Christmas party will take place at the end of term'. Affirmations about the hereafter are of an entirely different order – they point to a profound personal commitment which gives shape to an individual's entire life. Thus, if I say to someone who believes in the Last Judgement 'I don't share your belief', I would not be contradicting him in the ordinary way. I would be saying that I don't share his world-view. As Wittgenstein explains (1966, p. 53):

Suppose that someone believed in the Last Judgement, and I don't, does this mean that I believe the opposite to him, just that there won't be such a thing? I would say: 'not at all, or not always.'

Suppose I say that the body will rot, and another says:

'No. Particles will rejoin in a thousand years, and there will be a Resurrection of you.'

If some said: 'Wittgenstein, do you believe in this?' I'd say: 'No.' 'Do you contradict the man?' I'd say: 'No.' If you say this, the contradiction already lies in this. Would you say: 'I believe the opposite', or 'There is no reason to suppose such a thing'? I'd say neither.

Suppose someone were a believer and said: 'I believe in a Last Judgement,' and I said: 'Well, I'm not so sure. Possibly.' You would say that there is an enormous gulf between us. If he said 'There is a German aeroplane overhead,' and I said 'Possibly, I'm not so sure,' you'd say we were fairly near. It isn't a question of my being anywhere near him, but on an entirely different plane, which you could express by saying: 'You mean something altogether different, Wittgenstein.' The difference might not show up at all in any explanation of the meaning.

Why is it that in this case I seem to be missing the entire point?

Suppose somebody made this guidance for this life: believing in the Last Judgement. Whenever he does anything, this is before his mind.

The point of Wittgenstein's discussion of religious utterances is to show that they are not simple assertions of fact; instead they are existentially meaningful claims which reflect the deep concerns of the religious believer. To treat them as ordinary descriptive statements is to misconstrue their real nature.

Religion and Divine Discernment

Related to the existential interpretation of religion is the argument that religious belief has its own particular character, rendering it immune to straightforward analysis. Some writers such as Ian Ramsey, have suggested that a religious situation i characterized by a discernment which is fuller and more complete than ordinary perception. In such cases, the situation comes alive the penny drops, the ice breaks. According to Ramsey, such depth-discernment is not uniquely religious – it is paralleled by everyday events of an extraordinary nature. For example, he writes, imagine the setting of a courtroom. Here the situation is as impersonal as possible: a mere façade of human existence. Yet if one day the judge entered and found that the accused was his long-lost wife, he would be overwhelmed – an otherwise formal situation would have 'come alive'. Or to take another of Ramsey's examples: if at a dinner party one's jacket splits unexpectedly up the back or if someone sits sedately on a chair which collapses beneath her, the party would completely change, it would take on 'human warmth', 'the ice would break'.

In religious situations such discernment takes on even greater significance. Belief in God, he argues, arises from cosmic disclosures – experiences in which the universe comes alive, where ordinary existence takes on depth. Such situations can occur on occasions of various kinds: by a fireside, on a country walk, by a wind-swept river, in a city, while reading the Bible or attending Mass. There is simply no situation which cannot in principle give rise to a cosmic disclosure. In such contexts of discernment, religious commitment is evoked which is all-embracing; it is life-enriching, central and personally engaging as it gathers together and structures the believer's relationships, feelings and attitudes.

Since religious belief arises from situations of discernment and total commitment, Ramsey maintains that the language of belief is logically peculiar. In particular, religious discourse is characterized by negative terminology. The term 'mutable', for example, refers to the changeable features of ordinary experience; when negated the term 'immutable' attempts to evoke the discernment of what is changeless. Such negation highlights the fact that the divine lies outside the language of what undergoes change – such terminology is inadequate when referring to ultimate reality. Negative language thus emphasizes that ordinary perception is inadequate when talking about God. Turning to positive descriptions, such language also has a peculiar character. We view the meaning of the word 'perfect' as it is used in statements like 'God is perfect' by the presentation of situations characterized by varying degrees of imperfection. It is hoped that at some point depth-discernment will occur and one will be led to see what such a description signifies. Positive language does not exhaust the true reality of the divine.

Religious language then – both negative and positive – is rooted in discernment and seeks to evoke a religious commitment. When God is described as infinitely wise or infinitely good, the terms 'wise' and 'good' are drawn from ordinary human experience, but the qualifier 'infinitely' asks us to take such terminology to the lengths at which a characteristically religious discernment takes place. Distinguishing the particular logical behaviour of theological terms helps avoid the sort of difficulties that writers like Ayer and Flew have raised. As Ramsey explains (1969, p. 186), 'If we misunderstand the logical structure of a theological phrase, we can be guilty of the most absurd mistakes. Indeed, the very fun poked at theology often measures the logical blunder which has been committed; as the joke cracked by the school cleaner – regretting that children still haven't found the Least Common Multiple after so many years of searching – is a measure of her misreading of mathematics.' It is just such a blunder that Ayer and Flew make in misreading the true function and logical character of religious discourse.

Religious Belief as Interpretation

A similar account of religious statements is given by John Wisdom in his famous parable of the gardener. For Wisdom theological discourse has an attention-drawing function; what is important for the believer is the recognition of a particular pattern in the world. In the debate between the believer and the unbeliever, it is not a question of one person having more facts than another. Rather, their disagreement is about how the facts should be interpreted. To bring out this point, Wisdom tells a tale about two individuals who disagree about whether a gardener comes to tend a neglected garden (1953b, pp. 154–5).

> Two people return to their long neglected garden and find among the weeds a few of the old plants surprisingly vigorous. One says to the other 'It must be that a gardener has been coming and doing something about these plants.'

Upon inquiry they find that no neighbour has ever seen anyone at work in their garden.

The first man says to the other 'He must have worked while people slept'. The other says, 'No, someone would have heard him and besides, anybody who cared about the plants would have kept down these weeds'. The first man says 'Look at the way these are arranged. There is purpose and a feeling for beauty here. I believe that someone comes, someone invisible to mortal eyes. I believe that the more carefully we look the more we shall find confirmation of this.' They examine the garden ever so carefully and sometimes they come on new things suggesting that a gardener comes and sometimes they come on new things suggesting the contrary and even that a malicious person has been at work. Besides examining the garden carefully they also study what happens to gardens left without attention. Each learns all the other learns about this and about the garden. Consequently, when after all this, one says 'I still believe a gardener comes' while the other says 'I don't' their different words now reflect no difference as to what they have found in the garden, no difference as to what they would find in the garden if they looked further and no difference about how fast untended gardens fall into disorder. At this stage, in this context, the gardener hypothesis has ceased to be experimental, the difference between one who accepts and one who rejects it is now not a matter of the one expecting something the other does not expect. What is the difference between them? The one says 'A gardener comes unseen and unheard. He is manifested only in his works with which we are all familiar', the other says 'There is no gardener' and with this difference in what they say about the gardener goes a difference in how they feel towards the garden, in spite of the fact that neither expects anything of it which the other does not expect.

Wisdom is here seeking to show by means of this analogy that the theist and the atheist do not disagree about empirical facts, or about any observations they could make in the future. They are instead reacting in different ways to the same facts. They are not making mutually contradictory claims about the empirical world but are expressing different feelings about it. Understood in this way, we can no longer say that one is right and the other wrong; they both feel about what they experience in the ways that their assertions indicate. But such expressions of feelings do not constitute claims in an ordinary sense. According to Wisdom, there is no disagreement about the empirical facts – the dispute centres on their interpretation.

A variant of this position is offered by John Hick in an account of religious experience as a form of 'seeing-as' (1985, pp. 16–27). For Hick (whose account is indebted to Wittgenstein) there are two senses of the word 'see'. If I am looking at a picture of a face, for example, I see what is physically present on the paper. But in another sense of 'see' I see the parts of a face. This second sense of seeing involves understanding and interpretation. This interpretive activity is particularly evident when we look at a puzzle picture, such as the following illustration:

Looked at from one angle, this is a drawing of a duck; from another – when the paper is on its side – it is of a rabbit.

Related to the process of 'seeing' is the notion of 'experiencing-as'. In our everyday perception of our environment, we use several sense organs at once (not simply sight); 'experiencing-as' involves a multidimensional awareness. Like 'seeing-as', 'experiencing-as' is an interpretive mode of cognition which operates even in commonplace situations. If, for example, a stone-age savage were shown knives and forks, he would not experience them as such because of his lack of the concept of eating at a table with manufactured implements. As far as religious belief is concerned, religious experience should be seen in similar terms

Throughout history human beings have displayed a tendency to experience individuals, places and situations as having religious meanings. It is a particular feature of monotheistic religions, for example, to interpret any human situation as one in which the unseen presence of God is manifest.

Such 'experiencing-as' in religious terms is very much like the example of the puzzle-picture of a duck-rabbit. The same phenomenon can be perceived non-religiously. Thus a secular historian describing the events recorded in Hebrew scripture would speak of the rise and fall of empires, of economic, political and cultural factors, but would not conceive of God as an agent in ancient Near Eastern history. It is clear then that the way in which the believer or the non-believer sees the world depends on the system of concepts used. Such a view helps to explain why it is that the same features can be experienced in such radically different ways. Furthermore, it illustrates how it is that there is not simply one form of religious experience. Given the different conceptual frameworks of different religious systems, Hick writes (1985, p. 27) 'the world can be experienced as God's handiwork, or as the battlefield of good and evil, or as the cosmic dance of the Shiva'. These are simply different forms of 'experiencing-as' which constitute the core of the religious response.

Religious Beliefs as 'Bliks'

Another way of highlighting the interpretive nature of religious beliefs is to see them as centrally important presuppositions which have a profound effect on the life of the believer. R. M. Hare refers to such beliefs as *bliks* which are neither assertions nor a system of assertions, but rather frameworks for evaluation or explanation. The statements by which believers express their religious *bliks* – such as 'God exists' or 'God loves us as a father loves his children' – cannot be settled by reference to what happens in the world. Though they appear to be compatible with every state of affairs (and in this sense cannot be verified or falsified), this does not mean they are unimportant in the life of the devout.

To illustrate the function of *bliks*, Hare uses the example of a student who is convinced that all the professors in his college are intent upon murdering him. It is of no use trying to allay his suspicions by introducing him to numerous kindly professors – he will only see devious cunning in their apparent friendly attitudes. In other words, his belief is not open to confirmation or refutation by experience; his attitude is governed by an irrational *blik*. Those who try to persuade him to see sense similarly have a *blik* – the difference is that their *blik* is rational. As Hare explains (1964, p. 100), 'It is important to realize that we have a sane one, not no *blik* at all; for there must be two sides to any argument – if he has a wrong *blik*, then those who are right about professors must have a right one.'

Another instance Hare offers (1964, p. 100) of a sane *blik* is the belief in the rigidity of the steel in one's car. This is based on the assumption that the physical world has a stable character – objects do not suddenly appear or disappear or are transformed into something else:

> When I am driving my car, it sometimes occurs to me to wonder whether my movements of the steering-wheel will always continue to be followed by corresponding alterations in the direction of the car. I have never had a steering failure, though I have had skids, which must be similar. Moreover, I know enough about how the steering of my car is made, to know the sort of thing that would have to go wrong for the steering to fail – steel joints would have to part, or steel rods break, or something – but how do I know that this won't happen? The truth is, I don't know; I just have a *blik* about steel and its properties, so that normally I trust the steering of my car; but I find it not at all difficult to imagine what it would be like to lose this *blik* and acquire the opposite one.

The important point to note is that our entire interaction with the world – as in the case of driving one's car – is dependent on such *bliks* and the difference between *bliks* cannot be settled by observation.

Given the inevitability of having such unassailable assumptions, how is one to differentiate between right and wrong *bliks*? If experience can never yield confirmation or disproof of *bliks*, there appears to be no way to speak of them as appropriate or inappropriate. Yet it is just such a distinction that Hare makes when discussing the lunatic who believes all professors wish to murder him. The answer to this question is supplied by Basil Mitchell who recounts his own parable: a member of the resistance movement in an occupied country meets a stranger who claims to be a supporter of the resistance, whom he trusts. The stranger urges the partisan to have faith in him whatever may happen. Sometimes the stranger is seen aiding the resistance; at other times he appears to collaborate with the enemy. Nevertheless the partisan continues in his trust. He admits that at times the stranger appears to act against the resistance movement. But he has faith none the less. 'It is here,' writes Mitchell (1964, p. 105), 'that my position differs from Hare's. The partisan admits that many things may and do count against his belief; whereas Hare's lunatic who has a *blik* about professors doesn't admit that anything counts against his *blik*. Nothing can count against *bliks*. Also the partisan has a reason for having in the first instance committed himself, viz. the character of the stranger; whereas the lunatic has no reason for his *blik* about professors – because, of course, you can't have reasons for *bliks*.' In Mitchell's parable the partisan's belief is rooted in the depth of the impression the stranger makes on him; this is entirely different from Hare's example. Yet despite this important distinction, both Hare and Mitchell maintain that religious claims are meaningful and influential, profoundly shaping the life of those who subscribe to them.

Religious Belief as Parable

Another conception of the function of religious discourse has been offered by R. B. Braithwaite who asserts that religious language has primarily an ethical role. The purpose of religious statements, he believes, is to express and record a commitment to a particular way of life. For a Christian, for example, to assert that 'God is love' is his indication to follow a loving way of life. Obviously a religious statement is intended to be more than a moral claim, but Braithwaite contends (1955), that the purpose of the stories in a religion is to commend moral behaviour. Indeed, it is not even necessary that such stories are true – the connection between religious stories and the religious way of life is a psychological and causal one. It is an empirical psychological fact that many people find it easier to resolve upon and to carry through a course of action which is contrary to their natural inclinations if this policy is associated in their minds with certain stories.

Religious statements thus function as an expression of an intention to act in certain ways under special circumstances. It is therefore a mistake to think – as Ayer and Flew appear to do – that the important feature of religious language is its alleged descriptive content. The role of religious statements is to provide psychological strength in times of weakness and temptation. Religious language serves the dual function of enabling human beings to make common commitments to a way of life and strengthening them in their resolve. Our religious beliefs in this way reflect our moral aims and aspirations.

Following Braithwaite, T. R. Miles insists (1959) (see also J. Campbell, 1971, pp. 53–7) that the language of religious stories or parables is meaningful and important. A parable, he notes, has three essential characteristics: (1) the question of its literal truth or falsity is not significant; (2) it contains for the most part empirical assertions; (3) it conveys a message. These three characteristics, he believes, are found in the language of the Bible. In Genesis, for example, we read: 'In the beginning God created the Heaven and the Earth.' It makes no difference whether the creation account is literally true – by means of this story timeless truths are delineated. Within the context of parable language, the Genesis account does contain empirically verifiable statements – the words are linked with our experience of craftmanship. But the important feature of the story is that it forces us to look at the world in a new way – it leads to the recognition that everything is part of the divine purpose and that God is seen in all things that happen. These aspects of the parable lead to the moral conclusion that one's highest duty is to God's will. Such a parable has deep significance in the life of the believer.

Why it might be asked do we accept one parable rather than another? The answer, Miles argues, lies with personal conviction rather than rational discussion. We might, for example, choose one parable rather than another because of its connection with moral beliefs – a particular parable could commit us to moral positions we wish to adopt. Given such a personal preference, what sort of dispute exists between people who hold different parables and what occurs when someone substitutes one set of parables for another? According to Miles, all people accept parables of one sort of another. The theist and the atheist differ not in the facts they have at their disposal but in the parables they tell about them. Disagreement over the choice of parables is thus not a factual disagreement but is like a disagreement over a moral position. Even though reasons can be offered to support one's viewpoint, the choice of parables is ultimately a matter of subjective preference. To speak to God as a loving father, for example, can lead to the adoption of altruistic attitudes and actions; to hold to a parable that life is without purpose and meaning may lead to acts of selfishness.

The Nature of Religious Claims and Verification in an Afterlife

These various ways of trying to make sense of religious beliefs though they differ in certain respects are all attempts to confront the challenge of a positivistic critique of religion. Ayer and Flew reduce all religious statements to a single type, thereby calling into question their factual significance. Meaningful statements are defined as those open to empirical testing. The writers we have surveyed, however, stress that this conception of religion is too narrow. In their different ways these philosophers and theologians highlight the interpretive character of religious claims. Religious belief is realist in that it points to an objective transcendental world, but it derives from situations of discernment and patterning. Such trans-empirical reality is not mirrored by religious statements; rather it is evoked through various types of situations. Religious experience and the systems to which it gives rise call for the active engagement of the believer.

Here we can see an intimate relation between theology and the other areas discussed in this book. As we have seen, there appears to be a crucial interrelationship between poets and nature – it is a mistake to think that poetry simply mirrors the features of the natural world. So too in fiction; it is impossible to transcend the limitations of one's senses and intellect in utilizing a fictional model to represent reality. In addition one is inevitably constrained by the artistic conventions which the writer consciously or unconsciously employs in making manifest the order of the external world. Similarly the film is a carefully constructed illusion – a product of a system of carefully constructed conventions. In our encounter with reality, it is also the case that one's conception of the real is to a large measure socially conditioned. Even science appears not to be a neutral discipline as might be expected; the activity of research is dependent on scientific conventions as well as the personal inclinations, interests and concerns of the individual scientist. All of these spheres of human activity presuppose an inextricable connection between the perceiver and the perceived; observers do not simply measure and record facts. The religious believer thus does not stand alone in finding meaning and purpose through a process of reflection and interpretation – he is linked in a common human enterprise with all those who are engaged in an exploration of the real.

It might be objected, however, as Michael Leahy does in the philosophy chapter (pp. 167), that such a conception of religious belief robs religion of its significance since it involves a 'metaphorical redescription' of religious language. But it is a mistake to think that this view reduces religious statements to metaphor. Although the interpretive understanding of religion highlights the fact that religious claims are unlike ordinary statements in that they cannot be demonstrated to be true or false in this earthly life, it nevertheless conceives of religious claims as pointing to a transcendental reality. And as Hick has pointed out (1963, pp. 100–6; 1985, pp. 110–25), religious assertions could at least in theory be susceptible of verification or falsification in an afterlife. If there is a hereafter, it is possible to conceive the sort of experiences which would tend to confirm religious beliefs. To illustrate this point Hick tells a parable about two people who are travelling together along a road. One of them believes that it leads to a Celestial City; the other thinks it goes nowhere. But there is only one road, they must both travel on it.

Neither has been this way before, so they cannot say what they will find around each new corner. During their journey they meet

206

with moments of refreshment and delight as well as with hardship and disaster. The traveller who thinks of her journey as a pilgrimage to the Celestial City interprets the pleasant parts as encouragements and the obstacles as trials and lessons of endurance prepared by a sovereign of the city and designed to make of her a worthy citizen when she arrives there. The other disagrees – he sees the journey as unavoidable and aimless, for him there is no Celestial City, no all-encompassing purpose. During the course of their journey, the disagreement between them is not an experiential one; nevertheless when they turn the last corner, it will be apparent which one of them has been right all along.

This parable points to the ambiguous character of our present existence. From our earthly standpoint the difference between the theist and the atheist cannot be resolved by an appeal to empirical features of the world. In the main they do not have divergent expectations of the course of temporal history. But the believer does expect and the non-believer does not that when human history is completed it will be seen to have led to a particular end-state and to have fulfilled a specific purpose – that of creating 'children of God'. Our experience of the world in some ways seems to support and in other ways to contradict religious faith. Some events suggest that there is an unseen benevolent intelligence at work; other events point in the opposite direction. Our environment is religiously ambiguous. But in the hereafter (if it exists) such ambiguity would be transcended. As Hick explains (1963, p. 103),

> The system of ideas which surrounds the Christian concept of God, and in the light of which that concept has to be understood, includes expectations concerning the final fulfilment of God's purpose for mankind in the 'Kingdom of God'. The experience which would verify Christian belief in God is the experience of participating in that eventual fulfilment.

Such a situation is analogous to that of a small child who looks forward to adult life and having reached it looks back upon childhood. When he reaches adulthood, he is able to know that he has reached it – his understanding of maturing grows as he matures. This is similar to the realization of the divine purpose for human life. When we finally reach such a state, the problem of recognizing it will have disappeared in the process. The movement towards this end-state involves a gradual trans- formation of the final unambiguous situation which is tradi- tionally symbolized as heaven. In that state, Hick writes (1985, pp. 117–18),

> one's God-consciousness will be at a maximum. One will be continuously aware of living in the divine presence; and that awareness will no longer be in tension with the circum- stances of sin and suffering, ugliness and deprivation, which at present leave room for rational doubt. We are contemplat- ing an experience of progressive sanctification ... accom- panied by an increasingly powerful and pervasive sense of existing in the presence of an invisible transcendent power who knows us, who loves us, and who can be seen to be drawing us towards a perfection in which we are to dwell in joyous communion with that transcendent reality.

Such would be the process of verification which in an afterlife would confirm the truth of a religious belief which in our earthly life we are unable to demonstrate as true.

Summary

As in other spheres of inquiry in this book, positivism presents a forceful challenge to the validity of the theological enterprise. In particular, logical positivism constitutes a direct attack on relig- ious belief. Philosophers like Ayer and Flew dismiss religious discourse as devoid of factual content. Statements like 'God exists', 'God loves his children as a loving father', are seen as nonsensical utterances – in principle they are no different from meaningless sentences like 'The Wobbleness Wobbled'. Yet since the publication in 1936 of Ayer's classic presentation of this position in *Language, Truth and Logic*, theologians and philoso- phers of religion have attempted to rescue religious discourse from such an assault. In various ways they have emphasized the interpretive function of religious belief. Religious belief, they stress, is based on a depth of discernment related to a individual's existential predicament. Theological claims serve as absolute presuppositions which profoundly shape an individual's life and such all-absorbing dedication is frequently connected with the stories or parables which feature as central to particular traditions. Religious faith then is a form of 'experiencing-as' – experiencing life as infused with a divine presence. In our present life this religious vision is inevitably based on a personal response to the features of the world which are themselves ambiguous and this ambiguity makes it impossible to determine with certainty whether such religious interpretation is valid. Yet if there is a hereafter, all will be revealed – then the devout will know whether the transcendental world in which they have put their faith is really real after all.

Inconclusion

Although it is, in general, quite true that we select only facts which have a bearing upon some preconceived theory, it is not true that we select only such facts as confirm the theory and, as it were, repeat it; the method of science is rather to look out for facts which may refute the theory. This is what we call testing a theory – to see whether we cannot find a flaw in it.

K. R. Popper, *The Open Society and its Enemies* (1966)

The research worker is a solver of puzzles, not a tester of paradigms ... he is like the chess player who, with a problem stated and the board physically or mentally before him, tries out various alternative moves in the search for a solution. These trial attempts, whether by the chess player or by the scientist, are trials only of themselves, not of the rules of the game. They are possible only so long as the paradigm itself is taken for granted.

T. Kuhn, *The Structure of Scientific Revolutions* (1962)

When each of the contributors had read in draft form all the essays that were to constitute this book we had a long discussion about the individual chapters and about their collective effect. The editors studied a transcript of this conversation and also solicited further brief written comments from the essayists, thinking that some might wish to offer minor reservations or adjustments of emphasis in the light of the reactions they had heard.

What follows is a selection of the views that emerged from these procedures. The ordering of the material is necessarily arbitrary but the first section, *Reflections*, is primarily concerned with retrospective comment on the various essays while the second, *Questions Arising*, begins to pursue some of the conceptual

210

issues posed by the collection as a whole. Its open-endedness and shifts of direction reflect the discussion that gave rise to it. Where in the paragraphs that follow there is a reference to a discussion, it is this collective dialogue that is being referred to. All those who contributed to the book are represented, but in the second section no attributions are made.

Reflections

Physicist: I feel that we may have to some extent misrepresented science in our attempt to emphasize the characteristics it shares with other disciplines. Despite all the subtleties of interpretation and convention that have to be borne in mind we would still want to say that scientific statements are *true*. A scientific prediction is a *hard* prediction. If a theory has been well established for a long time, then its predictions are, to all intents and purposes, *true*.

The claims of science, like those of theology, are in some sense universal – they transcend the merely empirical. In both disciplines the nature of these claims has had to be modified. Nevertheless, science is still to be distinguished from (say) literature or sociology in that its truth claims are of a higher order.

Theologian: It may prove helpful in our consideration of the various chapters to bear in mind that there are three important theories of truth. The *correspondence* theory holds that a statement is true if, and only if, it corresponds with the facts. This is the notion of truth that is of particular relevance in scientific inquiry. The *coherence* theory maintains that truth is equivalent to systematic coherence. A statement is true if it logically coheres with other statements within some systematic whole – such a notion is especially applicable in the field of mathematics. The *pragmatic* theory of truth emphasizes the importance of truth understood functionally. A statement, on this view, is true not because it corresponds with the facts, or because it is systematically coherent with other statements, but because it is made true by events – because it works in the lives of those who believe in it. Some religious believers may want to subscribe to this view of

211

truth, asserting that a particular religious belief is true because it is meaningful in their own lives. We should be careful to distinguish which of these senses of truth we are referring to in our discussion.

Literature specialist: Current literary theory has thrown up a suggestive metaphor concerning the difficulties of defining and exploring reality. Thirty years ago the emphasis in academic criticism would have been very much upon the text as the repository of meaning. It was held to be the reader's responsibility to come to terms with the words upon the page and the various kinds of significance inherent in them. The text became, in effect, a fixed entity, the reality to be explored. More recently, however, an entirely different account of the reading process has been proposed. In this model the emphasis is not on the printed page but on the variety of reactions that it might elicit from different readers. It can be argued that there is no stability, in a sense no reality, in the text at all. The 'meaning' associated with it can only exist as engendered in the minds of particular individuals. The text itself, and by extension the author of the text are drained of authority.

It doesn't seem difficult to dispose of the arguments at either extreme of the dispute this theory has engendered. A text without a reader is inert – merely ink on paper. It can disclose meaning only when read, and that meaning will indeed be brought to life in and by the reader's own mind. On the other hand the meaning we are talking about derives, by definition, from the text – it is the product of a reading. And a reading is impossible without a text just as it is impossible without a reader. The meaning, the essential 'reality', of the work is the product of a transaction between reader and text.

This transactional model is interesting in several ways. The reader, or observer, is crucial to the process described. Since readers differ, an element of indeterminacy will be involved. In theory this element might be so pronounced that there would be as many readings as there were readers. In practice a remarkable measure of agreement is achieved. Those interested enough to read, say, *Hamlet* seriously are very largely in accord as to its literary status and its approximate 'meaning'. Moreover the

212

tend to revise an initial personal response by comparing notes with other readers and considering the recorded comments of critics from earlier times. What is in view is not some final and complete interpretation of *Hamlet*. Rather the sense is that one aspect of the play's meaning is its capacity to inspire dispute and reinterpretation. Establishing the meaning of this, or any other, work of art becomes a collective enterprise.

A kind of relativity is involved. In the lengthening perspective of the academic study of literature it becomes easier to see how Coleridge's *Hamlet* (to pursue the example) will differ from Dr Johnson's, or Bradley's, or Wilson Knight's. Each writes from a different temporal, social, political and intellectual perspective. *Hamlet* changes with time and so does its audience.

Art historian: I would like to make one brief comment on the discussion we had. From the seventeenth century onwards, and particularly as a result of the work of Descartes and Newton, it was generally assumed that the natural sciences were the paradigm of certain knowledge. It took a heterodox figure like Vico to turn this principle completely upside down, and assert the *verum factum* principle: that is, the only things that we could accept as *true* were what we ourselves had *made*, and in particular our systems of language and rhetoric. Vico is the first (but by no means the last) thinker to propound the view that the 'reality' of human history and human society could be discovered by a kind of etymology – taking our language systems back to first principles. Nietzsche was the subsequent thinker who made the most extreme claims for this point of view.

It seems to me that there is a surprising convergence between all our contributions, in that none of them accept the Cartesian view of knowledge and pretty well all of them implicitly accept the *verum factum* principle. I am inclined to feel that a pass has been sold somewhere! I would draw a broad distinction between the issue of *representation* – which might well extend from still or moving images, through poetry, and literature in general, to models of the atom or the genetic code – and an issue which we have not really faced *precisely because our contributions derive from separate disciplines*. These subject areas are pseudo-entities, which reflect academic practice, but do not in fact correspond with whatever options might be necessary to 'explore reality' at all effectively.

Philosopher: The discussion was disappointing in that most of the contributors did not seem to appreciate that I was offering them *overall* a lifeline. The emphasis in several of the essays on subjectivity, provisionality, paradox and so on could seem to imply an evasiveness or loss of nerve. Some readers may be tempted to revert to the persuasive, apparently commonsensical, assumptions about reality that I tried to dispose of in the opening chapter. My aim was to present an alternative theory which would define even the more diffident contributors as potential purveyors of REALITY. Because it is *created* it is, truly, provisional, paradoxical and so forth.

The objection to my view is that I seem to say that there is *nothing* beyond what we conceptualize. My simple defence (for discussion purposes) would be as follows: to raise the very question – there must be something beyond our interpretations, our subjective views, so what is it (because *that* is reality)? – is to conceptualize upon the theme of 'something'. We are in the realm of questions that *cannot* (not must not) be asked. These are questions that are nonsensical – as nonsensical, though not obviously so, as the question 'Is blue hard or soft?' The religious believer will be inclined to invoke God; but to do so is to miss the point, since the problem is simply pushed to another (putative) level of conceptualization.

Questions Arising

The philosopher's comment was partly a response to recurrent protests in our final discussion. 'Are we not trying to get at an external reality that is not simply the sum of all our disciplines? 'It makes no sense to say that Newton's laws only became true when Newton formulated them.' Some, at least, of the protesters would not be grateful for the particular philosophical lifeline offered to them. A recurring objection would be that the 'creation' of reality thus allowed for is in practice frequently brought about precisely through the attempt, however deluded, to reach reality conceived of as 'external' and 'objective'. As one of the scientists remarked: 'We never reach the end, but we proceed in the direction of an end.' A belief in such an end may be a necessary factor in the drive towards 'exploration'.

There are notable similarities between the essays – for example, a recurring emphasis on convention, on interpretation, on the role of the observer, on the supersession of old theories or modes by new ones. Are these similarities a common reaction against the positivistic views summarized in the introduction (the only chapter we all saw in advance)? If not, how did they come about? Are they no more than an interesting coincidence? Do they suggest an intriguing general unanimity among the disciplines concerned? Do they derive partly from cross-reference between different fields of study?

It has always seemed natural and helpful to borrow concepts from one discipline to shed light upon another. Often the outcome is a metaphor. For example, it is thanks to Darwin that literary critics talk about the 'evolution' of the novel. Is not cross-relation of this kind a major factor in keeping diverse disciplines loosely in step? Does it not suggest a reassuring measure of mutual corroboration and reinforcement between them?

Conversely, might not casual borrowings of this kind prove misleading? Is there not a risk that vague notions of (say) 'relativity' or 'uncertainty' will be invoked in areas remote from the field of inquiry for which the theory was devised? But surely it is fair to claim that these particular theories do, in broad terms, powerfully demonstrate the limitations of common sense? Is not a bemused acknowledgement of these limitations a characteristic of the contemporary response to reality? More specifically, were not these theories drawn upon because they filled a gap? Was there not a demonstrable need, in a variety of disciplines, to illustrate the difficulty of finding detached ground from which to observe, or the difficulty of observing at all without interfering with the phenomena under examination? Did not the search for an appropriate metaphor precede, and explain, the borrowing?

But even if that were the case, might not the effects of the borrowing be dubious? Metaphors can confine or distort one's thinking. Might not a vague notion that 'relativity' or 'uncertainty' have been scientifically proved to lie at the heart of things give rise to unjustified doubt or defeatism?

There was repeated reference in our discussion to cultural or intellectual determinism. Why were Mendel's observations unregarded for many years? They were premature – but what does it mean to say that a scientific discovery is 'premature'? Presumably the suggestion is that no conceptual framework yet exists within which it could be developed. An age, like an individual, is subject to certain preconceptions and limitations which it cannot transcend. History makes certain things possible and rules out others. Within a given period only certain things can be thought. But are generalizations of this kind as formidable as they seem at first glance? Do they have any predictive power? Do they not drift towards a tautology: 'An age cannot know more than it is capable of knowing'? In any case how can it come about that a premature discovery is even possible?

Language was often cited as a determining influence. How can we conceptualize about something we cannot define? But is there not a danger of being too defeatist here? We can and do adapt old words, invent new ones, borrow from other languages, resort to metaphor. Mathematics is a rich language – one that will cope, for example, with the movement of electrons, which emerges as paradoxical only when described in words. Pictorial representation, gesture, music are among the other languages available to us. But do the variety and the versatility of our languages affect the essential issue? The fact that we can only get at reality through the medium of language makes it inevitably a human construct.

Since each succeeding age has available to it, at least in theory, not only its own discoveries but those of previous centuries, is it not reasonable to look for progress? Should not our notions of reality be superior to those of, say, the eighteenth century? Certainly we can see more and see further (technologically assisted); we know more and can do more. But have not gains of this kind produced, not greater wisdom, insight, confidence, but a heightened sense of our ignorance and our inadequacies?

Has it not emerged that the knowledge of an age is directly related to its needs and capacities? If this is the case, does it make sense to invoke the idea of progress? Can one even say, for example, that those who used to believe that the earth was flat were wrong? In one sense clearly they *were* wrong: the earth is not flat. On the other hand the contrary view was not merely a crude guess; all sorts of supporting evidence made it plausible. Everyday observation and intuition tell us that the earth is flat. Roads can be built and considerable journeys undertaken on the assumption of flatness.

But is there a contrast to be drawn between the limitations of this belief and those of (say) Newtonian physics? Newton's laws still hold good provided, for example, that the objects concerned are not travelling too fast. Flat earth calculations will not enable one to travel from New York to Fiji. On the other hand, is our new-found interest in astronomical speeds and distances categorically different from the move towards longer terrestrial journeys a few hundred years ago? Can any 'world-view' do more than meet the challenges of its own time? And if it does so, can it reasonably be judged inferior to any other?

Within the arts the idea of progress seems to make little sense. Who would claim that Shakespeare or Mozart has been improved upon? What does happen is that boundaries and objectives are modified by fashion and, more obviously, by technological change. Photography impinges on painting, film on literature, television on film. How far would it be true to say that an art form surrenders some part of its territory when a new form seems to do certain things better?

Did not many of the difficulties that emerged in discussion stem from the fact that we were looking to generalize about intellectual enterprises very different in kind? The natural sciences deal in phenomena that can be weighed, measured, counted or calculated and hence make claims that are open to objective testing and possible falsification. At the other extreme literature, philosophy and theology deal in abstractions. How far can comparison usefully go between disciplines so diverse? Samples have been brought back from the surface of the moon for scientific analysis. The analyst could reasonably think that he or she had come far closer than anyone in previous generations to the 'reality' of the moon. But such investigation takes us, if anything, further away from the moon as celebrated in poetry, painting and music. Is the planet not an *idea*, as well as being an aggregation of physical substances? In other words, is there not more than one kind of reality involved? A poet, for example, might want to argue that the samples will tell us no more about the *real* moon than a lock of hair would tell us about the personality of a human being.

It would seem that human activity is governed by conventions of various kinds. Once a satisfactory convention has been evolved, why should it ever be replaced? How is one to account for novelty? In some cases, of course, external pressures will be at work: units of currency may be revalued because of inflation; a ball of a different colour may be used if a game is played under floodlights. But where a given system or sub-system is functioning efficiently and is not subject to outside pressure, why should one convention give way to another? Why did Western painting strive after a third dimension? Why did the proscenium arch become central to drama and then lose its supremacy? What is the driving force towards change? Is it inherent in the human species, or is it a cultural characteristic found in the West rather than in the East? Chinese art and science have seemed much less subject to such pressures.

Is there a concealed arrogance or solipsism in the frequent assumption that the human mind makes what it can of a passive universe? In *The Winter's Tale* Perdita rejects certain flowers whose mixed colour has been artificially produced by grafting. Polixenes rebukes her:

> Yet nature is made better by no mean
> But nature makes that mean: so, over that art,
> Which you say adds to nature, is an art
> That nature makes.

Man cannot impose himself on nature: he can only make use of the possibilities inherent in it. Could not the argument be taken a stage further? Is not the very desire for change – in this case for change in the colouring of the flowers – a natural instinct? In the search for novelty could man act unless he was acted upon by some innate drive or appetite?

Does not the methodology of this book leave theology particularly exposed? Should not the theologian transcend the kinds of uncertainty that representatives of other disciplines can freely acknowledge? One answer would be that such uncertainties can

218

be transcended only by faith and that faith has nothing to do with empirical testing and factual evidence. Religious statements are factual claims (not mere metaphors) but are unverifiable in this world. The theologian cannot deal in 'proof'.

Can theology in fact reasonably be seen as a discipline among other disciplines? In all other cases it would seem that the fallibility, or limitations, of the mode of thought concerned can be more easily demonstrated than its potential completeness. For example, physics is 'based' upon mathematics. Mathematics, while consistent with the laws of logic, cannot be wholly derived from them. Gödel has shown (in his 'On formally undecidable propositions of *Principia Mathematica* and related systems') that no proof of the consistency of any deductive system which was rich enough for the expression of arithmetic, could be represented within the system. Any such system must involve propositions that the system itself lacks the means to demonstrate. In a sense, then, Gödel showed that arithmetic is incomplete. But if arithmetic has holes in it, so also does physics. We can *never*, in the nature of things, account wholly and completely for natural phenomena.

Religion, then, could be seen as a unique means of moving towards an ultimate reality – towards God himself, who lies beyond the limitations of our flawed reasoning powers: the God of the mystics, who is encountered in silence, while reason is laid to rest.

This is, of course, dangerous ground and makes theology a dangerous discourse.

Further Reading and Filmography

Chapter 1
Introduction

See further reading list for Chapter 8 (Philosophy) which also covers this chapter.

Chapter 2
Literature

Further reading in this area could most profitably take the form of close study of the works discussed in detail.

Chapter 3
Sociology

Berger, P. L., *Invitation to Sociology* (Harmondsworth: Penguin, 1966)
Berger, P. L. and Luckmann, T., *The Social Construction of Realit* (New York: Anchor Books, 1967).
Campbell, T., *Seven Theories of Human Society* (Oxford: Clarendor 1981).
Goffman, E., *The Presentation of Self in Everyday Life* (New York Anchor Books, 1959).
Linton, R., *The Study of Man* (New York: Appleton-Century-Croft 1964).
Sapir, E., *Culture, Language, and Personality* (Berkeley, Calif.: Unive sity of California Press, 1956).

Chapter 4
Biology

Goldstein, M. and Goldstein, I. F., *How We Know: an Exploration of the Scientific Process* (New York: Plenum Press, 1978).

Iltis, H., *Life of Mendel*, translated by E. and C. Paul (London: Allen & Unwin, 1932).

Judson, H. F., *The Eighth Day of Creation* (New York: Simon & Schuster, 1979).

Olby, R., *The Path to the Double Helix* (London: Macmillan, 1974).

Orel, V., *Mendel* (Oxford: Oxford University Press, Past Masters series, 1984).

Watson, J. D., *The Double Helix: A Personal Account of the Discovery of the Structure of DNA* (New York: Atheneum, 1968).

Yanchinski, S., *Setting Genes to Work: The Industrial Era of Biotechnology* (Harmondsworth: Penguin, 1985).

Ziman, J., *Reliable Knowledge: An Exploration of the Grounds for Belief in Science* (Cambridge: Cambridge University Press, 1978).

Chapter 5
Art

Alpers, S., *The Art of Describing – Dutch Art in the Seventeenth Century* (London: Murray, 1983).

Baxandall, M., *Painting and Experience in Fifteenth-Century Italy* (Oxford: Oxford University Press, 1972).

Bryson, N., *Vision and Painting – The Logic of the Gaze* (London: Macmillan, 1983).

Fried, M., *Absorption and Theatricality – Painting and the Beholder in the Age of Diderot* (Berkeley, Calif.: University of California Press, 1980).

Mitchell, W. J. M. (ed.), *The Language of Images* (Chicago: University of Chicago Press, 1980).

White, J., *The Birth and Rebirth of Pictorial Space* (London: Faber, 1972).

Chapter 6
Physics

Berstein, J., *Einstein* (London: Fontana/Collins, 1973).

Einstein, A., *Relativity* (London: Methuen, 1960).

Einstein, A. and Infeld, L., *The Evolution of Physics* (Cambridge: Cambridge University Press, 1971).

Feynman, R., *The Character of Physical Law* (London: BBC, 1965; Cambridge, Mass.: MIT Press, 1967).

Gamow, G., *Mr. Tomkins in Paperback* (Cambridge: Cambridge University Press, 1978).

Polkinghorne, J. C., *The Quantum World* (Harmondsworth: Penguin, 1986; Princeton, NJ: Princeton University Press, 1985).

Chapter 7
Film

The following list gives minimal information about the films mentioned in this chapter: title (plus original title if different from that used in the text), country of production, year of first release, production company (p.c.), director (d.), scriptwriter (sc.), photographer (ph.), leading players (l.p.), original length in minutes (or reels for silent films where the precise length is unknown – a reel of silent film lasts between twelve and fifteen minutes), and other credits where these seem relevant.

Annapurna (*Victoire sur l'Annapurna*), France, 1953, ph. Marcel Ichac, 56 minutes.

The Birds, USA, 1963, p.c. Universal, d. Alfred Hitchcock, sc. Evan Hunter, ph. (Technicolor) Robert Burks, special effects Lawrence A. Hampton, l.p. Tippi Hedren, Jessica Tandy, Rod Taylor, 120 minutes.

Chronicle of Anna Magdalena Bach (*Chronik der Anna Magdalena Bach*), Germany/Italy, 1968, d. Jean-Marie Straub, sc. J.-M. Straub/ Danièle Huillet, ph. Ugo Piccone, sound Louis Hochet/Lucien Moreau, l.p. Gustav Leonhardt, Christiane Lang, 93 minutes.

Citizen Kane, USA, 1941, p.c. RKO Radio Pictures, d. Orson Welles, sc. Herman J. Mankiewicz/O. Welles, ph. Gregg Toland, music Bernard Herrmann, special effects Vernon L. Walker, l.p. Orson Welles, Dorothy Comingore, Everett Sloane, Joseph Cotton, 119 minutes.

The Cobweb, USA, 1955, p.c. MGM, d. Vincente Minnelli, sc. John Paxton, ph. (Cinemascope, Eastmancolor) George Folsey, drawings David Stone Martin, music Leonard Rosenman, l.p. Richard Widmark, Lauren Bacall, Charles Boyer, Gloria Graham, Lillian Gish, John Kerr, Susan Strasberg, Oscar Levant, Fay Wray, 124 minutes.

Intolerance, USA, 1916, p.c. Wark Producing Corp., d. D. W. Griffith, sc. D. W. Griffith, ph. G. W. Bitzer, l.p. Lillian Gish, Mae Marsh, Robert Harron, Fred Turner, Sam de Grasse, Vera Lewis, Miriam Cooper, Walter Long, Ralph Lewis, Howard Gage, Margery Wilson,

222

Eugene Pallette, Spottiswood Aitken, Josephine Crowell, Constance Talmadge, Elmer Clifton, Alfred Paget, Seena Owen, Tully Marshall, George Siegmann, Elmo Lincoln, 14 reels.
Scarlet Street, USA, 1945, p.c. Diana Productions, d. Fritz Lang, sc. Dudley Nichols, ph. Milton Krasner, paintings John Decker, music Hans J. Saller, l.p. Edward G. Robinson, Joan Bennett, Dan Duryea, 102 minutes.
Toni, France, 1934, p.c. Films d'Aujourd'hui, d. Jean Renoir, sc. J. Renoir/Carl Einstein, ph. Claude Renoir, sound Barbishanian/Sarrazin, music Paul Bozzi, l.p. Charles Blavette, Jenny Hélia, Célia Montalvan, Edouard Delmont, Andrex, 95 minutes.
True Heart Susie, USA, 1919, p.c. D. W. Griffith for Paramount-Artcraft, d. D. W. Griffith, sc. Marion Fremont, ph. G. W. Bitzer, l.p. Lillian Gish, Robert Harron, Wilber Higby, Loyola O'Connor, George Fawcett, Clarine Seymour, Kate Bruce, Carol Dempster, 6 reels.

Chapter 8
Philosophy

Aristotle, 'On the art of poetry', in T. S. Dorsch (trans. and ed.), *Classical Literary Criticism* (London: Penguin, 1965) pp. 29–75.
Carr, E. H., *What is History?* (London: Penguin, 1961).
Gombrich, E. H., *Art and Illusion*, 5th edn (London: Phaidon, 1977).
Hacking, I. (ed.), *Scientific Revolutions* (New York: Oxford University Press, 1981).
Rorty, R., *Philosophy and the Mirror of Nature* (Princeton, NJ: Princeton University Press, 1980).
Ryle, G., *The Concept of Mind* (London: Hutchinson, 1949).
Winch, P., *The Idea of a Social Science and its Relation to Philosophy* (London: Routledge & Kegan Paul, 1958).

Chapter 9
Theology

Ayer, A. J., *Language, Truth and Logic* (New York: Dover, 1952).
Flew, A. and MacIntyre, A. (eds), *New Essays in Philosophical Theology* (New York: Macmillan, 1964).
Hick, J., *Problems of Religious Pluralism* (London: Macmillan, 1958).

Ramsey, I., *Religious Language* (London: SCM, 1969).
Wisdom, J., *Philosophy and Psychoanalysis* (Oxford: Blackwell, 1953).
Wittgenstein, L., *Lectures and Conversations on Aesthetics, Psychology and Religious Belief*, ed. C. Barrett (Oxford: Blackwell, 1966).

Bibliography

Chapter 1
Introduction

Briggs, A. (1954), *Victorian People* (London: Odhams).

Carr, E. H. (1961), *What is History?* (London: Penguin).

Comte, A. (1974), *Cours de Philosophie Positive*, translated by H. Martineau as *The Positive Philosophy* (New York: AMS).

Dickens, C. (1907), *Hard Times* (London: Dent).

Gombrich, E. H. (1977), *Art and Illusion*, 5th edn (London: Phaidon).

Hacking, I. (ed.) (1981), *Scientific Revolutions* (New York: Oxford University Press).

Hume, D. (1902), 'Of miracles' and 'Of a particular providence and of a future state', in L. A. Selby-Bigge (ed.), *Hume's Enquiries*, 2nd edn (Oxford: Clarendon), pp. 109–48.

Moore, W. (1955), *Bring the Jubilee* (London: Heinemann).

Nidditch, P. H. (ed.) (1968), *The Philosophy of Science* (New York: Oxford University Press).

Popper, K. (1966), *The Open Society and Its Enemies*, 5th edn, 2 vols (London: Routledge).

Rorty, R. (1980), *Philosophy and the Mirror of Nature* (Princeton, NJ: Princeton University Press).

Rorty, R. (1982), *The Consequences of Pragmatism* (Minneapolis, Minn.: University of Minnesota Press).

Thompson, F. M. L. (1963), *English Landed Society in the Nineteenth Century* (London: Routledge & Kegan Paul).

Williams, B. (1985), *Ethics and the Limits of Philosophy* (London: Fontana/Collins).

Yee, Chiang (1937), *The Silent Traveller* (London: Country Life Books).

Chapter 2
Facts and Fictions

Gardner, M. (ed.) (1965), *The Annotated Alice: Alice's Adventures in Wonderland and Through the Looking-Glass by Lewis Carroll* (London: Penguin).

Reeves, J. (ed.) (1954), *Selected Poems of John Clare* (London: Heinemann).

Tibble, J. W. (ed.) (1935), *The Poems of John Clare* (London: Dent).

White, Gilbert (1906), *The Natural History of Selborne* (London: Dent).

'Sorrow-acre' is to be found in Isak Dinesen's *Winter's Tales*. This, and all the other works mentioned in the chapter, save those listed above, can be read in a variety of editions between which it would be pointless to adjudicate.

Chapter 3
Sociology

Aristotle (1952), *The Politics*, translated by Ernest Barker (Oxford: Clarendon).

Berger, P. L. (1966), *Invitation to Sociology* (Harmondsworth: Penguin).

Berger, P. L. and Kellner, H. (1974), 'Marriage and the construction of reality', in R. L. Coser (ed.), *The Family*, 2nd edn (London: Macmillan), pp. 157–74.

Cohen, S. and Taylor, L. (1978), *Escape Attempts: The Theory and Practice of Resistance to Everyday Life* (Harmondsworth: Penguin).

Dumont, L. (1972), *Homo Hierarchicus: The Caste System and Its Implications* (London: Paladin).

Durkheim, E. (1964), *The Rules of Sociological Method* (New York: Free Press).

Geertz, C. (1973), *The Interpretation of Cultures* (New York: Basic Books).

Goffman, E. (1969), *Where The Action Is: Three Essays* (London: Allen Lane).

Huxley, J. (1955), *Evolution: The Modern Synthesis* (London: Allen & Unwin).

Linton, R. (1964), *The Study of Man* (New York: Appleton-Century-Crofts).

MacIntyre, A. (1962), 'A mistake about causality in social science', in

P. Laslett and W. G. Runciman (eds), *Philosophy, Politics, and Society*, Second Series (Oxford: Blackwell).

Marwick, A. (1981), *Class: Image and Reality in Britain, France and the USA since 1930* (London: Fontana/Collins).

Marx, K. (1962), 'The eighteenth Brumaire of Louis Bonaparte', in K. Marx and F. Engels, *Selected Works in Two Volumes* (Moscow: Foreign Languages Publishing House).

Marx, K. and Engels, F. (1963), *The German Ideology* (New York: International Publishers).

Mead, G. H. (1967), *Mind, Self, and Society* (Chicago: University of Chicago Press).

Mead, M. (1963), *Sex and Temperament in Three Primitive Societies* (New York: Morrow).

Merton, R. (1964), 'The role set', in L. A. Coser and B. Rosenberg (eds), *Sociological Theory* (New York: Macmillan), pp. 376–87.

Orwell, G. (1954), *Nineteen Eighty-Four* (Harmondsworth: Penguin).

Reid, I. (1977), *Social Class Differences in Britain* (London: Open Books).

Robertson, I. (1981), *Sociology*, 2nd edn (New York: Worth Publishers).

Russell, E. S. (1946), *The Directiveness of Organic Activities* (Cambridge: Cambridge University Press).

Sapir, E. (1956), *Culture, Language, and Personality* (Berkeley, Calif.: University of California Press).

Steiner, G. (1969), *Language and Silence* (Harmondsworth: Penguin).

Chapter 4
Biology

Allen, G. E. (1975), *Life Science in the Twentieth Century* (New York: Wiley).

Bateson, W. (1913), *Mendel's Principles of Heredity*, 2nd edn (Cambridge: Cambridge University Press).

Birkett, C. (1979), *Heredity, Development and Evolution* (London: Macmillan).

Fisher, R. A. (1936), 'Has Mendel's work been rediscovered?', *Ann. Sci.*, vol. 1, pp. 115–37.

Focke, W. O. (1881), *Die Pflanzenmischlinge* (Berlin: Bornträger).

Gabriel, M. S. and Fogel, S. (1955), *Great Experiments in Biology* (Englewood Cliffs, NJ: Prentice-Hall).

Goldstein, M. and Goldstein, I. F. (1978), *How We Know; an Exploration of the Scientific Process* (New York: Plenum Press).

Iltis, H. (1932), *Life of Mendel*, translated by E. and C. Paul (London: Allen & Unwin).

Judson, H. F. (1979), *The Eighth Day of Creation* (New York: Simon & Schuster).

Kuhn, T. S. (1962), *The Structure of Scientific Revolutions* (Chicago: University of Chicago Press).

Medvedev, Z. A. (1969), *The Rise and Fall of T. D. Lysenko* (translated by I. M. Lerner) (New York: Columbia University Press).

Olby, R. (1974), *The Path to the Double Helix* (London: Macmillan).

Orel, V. (1984), *Mendel* (Oxford: Oxford University Press, Past Masters series).

Price, D. J. de S. (1963), *Little Science, Big Science* (New York: Columbia University Press).

Schrödinger, E. (1944), *What is Life?* (Cambridge: Cambridge University Press).

Stent, G. S. (ed.) (1981), *The Double Helix: a new critical edition* (London: Weidenfeld & Nicolson).

Sturtevant, A. H. (1965), *A History of Genetics* (New York: Harper & Row).

Watson, J. D. (1968), *The Double Helix: A Personal Account of the Discovery of the Structure of DNA* (New York: Athenaeum).

Watson, J. D. and Crick, F. H. C. (1953), 'A structure for deoxyribose nucleic acid', *Nature*, vol. 171, pp. 737–8.

Wilson, E. B. (1896), *The Cell in Development and Heredity* (New York: Macmillan).

Yanchinski, S. (1985), *Setting Genes to Work: The Industrial Era of Biotechnology* (Harmondsworth: Penguin).

Ziman, J. (1978), *Reliable Knowledge: An Exploration of the Grounds for Belief in Science* (Cambridge: Cambridge University Press).

Chapter 5
Art

Alberti (1977), *On Painting*, translated and with an introduction by John R. Spencer (New Haven, Conn.: Yale University Press).

Alpers, S. (1983), *The Art of Describing – Dutch Art in the Seventeenth Century* (London: Murray).

Apollinaire, G. (1972), *Apollinaire on Art – Essays and Reviews 1902–1918*, edited by Leroy C. Breunig and translated by Susan Suleiman (New York: Viking).

Bryson, N. (1983), *Vision and Painting – The Logic of the Gaze* (London: Macmillan).

Damisch, H. (1976), 'Equals infinity', translated by R. H. Olorenshaw, *20th Century Studies*, 15/16, pp. 56–81.

Gombrich, E. H. (1963), *Meditations on a Hobby Horse* (London: Phaidon).

Gombrich, E. H. (1980), 'Standards of truth', in W. J. T. Mitchell (ed.), *The Language of Images* (Chicago: University of Chicago Press), pp. 181–217.

Kemp, M. (1984), 'Construction and cunning: the perspective of the Edinburgh Saenredam', in *Dutch Church Painters* (Edinburgh: National Galleries of Scotland).

Kemp, W. (1985), 'Death at work: a case study in constitutive blanks in nineteenth-century painting', *Representations*, 10, pp. 102–23.

Ruskin, J. (1903), *Modern Painters*, I (London: George Allen).

White, J. (1972), *The Birth and Rebirth of Pictorial Space* (London: Faber).

Chapter 6
Physics

Bernstein, J. (1973), *Einstein* (London: Fontana/Collins).

Sambursky, S. (1974), *Physical Thought from the Presocratics to the Quantum Physicists* (London: Hutchinson).

Chapter 7
Film

Aristotle (1965), 'On the art of poetry', in T. S. Dorsch (trans. and ed.), *Classical Literary Criticism* (Harmondsworth: Penguin), pp. 29–75.

Arnheim, R. (1933), *Film*, translated by L. M. Sieveking and I. F. D. Morrow (London: Faber).

Arnheim, R. (1975), *Film als Kunst*, with a foreword to the new edition (Munich: Carl Hanser).

Barnouw, E. (1981), *The Magician and the Cinema* (London: Oxford University Press).

Bazin, A. (1967), *What is Cinema?*, essays selected and translated by Hugh Gray (Berkeley, Calif.: University of California Press).

Bazin, A. (1971), *What is Cinema?*, Volume 2, translated by Hugh Gray (Berkeley, Calif.: University of California Press).

Bordwell, D. (1985), *Narration in the Fiction Film* (Madison, Wis.: University of Wisconsin Press).

Burch, N. (forthcoming), *La Lucarne de l'infini* (to be published in both French and English).

Genette, G. (1969), 'Vraisemblance et motivation', in *Figures*, t. II (Paris: Seuil), pp. 71–99.

Heath, S. (1976), 'Narrative space', *Screen*, vol. 17, no. 3, pp. 68–112, reprinted in *Questions of Cinema* (London: Macmillan, 1981), pp. 19–75.

Jakobson, R. (1971), 'On realism in art', in L. Matejka and K. Pomorska (eds), *Readings in Russian Poetics: Formalist and Structuralist Views* (Cambridge, Mass.: MIT Press), pp. 38–46.

Kuleshov, L. (1974), *Kuleshov on Film; Writings by Lev Kuleshov*, selected, translated and edited by R. Levaco (Berkeley, Calif.: University of California Press).

Lukács, G. (1963), *Ästhetik*, Teil I: *Die Eigenart des Ästhetischen*, two vols (Neuwied am Rhein: Luchterhand).

MacCabe, C. (1974), 'Realism in cinema: notes on some Brechtian theses', *Screen*, vol. 15, no. 2, pp. 7–27, reprinted in *Theoretical Essays: Film, Linguistics, Literature* (Manchester: Manchester University Press, 1985), pp. 33–57.

McLean, A. (1965), *American Vaudeville as Ritual* (Lexington, Ky: University of Kentucky Press).

Norris, F. (1899), *McTeague, A Story of San Francisco* (New York: Doubleday & McClure).

Pliny the Elder (C. Plinius Secundus) (1896), *The Elder Pliny's Chapters on the History of Art*, translated by K. Jex-Blake (London: Macmillan); reprinted 1968 (Chicago: Argonaut Inc.).

Pudovkin, V. I. (1929), *Film Technique: Five Essays and Two Addresses*, translated by I. Montagu (London: Gollancz).

Salt, B. (1984), *Film Style and Technology: History and Analysis* (London: Starword).

Straub, J.-M. (1970), 'Entretien avec Jean-Marie Straub et Danièle Huillet', *Cahiers du cinéma*, no. 223, pp. 53–5.

White, J. (1957), *The Birth and Rebirth of Pictorial Space* (London: Faber).

Wood, N. (1984), 'Towards a semiotics of the transition to sound: spatial and temporal codes', *Screen*, vol. 25, no. 3, pp. 16–24.

Chapter 8
Philosophy

Aristotle (1965), 'On the art of poetry', in T. S. Dorsch (trans. and ed.), *Classical Literary Criticism* (London: Penguin), pp. 29–75.

Briggs, A. (1954), *Victorian People* (London: Odhams).

Carr, E. H. (1961), *What is History?* (London: Penguin).

Carroll, L. (1962), *Through the Looking-Glass*, with *Alice's Adventures in Wonderland* (London: Penguin).

Comte, A. (1974), *Cours de Philosophie Positive*, translated by H. Martineau as *The Positive Philosophy* (New York: AMS Press).

Descartes, R. (1960), *Meditations*, with *Discourse on Method* (Indianapolis, Ind.: Bobbs-Merrill).

Dickens, C. (1907), *Hard Times* (London: Dent).

Eliot, G. (1961), *Adam Bede* (New York: New American Library).

Fowles, J. (1977), *The French Lieutenant's Woman* (London: Triad/ Granada).

Gombrich, E. H. (1977), *Art and Illusion*, 5th edn (London: Phaidon).

Hacking, I. (ed.) (1981), *Scientific Revolutions* (New York: Oxford University Press).

Hume, D. (1902), 'Of miracles' and 'Of a particular providence and of a future state', in L. A. Selby-Bigge (ed.), *Hume's Enquiries*, 2nd edn (Oxford: Clarendon), pp. 109–48.

Hume, D. (1963), 'Of the standard of taste', in *Essays: Moral, Political and Literary* (Oxford: Clarendon Press), pp. 231–55.

Hume, D. (1947), *Dialogues Concerning Natural Religion*, 2nd edn, edited by N. Kemp-Smith (London: Nelson).

James, H. (1968), 'The art of fiction', in *The Portable Henry James* (New York: Penguin/Viking).

Joyce, J. (1977), *A Portrait of the Artist as a Young Man* (London: Grafton).

Joyce, J. (1986), *Ulysses*, corrected edition (London: Penguin).

Kafka, F. (1961), *Metamorphosis and Other Stories*, translated by W. and E. Muir (London: Penguin).

McGinn, C. (1983), *The Subjective View* (Oxford: Clarendon).

Moore, W. (1955), *Bring the Jubilee* (London: Heinemann).

Nidditch, P. H. (ed.) (1968), *The Philosophy of Science* (New York: Oxford University Press).

Popper, K. (1959), *The Logic of Scientific Discovery* (London: Hutchinson).

Popper, K. (1966), *The Open Society and its Enemies*, 5th edn, 2 vols (London: Routledge & Kegan Paul).

Rorty, R. (1980), *Philosophy and the Mirror of Nature* (Princeton, NJ: Princeton University Press).

Rorty, R. (1982), *The Consequences of Pragmatism* (Minneapolis, Minn.: University of Minnesota Press).

Ryle, G. (1949), *The Concept of Mind* (London: Hutchinson).

Sartre, J.-P. (1965), *Nausea*, translated by R. Baldick (London: Penguin).

Thompson, F. M. L. (1963), *English Landed Society in the Nineteenth Century* (London: RKP).

Strindberg, A. (1976), *Miss Julie*, with other plays, translated by M. Meyer (London: Eyre Methuen), pp. 91–146.

Williams, B. (1973), *Problems of the Self* (Cambridge: Cambridge University Press).

Williams, B. (1985), *Ethics and the Limits of Philosophy* (London: Fontana/Collins).

Winch, P. (1958), *The Idea of a Social Science and its Relation to Philosophy* (London: RKP).

Wisdom, J. (1953), 'Gods', in J. Wisdom, *Philosophy and Psychoanalysis* (Oxford: Blackwell).

Wittgenstein, L. (1958), *Philosophical Investigations*, 2nd edn (Oxford: Blackwell).

Wittgenstein, L. (1966), *Lectures and Conversations on Aesthetics, Psychology and Religious Belief*, edited by C. Barrett (Oxford: Blackwell).

Wordsworth, W. (1944), *The Poetical Works*, edited by E. de Selincourt, Vol. 2 (Oxford: Clarendon Press).

Yee, Chiang (1937), *The Silent Traveller* (London: Country Life Books).

Zola, E. (1981), *Therese Raquin*, translated by L. Tancock (Harmondsworth: Penguin).

Chapter 9
Theology

Ayer, A. J. (1936), *Language, Truth and Logic* (New York: Dover, 1952 edn).

Braithwaite, R. B. (1955), 'An Empiricist's view of the nature of religious belief' (Cambridge: Cambridge University Press); reprinted in J. Hick (ed.), *The Existence of God* (London: Macmillan, 1964), pp. 229–52.

Campbell, J. (1971), *The Language of Religion* (London: Collier-Macmillan).

Flew, A. (1964), 'Theology and falsification', in Flew and MacIntyre (eds), op. cit.

Flew, A. and MacIntyre, A. (eds) (1964), *New Essays in Philosophical Theology* (New York: Macmillan).

Hare, R. M. (1964), 'Theology and falsification', in Flew and MacIntyre (eds), op. cit.

Hick, J. (1963), *Philosophy of Religion* (Englewood Cliffs, NJ: Prentice-Hall).

Hick, J. (1985), *Problems of Religious Pluralism* (London: Macmillan).

Leon, P. (1955), 'The meaning of religious propositions', *The Hibbert Journal*, vol. LIII, p. 153.

MacKinnon, D. M. (1964), 'Death', in Flew and MacIntyre (eds), op. cit.

Miles, T. R. (1954), *Religion and the Scientific Outlook* (New York: Humanities Press).

Mitchell, B. (1964), 'Theology and falsification', in Flew and MacIntyre (eds), op. cit.

Ramsey, I. (1969), *Religious Language* (London: SCM).

Wisdom, J. (1953a), 'Gods', in Wisdom, op. cit.

Wisdom, J. (1953b), *Philosophy and Psychoanalysis* (Oxford: Blackwell).

Wittgenstein, L. (1966), *Lectures and Conversations on Aesthetics, Psychology and Religious Belief*, edited by C. Barrett (Oxford: Blackwell).

Index

Index

Index

Pliny 84, 145, 146
poetry 13–23, 168–9
Pope, Alexander 14–15
Popper, Karl 12, 172, 210
portraiture 181
positivism 4–11, 130; logical 4, 192–3, 208; and science 6–8
post-modernism 173
progress 216–17; and science 68–71
Ptolemy 111, 112–14, 116, 118

quantum theory 110, 131–42, 143

racial stereotyping 48–9
Ramsey, Ian 196–7, 198
realism: in the arts 3, 146–7
reductionism 123
Reeves, James: *Selected Poems of John Clare* 20
relativity 110, 122; special relativity 124–31
religious belief 191–4
Renaissance painting 86–92, 102
Renoir, Jean 158; *Toni* 160–1
replication 146
revolution 43–4
role-playing 51–4
Romanticism: poetry 15, 20–1
Rossellini, Roberto 158
Ruskin, John: 'pathetic fallacy' 14, 169; *Modern Painters* 106

Saenredam, Pieter: *Interior of St Bavo's Church at Haarlem* 93, 94–6, 100
Sapir, E. 45
Sartre, Jean-Paul: *Nausea* 188
scepticism 9–10, 11
Schrödinger, Erwin 136–7
science: and positivism 6–8; and reality 63–5, 78; and progress 68–71; physics 109–44; methodology 172; truth of 211
selectivity 3, 170, 171–2, 184
self 173–6, 188
sexual stereotyping 48
Snow, Michael 163
society 37–55; and language 41–7;

sub-cultures 47–52; hierarchy in 49–50; individual in 52–5
speech, *see* language
Steiner, George 45, 46
Straub, Jean-Marie: *Chronicle of Anna Magdalena Bach* 163–5
Strindberg, Auguste: *Miss Julie* 178
subjectivity 2, 169, 176–7; poetry 13–23; novel 23–6, 29; and religion 191–2
symbols 41–2

Tetley, John: *Banqueting House Interior, Hackfall* 97, 98–9
theology 186–7, 191–209, 218–19
Toland, Gregg 158
Toni 160–1
Trollope, Anthony 188
trompe-l'oeil 5, 85, 148
True Heart Susie 153
truth, theories of 211–12

uniforms 179–80

verisimilitude 147–8, 149; cinematic 151–7
Vico, Giovanni Battista 213
Visconti, Luchino 158
vocabulary, *see* language

Watson, James 73–7
wave motion 132–3
Welles, Orson 158: *Citizen Kane* 152
Welsby, Chris 163
White, Gilbert: *Natural History of Selborne* 17–18, 169, 170
Wisdom, John: *Gods* 187, 198–200
Wittgenstein, Ludwig 190, 195–6, 200
Wordsworth, William 168–9; *The Tables Turned* 15; *The Prelude* 15; *Tintern Abbey* 21, 22, 169, 172, 176; *Immortality* 21–2; *The Excursion* 22, 172
Wyler, William 158

Yee, Chiang: *Cows in Derwentwater* xvii, 6

Zola, Emile 189